The Establishment of Marxist Regimes

The Establishment of Marxist Regimes

Bogdan Szajkowski

Lecturer in Comparative Social
Institutions, University College, Cardiff

Butterworth Scientific
London   Boston   Sydney   Wellington   Durban   Toronto

First published 1982

© **Butterworth & Co (Publishers) Ltd 1982**

British Library Cataloguing in Publication Data
Szajkowski, Bogdan
    The establishment of Marxist regimes.
    1. Communist state
    I. Title
    321.92 D847

    ISBN 0-408-10834-7
    ISBN 0-408-10833-9 Pbk

Photoset by Butterworths Litho Preparation Department
Printed in Great Britain by The Thetford Press Ltd, Thetford, Norfolk

For Nadia

Preface

In the last decade there has been a considerable increase in the number of scholarly works devoted to communist studies. The same period has also witnessed a steady growth in the number of regimes that adhere to the principles of scientific socialism. Yet the coming to power of Marxist regimes has been given little attention in the literature. No major comparative work devoted to the subject appears to have been published since 1975.

This study aims at filling a major gap in the literature on this subject. It is a first endeavour to describe and analyse in broad terms the establishment of all professedly Marxist regimes. It should be stressed that what follows is not an attempt to present an exhaustive account of the emergence of these regimes. In-depth case studies of how they emerged, and in many cases ceased to exist, would have resulted in many volumes of written work. Here, essentially, an historical map has been created. Such an approach best illustrates the main arguments advanced in this study.

The first chapter sets out the criterion for the inclusion of a particular regime in this study; namely, its ability to be recognized as an independent state in international law and its self-ascription as Marxist. It also briefly discusses the terminology which has been used by scholars in describing the coming to power of Marxist regimes. Since none of the terms presently used appears to define adequately the varying processes which brought to power the Marxist regimes, it is suggested that these are best summarized by the term 'establishment'. Such a term encompasses both the multiplicity of factors involved in the coming to power and the time-scale during which these processes take place.

Chapters 2 and 3 are devoted to the critical review of literature and to the various typologies of 'communist takeovers', respectively. Chapters 4, 5 and 6 discuss the establishment of the Marxist regimes during three clearly identifiable periods. The first period between 1917 and 1924 is linked directly with the Bolshevik revolution and its immediate consequences on the peripheries of the former tsarist empire. The establishment of the Marxist regimes during the second period between 1939 and 1957 reflect the extension of the 'socialist commonwealth' in the aftermath of the Second World War. The third period between 1959 and 1979 is linked with the surging national liberation movements in Asia, Africa and the Caribbean, which had hitherto been latent. Finally, Chapter 7 surveys the whole historical nexus of the overall establishment process. It also suggests a new approach to the subject area, one which concentrates on the analysis of the time and geographical context as well as on the causes which led to the emergence of these regimes.

This project has in many different ways proved a challenging undertaking. The search for relevant and sometimes quite obscure material required a good deal of perseverance. I have found all this rewarding in various ways, though the scope of the project appeared at times daunting and overwhelming.

I should like to thank warmly my friend and colleague Michael Waller for reading the manuscript and for his most useful comments and suggestions.

My deep gratitude also goes to my wife Martha, for her encouragement and tolerance, and for keeping our children away from my desk during the long hours of writing this book. This study would have never been completed without her help.

Bogdan Szajkowski

University College,
Cardiff

Contents

Chapter 1

The process of establishment

The subject of this book is the establishment of Marxist regimes and its object is to identify and analyse in broad terms the components of the different establishment processes of these regimes and to suggest a new approach to their appraisal. The criterion for a particular regime's inclusion in this study, in addition to its ideological character, was also its ability to be recognized as an independent state in international law. For the purpose of this study the characteristics of statehood as defined in the Montevideo Convention of 1933 have been employed, according to which

The state as a person of international law should possess the following qualifications: (a) a permanent population; (b) defined territory; (c) a government; and (d) capacity to enter into relations with other states[1].

In view of the above, not included here are state governments in India[2] or provisional governments such as the Provisional Revolutionary Committee established in Białystok on 30 July 1920[3], the Provisional Revolutionary Government of the Republic of South Vietnam established on 8 June 1969[4] and the Provisional Democratic Government formed on 4 December 1947 by Markos Vafiadis, commander of the Democratic Army, the military wing of the Communist Party of Greece[5].

An explanation is due as to why the term 'establishment' is used here in preference to other terms[6]. The reason is that in a great many cases the way these regimes came to power are too diverse to be grouped together under one particular label. For example there was a *coup d'état* in Benin, a governmental crisis in Czechoslovakia, a nationalist war of independence in Angola, a presidential proclamation in Somalia, a revolution in Bavaria and an imposition of government in the People's Republic of Kampuchea. In all these cases and many others the end-product was a Marxist regime.

The term establishment encompasses the continuing process of laying down the roots of a Marxist regime until such a regime is able to function within its ascribed framework. The regimes with which this study is concerned were set up through varying processes, and consequently no uniform terminal point for the establishment process of these regimes could be determined. In some cases it was an official proclamation, in others the adoption of a new constitution, while in yet others it was a merger of different parties or the formation of a Leninist party. Since the establishment of the Bolshevik regime on 25 October 1917 in Russia, fifty-three Marxist regimes have come into being over the period of the past six decades.

Included here in the category of Marxist regimes are all those whose leaders profess to be Marxist in the sense that they subscribe to, or claim to subscribe to, a particular 'scientific theory' of the laws of the development of human society and human history. The political leadership of these countries claim that this 'scientific doctrine' consists of the discovery of objective causal relationships; it is used to analyse the contradictions which arise between goals and actualities in the pursuit of a common destiny. The acceptance by the ruling elites in these countries of this conceptual framework was a further criterion for inclusion in this book.

The author is quite aware of the problems of taking self-ascription as the basis for accepting a regime as Marxist. There is, of course, an important distinction between, on the one hand, China, Vietnam, Laos, Cambodia, Mozambique and Yugoslavia, where a long-established communist/nationalist party's accession to power was the result of a particular relationship between the party and an overwhelming number of peasantry in these countries, which matured over a period of time; and, on the other hand, states like Somalia, Ethiopia, the People's Democratic Republic of Yemen and Angola, where Marxism and its structures were accepted almost overnight in return for military hardware and economic survival kits; and Benin and the Congo, where Marxism was rather abruptly embraced by military governments.

It would seem that self-ascription as a multipurpose indicator in any comparative exercise is clearly more fruitful than basing such an exercise on models and categories shaped on the basis of an earlier situation and which, for that very reason, may not be capable of making sense of the new phenomena. Self-ascription, of course, also provides a hypothesis. In addition, common rhetoric is an important factor in politics affecting, in particular, the legitimacy of a leadership which espouses that rhetoric. It should also be emphasized that communism must be seen as a movement, and movements grow by a process of diffusion which involves not only proselytization but also self-ascription[7].

The regimes considered in this study are variously called People's Republic, People's Democratic Republic, Democratic Republic or Socialist Republic. These designations in general terms denote the economic and political structures of the respective societies and indicate the progression from one type of society to another. This progression relates to the stages in the revolutionary process, from bourgeois democratic revolution to socialist revolution, and consequently to the economic development of these societies, their state structure and the role of the state in the economy.

The essential stages of this progression may be summarized as follows. The first stage of the revolutionary process is that of popular anti-feudal, anti-imperialist or, as in the case of Eastern Europe during the Second World War, anti-fascist movements partially led by the working class which lays the foundations for the next stage, that of the popular democratic revolution. During this period the working class is not yet in complete control but shares power with the peasantry and the lower middle classes. Nevertheless, the political structure, described as a dictatorship of the workers and peasants, enables them to embark on radical economic reforms, among them agrarian reform and nationalization of the larger industries, transport and banking.

The gradual transformation of the popular democratic revolution, through the assumption by the proletariat of its leading role in the society, into the socialist revolution involves further reshaping of the political and economic structures. In particular, this means the attainment of the workers' (communist) party's supreme political power, the beginning of the collectivization of land, the reduction of the private sector by further socialization and the initiation of long-term economic planning.

The completion of the socialist revolution is characterized by the creation of an integral socialist economic system involving the abolition of the private sector and the total collectivization of agriculture. In addition, class struggle, so characteristic of the early stages of the revolutionary process, now disappears, and the workers, peasants and intelligentsia form a united people, a socialist nation. As a formal expression of the victory of socialism the name of the country is changed to a Socialist Republic.

The general scheme of the societies' development towards communism is, on the whole, reflected in the self-ascriptive terminology of the regimes included in this book. However, it should also be remembered that internal and external political factors may have influenced the choice of a particular description[8].

Excluded from this study are Marxist coalition governments formed with the participation of a Marxist party, namely Chile under the Popular Unity Government, the Democratic Republic of Madagascar, San Marino and Zimbabwe.

San Marino was governed by a coalition of the San Marino Communist Party (PCSM) and the San Marino Socialist Party without interruption from 1945 to 1957. The Great and General Council, composed of sixty deputies elected by universal suffrage, was until March 1957 in the hands of the communist–socialist majority, which held thirty-five seats, nineteen of which belonged to the communists. The Marxist regime was, however, a coalition of two left-wing and to a certain extent competing parties.

Similarly, in Chile, the Allende Popular Unity government inaugurated on 3 November 1970 was a coalition composed of six left-wing parties[9].

Madagascar since 1975 has been ruled by a Supreme Revolutionary Council presided over by Lieutenant-Commander Didier Ratsiraka. The Council's political organization is the National Front for the Defence of the Revolution, a broad coalition of Marxist and left-wing parties[10]. However, no single party has gained overall control over it.

The government of Zimbabwe consists of representatives of two former nationalist guerrilla forces, the Zimbabwe African National Union (ZANU) and the Zimbabwe African People's Union (ZAPU). In addition the coalition includes two unaffiliated representatives of the white community in Zimbabwe.

For lack of even the most essential data, also excluded from this study is the People's Socialist Republic of Nambuangongo, established around February 1961 in the Dembos forests in north-western Nambuangongo (between the rivers Loge and Dang) in the immediate wake of the 1961 rising in Luanda. The republic will probably remain the most curious and distant echo of the Bolshevik revolution. Therefore, in spite of the fact that it has not proved possible to unearth any data on this example, it does seem important that its existence should be put on record.

1 D. W. Greig, *International Law*, 2nd edn, p. 93
2 On Kerala and West Bengal see, for example, Donald S. Zagoria, 'Kerala and West Bengal', *Problems of Communism*. On the United Front Governments of West Bengal in 1967 and 1969–1970 see, for example S. Ray, 'Communism in India: Ideological and Tactical Differences Among Four Parties', *Studies in Comparative Communism*, v, Nos 2 and 3, Summer/Autumn 1972, 161–233. On Kerala see, for example, G. Heeger, 'The Sources of Communist Political Power in Kerala' in Thomas T. Hammond, *The Anatomy of Communist Takeovers*

3 For a short historical account of the Provisional Revolutionary Committee for Poland see M. K. Dziewanowski, *The Communist Party of Poland*, pp. 92–95. For texts of the decrees issued by the Committee see *Tymczasowy Komitet Rewolucyjny Polski*

4 For some details on the Congress of People's Representatives which established the Provisional Government see R. F. Staar, *Yearbook on International Communist Affairs – 1970*, pp. 721–725. The Twelve-Point Action Programme of the Provisional Revolutionary Government can be found in ibid, pp. 838–841

5 For a comprehensive account of this period see, for example, D. G. Kousoulas, *Revolution and Defeat: The Story of the Greek Communist Party*; C. M. Woodhouse, *The Struggle for Greece 1941–1949*

6 Thomas T. Hammond, in his book *The Anatomy of Communist Takeovers*, employs rather indiscriminately the term 'takeover' without even defining it. The closest he comes to a definition of the term is when he states: 'The reason for the use of "takeovers" is simply that the process whereby the Communists gained power often cannot accurately be described as a "revolution" (p. xvi). For the purpose of this study a revolution is understood as a popular movement whereby a significant change in the economic and social structure of a nation or society is effected. In such a movement the overthrow of an existing government and the substitution by another takes place at an early stage

7 For a discussion on this see M. Waller and B. Szajkowski, 'The Communist Movement: From Monolith to Polymorph' in *Marxist Governments: A World Survey* ed. by B. Szajkowski), Vol. 1, pp. 1–19.

8 For further discussion see I. Kovacs, *New Elements in the Evolution of Socialist Constitution*; Z. Mlynar, *K teorii socialisticke demokracie;* B. I. Schwartz, *China and the Soviet Theory of 'People's Democracy';* B.S. Man'kovski, *Norodno-demokratischeskie republike Tsentral'noi i Iugo Vostochnoi Evropy – gosudarsta sotsialistischeskogo tipa;* T. Szymczak, *Organy władzy i administracji europejskich panstw socjalistycznych*

9 Besides the Communist Party of Chile these were the Chilean Socialist Party, the Radical Party, the Christian Left, the Movement of United Popular Action and the Independent Popular Action

10 The Front includes six parties which support the Charter of the Malagasy Socialist Revolution: the Vanguard of the Malagasy Revolution (AREMA), the Independence Congress Party of Madagascar (AKFM), the Party of Proletarian Power (MFM), the Popular Movement for National Unity (VONJY) and the Malagasy Socialist Party

Chapter 2

A review of the literature

Before embarking on the analysis of the establishment of the fifty-three regimes to which this study is devoted it would perhaps be useful to glance at the literature already devoted to the subject. Practically all the books (with one notable exception) either do not deal with the subject-matter or look at it in a biased if not tendentious way. It seems that no comprehensive work dealing with all the regimes has emerged since 1917. Whether these regimes exist at present or are 'historical' communist regimes, their process of emergence is part of the subject-matter. It would appear that no rigorous study of the subject-matter really exists, and what has been written so far leaves much to be desired not only in terms of data but also in its intellectual quality.

One of the earliest works on this subject is Seton-Watson's *The Eastern European Revolution*[1]. Although undoubtedly a work of high scholarship when it was published, now most of it has tarnished through the passage of time. On the whole, the work is a characteristic reflection of literature on Eastern Europe written at the height of the cold war. In the author's own words, 'the purpose of this book is both to describe and analyse the Sovietisation of Eastern Europe'[2].

In that respect the book does not differ from practically all other works on this subject. It looks at the post-war developments in Eastern Europe from the point of view of Soviet power and one of its techniques – Sovietization. It tells us nothing about the rebuilding of social and political structures in societies ravaged by war, social processes and political mobilization. Although the book includes a wealth of data which is of enormous value even today, its interpretation is from a Western scholar's 'vantage point'. In some parts the material selected for the purpose of analysis seems to be highly unbalanced. For example, the section on Poland[3] consists basically of the story of Stanisław Mikołajczyk, his Peasants' Party, and his struggles with Stalin, Bierut and Gomułka. However important, Mikołajczyk's role in post-war Poland was only a part of the general picture. But by concentrating on this pro-Western politician and his defence, Seton-Watson fails to give any insight into the complex machinery he calls the seizure of power. The proposition that the Russian tanks produced a steamroller effect in Eastern Europe, and that in its aftermath came the communist regime, is simplistic and indefensible.

Burks' contribution, entitled 'Eastern Europe', to a book by Black and Thornton, *Communism and Revolution; the Strategic Uses of Political Violence*[4], suffers from similar limitations. It looks at the emergence of the communist regimes from the point of view of Soviet expansion, including an interesting survey of Russian attitudes towards Eastern Europe during the war. The main gist of this chapter is an analysis of the familiar techniques of the seizure of power which by 1964, when the book was published, became clichés or variations on the same theme.

Black's chapter entitled 'The Anticipation of Communist Revolutions' in the book mentioned above[5] is a first attempt to look at some communist revolutions in Asia (Gilan, Tannu Tuva, Vietnam and others) as well as in Eastern Europe. His contribution, however, is not really about 'seizure of power' or 'takeover' but communist revolutions in general, both successful and unsuccessful. Consequently the subject of the establishment of Marxist regimes is lost in the wider analysis of revolutions as a whole. But even here the clear pattern of looking at these developments from a cold-war perspective is unmistakably present, thus devaluing much of the analysis.

In 1975 Hammond published a collection of thirty-three papers in a bulky volume entitled *The Anatomy of Communist Takeovers*[6]. The title of the book gives a clear indication of the general treatment of the subject, although the editor never defines what is meant by 'takeover'. The papers included in the volume deal, however, with varieties of 'takeovers'; attempted, successful, unsuccessful, aborted and even a 'takeover that remained in limbo'[7]. The volume attempts to deal with almost the entire geographical spectrum, with the exclusion of Africa. Surprisingly, however, there are chapters on the Hungarian revolution of 1956, the 'Prague Spring' and the source of communist power in Kerala – all in the context of takeovers.

But the most unfortunate aspect of this volume (which is certainly useful as a reference work and introductory background reading) is that most of the contributors to it (notable exceptions being Boris Goldenberg writing on Cuba and Jurgen Domes on China) still look at the coming to power of the various communist regimes from the point of view of the extension of Soviet power. As in previous works, the emphasis here is again placed on the techniques of the takeovers. A serious gap is any mention of the Marxist regimes on the African continent and on the Saudi Arabian peninsula. A book published in 1975 should have included some reference to the then existing communist regimes in the Congo, South Yemen and Somalia. This omission is more than just an oversight or misunderstanding. Surprisingly inaccurate statements can also be found which, to some extent, demonstrate the book's general intellectual calibre. For example, on page 27 Hammond states: 'It is significant that every country that has ever become Communist was invaded by the Red Army except for three – Albania, Vietnam and Cuba.' Writing in 1974 he should surely have been aware that this was clearly not the case with several of the earlier regimes such as Hungary, Slovakia or Bavaria (incidentally all included in this volume). But that such a statement is expected to apply, for example, to China, the Congo or Somalia is curious indeed.

Overall, the volume lacks intellectual rigour. Most of the contributions are heavily biased and some inconsistent and confusing[8]. One should emphasize that the volume is basically about the technique of what Hammond terms 'takeovers' while the present study aims at examining and analysing how the communist regimes were established.

Soviet military, political and economic expansion through the creation of other communist regimes is the dominant theme of Hammond's article 'Moscow and Communist Takeovers' in the January–February 1976 issue of *Problems of Communism*[9]. The importance of this article seems to lie in the attempted clarification of the term 'Communist takeover'. According to Hammond:

> this term was chosen rather than the expression 'Communist revolution' because relatively few countries have become communist through genuine revolutions. Most of the Communist regimes in Eastern Europe, for example, came to power not through revolutions but through the intervention of the Red Army. The Communists in the Indian state of Kerala, on the other hand, won control of the state government in free elections. The word 'takeover' covers the whole spectrum of possible means of taking power both in indigenous revolutions, like those in Vietnam, and revolutions exported by the USSR, like those in the Baltic States and Poland. For the purpose of this discussion, a Communist takeover occurs whenever Communists gain control of a country by any means, whether native or foreign, peaceful or violent[10].

This is strange logic indeed.

The word 'takeover' normally implies the imposition of power through the use of force, and no doubt this is the implication in Hammond's analysis. In the language of political science and for most students of the discipline, free elections, whether in Kerala or Washington, are free elections and not takeovers. Also the term 'revolution' has by now acquired an established meaning in political science. Hammond's concept is not only confusing but its intellectual credibility is questionable to say the least. The passage quoted from the article adequately summarizes its general tenor and intellectual level. Overall the article is a general glance at the main arguments included in his book.

Gripp, in *The Political System of Communism*, devotes one chapter to the 'Coming of Power of Communist Parties'[11]. The title of the chapter suggests a partially new approach to the study of the establishment of the communist regimes, but unfortunately this is not the case. Gripp indeed looks at the individual communist parties' coming to power but his classification includes curiously misplaced examples. Thus, in a category of armed *coups* by native communists we find as examples China and Cuba. It would seem that he confuses communist-led guerrilla wars with armed *coups*. But Cuba does not warrant inclusion in this category in any case, since the communist input into guerrilla war was practically non-existent. Even more surprising is the inclusion of Albania and Yugoslavia in the category of 'non-violent actions' by native communists. Gripp seems to negate completely the partisan experience of both parties.

Further on in the chapter he falls into a well-known trap of describing Soviet techniques of takeover, and has to conclude that 'the importance of the USSR in communist parties' coming to power is obvious . . .'[12]. No attempt is made to describe or analyse the national liberation movements in Vietnam, Albania and Yugoslavia, all, according to Gripp, having come to power through non-violent actions. On the whole, however, Gripp attempts to present a more balanced view and analysis, although it includes several very basic errors and inaccuracies, as mentioned above.

Wesson, in *Communism and Communist Systems*, has devoted one chapter to 'The Rise of Communism'[13]. The chapter is useful introductory reading on the rise of the Marxist regimes in China, Vietnam and Cuba but gives a rather pedestrian account and very little analysis of Eastern Europe and Korea, which it terms 'Imposed Communism'. In spite of the fact that the book was published in 1978, the chapter makes no reference to the 'rise' of the communist regimes in Africa, South Yemen, Laos or Kampuchea, let alone any of the 'historical' regimes in the 1920s. His particular emphases are on methods of 'Communization' and therefore should be seen as another example of literature still influenced by the cold-war analysis.

Some of the most useful material, although only in part related to the subject-matter here, are the articles in McCauley's *Communist Power in Europe, 1944-1949*[14]. The book includes a detailed account and analysis of the emergence of five regimes in Eastern Europe. The articles on Poland, East Germany and Czechoslovakia are particularly illuminating.

On the whole, however, the literature on the establishment of Marxist–Leninist regimes is, at best, disappointing or, more to the point, unhelpful and tendentious, heavily reflecting the well-trodden cold-war path of analysis based on the extension of Soviet power.

It would have been more fruitful for the study and understanding of the processes that brought about the establishment of the Marxist regimes in fifty-three diverse societies if more emphasis were placed on the history of the respective nationalist movement and its links, if any, with indigenous communist groups or parties which might have had particular influence on it. The interrelation between all the components of the various processes appears to be as important as that of the principal one, the Soviet Union. Yet there appears to be no literature, for example, on relations between the various communist parties or governments in the immediate post-Second World War period. Another important discussion missing in the literature on this subject so far is a balanced account of communist activities at the grass-roots level prior to their assumption of power. In Chapters 4, 5 and 6 an attempt is made to remedy some of these omissions wherever there were sufficient data on which to draw.

1 Hugh Seton-Watson, *The Eastern European Revolution*
2 Ibid., p. viii
3 Ibid. pp. 171–179
4 Cyril E. Black and Thomas P. Thornton (eds), *Communism and Revolution; the Strategic Uses of Political Violence*
5 Ibid., pp. 417–448
6 Thomas T. Hammond, *The Anatomy of Communist Takeovers*
7 Ibid., p. 163
8 See, for example, D.J. Duncanson, 'Vietnam; From Bolshevism to People's War' and Dae-Sook Suh, 'A Preconceived Formula for Sovietization: The Communist Takeover of North Korea'
9 Thomas T. Hammond, 'Moscow and Communist Takeovers', *Problems of Communism*, January-February 1976, 48–67
10 Ibid., pp. 48–49

11 Richard C. Gripp, *The Political System of Communism*, pp. 19–39
12 Ibid., p. 32
13 Robert G. Wesson, *Communism and Communist Systems*, pp. 59–99
14 Martin McCauley, *Communist Power in Europe, 1944–1949*

Chapter 3

Why a typology?

Let us now turn our attention to the various typologies of the 'coming to power of communist states' or 'communist takeovers' that are suggested by the literature. It should be emphasized that these typologies have emerged from a literature that has concentrated mainly on the techniques of 'takeovers'.

It is perhaps important to state from the outset that it is not the intention here to attempt to offer an alternative typology but merely to list and compare those suggested thus far. The reasons for this reluctance to offer yet another typology will hopefully become obvious during the discussion in this chapter.

Seton-Watson, in his *Eastern European Revolution*, employs a three-stage typology of Sovietization[1]:

(1) The first stage is the genuine coalition, during which several political parties participate in national governments.
(2) The second stage is that of the bogus coalition. The governments still contain non-communist parties but these are represented by men chosen no longer by the Party membership but by the communists.
(3) The third stage is the 'monolithic' regime. An important feature of this stage is the forced fusion of the well-purged social democrats with the communists in a United Workers' Party.

In an enlarged and updated version of his *East European Revolutions* published in 1960 under the title *From Lenin to Khrushchev: The History of World Communism*[2] he suggests three ways in wich communist parties have come to power:

(1) By winning power principally by their own efforts (Russia, Yugoslavia, Albania, China).
(2) By obtaining power through armed intervention from outside (Azerbaijan, Armenia, Georgia, Mongolia, Baltic States, Poland, Romania, the German Democratic Republic, North Korea).
(3) by combining (1) and (2) above (Bulgaria, Hungary, Czechoslovakia).

A somewhat different typology is used by Burks[3] in categorizing the parties according to the type of process by which they came to power:

(1) Under enemy occupation a Party was built up and carried out guerrilla action, thus identifying the communist party with the national interest. After the withdrawal of occupational forces the communist guerrillas simply and automatically took over (Albania and Yugoslavia).

(2) In countries in which the communists enjoyed significant popular support and in which the Party had an important history, communists formed an anti-fascist coalition (Czechoslovakia and Hungary).

(3) The communist party had a long history and considerable popular support; but the State in question was on the Axis side during the Second World War and was therefore attacked and occupied by the Red Army, which then established a puppet government (Bulgaria).

(4) In states in which the communist party had little popular support a baggage-train government was brought in as part of the occupying Red Army (German Democratic Republic, Poland, Romania).

Dallin and Breslauer, in *Political Terror in Communist Systems*[4], also suggest three types of cases in which communist parties came to power:

(1) Through a *coup* and following civil war (Russia).

(2) Through armed struggle from expanding territoral bases (China, Yugoslavia, Albania, Cuba, Vietnam).

(3) Through the institution of regimes imposed with help from an external military force (most of Eastern Europe, Mongolia, North Korea).

Black[5], in analysing the revolutionary methods which the communists found most useful in achieving power, suggests four patterns according to the extent of political violence and outside assistance involved:

(1) In a violent domestic revolution the local communist party seizes power as a result of extended civil war and generally with assistance, short of armed occupation by a foreign communist state (Russia, China, Yugoslavia, Albania and North Vietnam).

(2) In a 'revolution from without' extensive political violence is likewise involved but the decisive influence is exerted by a foreign communist army which installs the local communists in power (Gilan, Tannu Tuva, Mongolia, Baltic States, Poland, Romania, Bulgaria, Hungary, Czechoslovakia, East Germany, North Korea, Kurdistan and Azerbaijan).

(3) In a 'revolution from above', a manipulative revolution, foreign communist influence is exerted by essentially non-violent means to assist a local communist party in establishing a position of decisive political influence[6].

(4) In an electoral revolution, a communist party is voted into office without any more than incidental political violence (Kerala, San Marino).

Gripp[7] suggests the following typology in which communist parties came to power:

(1) Independent action;
    (a) armed *coups* (USSR, China, Cuba);
    (b) non-violent action (Albania, Yugoslavia, North Vietnam, Czechoslovakia).

(2) Armed intervention;
    (a) nationwide occupation (Mongolia, Romania, Bulgaria, Hungary, Poland);
    (b) partial occupation (North Korea, German Democratic Republic).

Hammond's typology of communist takeovers consists of the following types[8].

(1) Outright annexation of territory by a communist state (Tannu Tuva, borderlands of the former tsarist empire, Baltic States, Kurile Islands, Tibet and other small areas).

(2) Installation of a communist regime outside Russia by the Soviet Army (Mongolia, Tannu Tuva, Poland, German Democratic Republic, Hungary, Bulgaria, Romania and North Korea).

(3) Counter-revolutions in heretical communist countries by the Soviet Army (German Democratic Republic, Hungary, Czechoslovakia).

(4) A revolution in the urban centres, based largely on the proletariat followed by conquest of the urban centres (Russia).

(5) A revolution in the countryside based mainly on the peasants followed by conquest of the urban centres (China, Yugoslavia, Albania, North Vietnam).

(6) A completely legal takeover through free elections (San Marino, Kerala and West Bengal).

(7) Semi-legal takeover through considerable popular support combined with armed threats (Czechoslovakia).

(8) A non-communist leader seizes power and then decides to adopt communism (Cuba).

As can be seen from the typologies listed above, there is a great deal of inconsistency and confusion. This is partly due to the fact that the authors of these classifications have tried to look at the subject from several diverse points of view (revolution, takeover, foreign policy issues) and have applied their categories to the subject, rather than the other way round. Thus they have tried to see if an analysis of the processes that brought about the communist regimes in societies differing in a multitude of ways could suggest similarities.

These similarities are rather general, and so perhaps they can only be couched in general terms. This is particularly so in view of the nature of the individual establishment processes which occur in a great variety of circumstances, with tactics dictated by those circumstances differing from country to country and from time to time. The obvious similarities are that these are revolutions (of various types) in which the communist groups or parties play an important, if not decisive, part. This, however, hardly necessitates a typology, and tells us little, if anything, about what generates these revolutions, the conduct of such events, the strength and composition of the various forces involved, the interaction between them and the many other factors which accompanied them.

Typologies tend to oversimplify the remarkable diversity of the processes by which the fifty-three Marxist regimes were established. As can be seen clearly from the individual studies in the next three chapters, the establishment of the regimes considered in this book has been in each and every case the result of a unique process determined by a multitude of factors, each of which needs to be examined in its own context.

1 Hugh Seton-Watson, *The Eastern European Revolution*, pp. 169–171
2 Hugh Seton-Watson, *From Lenin to Khruschev: The History of World Communism*, p. 330
3 R. V. Burks, 'Eastern Europe' in *Communism and Revolution; the Strategic Uses of Political Violence* (ed. by C. E. Black and T. P. Thornton), pp. 86–89
4 Alexander Dallin and George W. Breslauer, *Political Terror in Communist Systems*, p. 14
5 Cyril E. Black, The Anticipation of Communist Revolutions', in Black and Thornton (eds.), op.cit. (note 3), pp. 417–425

6 Black finds no example of a revolution from above 'but perhaps Cuba when events in that country run their course, will fulfil the requirements for this model', ibid., p. 422
7 R. C. Gripp, *The Political System of Communism*, p. 32
8 Thomas T. Hammond, 'A Summing Up' in *The Anatomy of Communist Take-overs* (ed. by Thomas T. Hammond), pp. 67–68

Chapter 4

The Russian revolution and its sequel

The history of the communist movement in the period from 1917 to 1924 is normally presented as the history of the formation of the Soviet Union after the success of the Bolsheviks in the Russian revolution. There is every reason for so presenting it. If, before 1917, the hub of theory and organization in the Marxist world was the German Social Democratic Party, here now was revolution itself, and the creation of a socialist order on the vast territories of the tsarist empire. Moreover, since the Soviet state, once established as a state, went on not only to incorporate almost all of that territory in itself but also to dominate – organizationally through the Comintern – the entire communist movement for some forty years, it is difficult not to view the 'October revolution' as the logical source of that domination. However, now that the communist movement has passed from the organizational unity of those forty years to a situation of considerable variety or variation, it is possible with the hindsight of history to see round the edges of the monolith of the early years of Soviet power and to present the revolutionary events of 1917-1924 in a rather different light.

For, precisely, these were revolutionary *events*, and not just a single event. And if the result was that they all were either engulfed in the creation of the Soviet state or else failed to establish a new order as the Bolsheviks had done in Russia, *at the time of their occurrence* these events were in most cases autonomous. The local Bolsheviks who established themselves in the Ukraine, Belorussia, Khorezm, Armenia, Tannu Tuva and other lands were not only in a sense part of the Russian revolution; in another equally important sense they were autonomous attempts to establish a socialist order on individual national territories. In most cases their subsequent incorporation within the Soviet Union was either resisted or met, at the most, with disappointed acquiescence. Moreover, the Bremen, Gilan, Hungarian, Slovak and Bavarian revolutionary events of the years 1918-1920 were so short-lived that they have been eclipsed by the creation and development of the Soviet Union and, in any case, had they been successful themselves might well have been caught up in that process. They were nonetheless events which, for the historian, can be disassociated from it.

The presentation of those events which follows therefore requires some words of explanation. The reader will doubtless be surprised to find the Bremen, Bratislava, Finnish and Estonian revolutionary upheavals being treated at the same level as the Bolshevik revolution in Petrograd. He will also, perhaps, be dismayed to find the Russian revolution itself *reduced* in status, and its treatment, in comparison with more usual treatments, severely telescoped and somewhat schematic. This reduction is deliberate. In any case, whoever wishes to read more about the Russian revolution has a vast literature at his disposal. Far less easily accessible and far less visible within the literature are treatments of those other revolutionary events which the writing of Soviet history, in the East as in the West, has deprived of their autonomy and interest in the history of the communist movement.

Let us now attempt to construct a historical map of the emergence of the Marxist regimes between 1917 and 1924.

1917, 25 October
The Military Revolutionary Committee of the Petrograd Soviet of Workers' and Soldiers' Deputies

The Bolsheviks' seizure of power in Russia is perhaps best symbolically summed up in the proclamation of the Military Revolutionary Committee issued on 25 October 1917:

> All railroad stations and the telephone, post and telegraph offices are ocupied. The telephones of the Winter Palace and the staff Headquarters are disconnected. The State Bank is in our hands. The Winter Palace and the Staff have surrendered. The shock troops are dispersed, the cadets paralyzed. The armoured cars have sided with the Revolutionary Committee. The Cossacks refused to obey the government. The Provisional Government is deposed. Power is in the hands of the Revolutionary Committee of the Petrograd Soviet of Workers' and Soldiers' Deputies[1].

By the time the Second All-Russian Congress of Soviets opened at 11 p.m. on 25 October the revolutionary forces were in full control of the capital. The following evening, the second and last meeting of the Congress adopted the decrees on peace and on the land, and approved the composition of the Council of People's Commissars – the Provisional Workers' and Peasants' Government – which in reality meant the establishment of the first Marxist regime.

At the time of its assumption of power the Provisional Workers' and Peasants' Government determined that it would exercise its authority until the convocation of the constituent Assembly, for which elections were fixed on 25 November 1917. In these elections the Bolsheviks secured 175 out of 707 seats, with the majority, 410, claimed by the Social Revolutionaries[2]. The remaining seats were distributed among the Kadets and other middle-class and conservative parties. These results made it certain that the Constituent Assembly would serve as a rallying-point for opposition to the Soviet regime.

The first and only meeting of the Assembly took place on 18 January 1918[3]. The meeting was suspended at 5 p.m. on 19 January, apparently at the request of the soldiers guarding the entrance to the building, who became tired[4]. It never met again. Later the same day it was dissolved by the Central Executive Committee of the Soviets of Workers', Soldiers' and Peasants' Deputies. This decision was confirmed on 23 January 1918 by the latter. At the closing session of the Congress on 31 January the assembled elegates unanimously approved a proposal to abandon the designation of 'Provisional Workers' and Peasants' Government' and to refer to the supreme power henceforth as the Workers' and Peasants' Government of the Russian Socialist Soviet Republic. Another resolution declared that the Republic was 'created on the basis of a voluntary union of the peoples of Russia in the form of a federation of the Soviet republics of these peoples'[5]. The first Marxist regime was subsequently referred to as the Russian Socialist Federative Soviet Republic (RSFSR).

These changes were subsequently embodied in the first constitution of the new regime published on 3 July 1918. On the same day it was submitted for approval to the Central Committee of the Party as a preliminary to its adoption on 10 July 1918 by the Fifth All-Russian Congress of Soviets. The constitution enunciated the federal character of the republic, which was named the Russian Socialist Federative Soviet Republic.

The RSFSR subsequently became a nucleus for unions with other republics, which eventually led to the creation of the Union of Soviet Socialist Republics (USSR) on 30 December 1922.

1917, 25 December
The Ukranian Soviet Republic

The Ukrainian Soviet Republic was proclaimed on 25 December 1917 by the All-Ukranian Congress of Soviets[6]. Its rule, however, lasted for only a few weeks. On 2 March 1918 the Ukrainian Soviet Government was forced to abandon Kiev when the German armies swept across the Ukraine.

Later that year within a few days of the German collapse, a Provisional Workers' and Peasants' Government of the Ukraine constituted itself at Kursk, in the RSFSR[7]. On 29 November 1918 it issued a manifesto announcing its assumption of power and the transfer of the land to peasants and the factories to the workers. A few days later, after a three-day general strike, a soviet seized power in Kharkov on 12 December. Around the same time local soviets seized power in Odessa (12 December), Ekaterinoslaw (26 December) and elsewhere, and the Red Army began its drive westward, capturing Kiev in February 1919. On 10 March 1919 a constitution of the Ukrainian Soviet Socialist Republic was officially adopted by the third All-Ukrainian Congress of Soviets. However, during the same year the Ukrainian Soviet regime was dissolved again when the anti-Bolshevik forces, under the command of General Denikin, occupied large sections of the Ukraine, including Kiev.

The third attempt to consolidate a Soviet regime in the Ukraine began after the defeat of Denikin in December 1919 and the recapture of Kiev by the Red Army. By February 1920 Soviet authority had been re-established in the main centres.

But this did not bring peace to the Ukraine. In 1920 another incursion into the Ukraine, this time by Polish armies supported by anti-Soviet nationalists, occupied Kiev for some six weeks in May–June 1920. With the thrusting back of the Polish invasion the Ukrainian Soviet regime reasserted its power throughout the country, though partisan activities against it continued for some months to come.

On 28 December 1920 the Ukrainian Soviet Socialist Republic concluded a treaty of alliance with the RSFSR, which provided essentially for military union between the two countries. The treaty laid a foundation for the eventual Union of Socialist Soviet Republics and the creation, on 30 December 1922, of the USSR[8].

1918, 28 January to 1918, 5 May
The Finnish Socialist Republic of Workers

The Republic was proclaimed on 28th January 1918 after the seizure of power in the industrial cities of southern Finland by the Red Guards[9]. The Finnish Red Guards received considerable military and political assistance from Russia, at least until the signing of the Treaty of Brest-Litovsk in March 1918, when Soviet Russia formally relinquished any remaining rights to invervene in Finnish affairs[10].

On 1 March the Soviet Government signed a treaty with the Finnish Socialist Republic of Workers. This was on the eve of the military evacuation required by the Russians under the Brest-Litovsk Treaty. In spite of the fact that a force of at least a thousand Red Army soldiers stayed behind, it must have been known to the Russian leaders that the Republic could not survive. Nevertheless the Soviet–Finnish treaty created a joint citizenship. The German army captured Helsinki on 5 May 1918 and the leaders of the Finnish Socialist Republic of Workers went to Russia, where in May 1918 they founded the Finnish Communist Party.

1918, 29 November to 1919, February
The Estonian Workers' Commune

The first phase in the establishment of the Marxist regime in Estonia came within days of the Bolshevik seizure of power in Petrograd. At that time the Estonian Bolsheviks had a considerable following in the country[11], including the control of several councils. After the October revolution power passed to the councils in the Baltic provinces. There was no open resistance to the Bolsheviks since the soldiers and sailors stationed there were among the first to recognize the new revolutionary leadership.

On 4 November 1917 the Executive Committee of the Tallin councils set up a Military Revolutionary Committee to exercise governmental authority over the country in the name of the revolutionary proletariat and peasantry. However, the Committee was swept away some six weeks later by the advancing German armies.

The second phase in the establishment of the Estonian Marxist regime began in November 1918, after the Soviet government decided to repudiate the Brest-Litovsk treaty in order 'to embark on the political and military struggle for the liberation of Estonia and Latvia from the yoke of German Imperialism'[12].

On 29 November 1918 Estonian Bolshevik units and Red Army forces occupied the north-eastern town of Narva and proclaimed a Soviet republic under the name of the Estonian Workers' Commune. The new republic, which was headed by the veteran

Estonian Communist leader Jaan Anvelt, was recognized by Moscow on 7 December 1918[13].

The government of the Estonian Workers' Commune had held office for some six weeks when it was overthrown by anti-Bolshevik Estonian and Russian units with the help of volunteers from Finland. Another attempt to recreate the Bolshevik regime was made on the offshore island of Saaremea, where a communist revolt was launched on 16 February 1919. The uprising was suppressed within a week.

1918, 16 December to 1919, 21 April
The Provisional Revolutionary Workers' and Peasants' Government of Lithuania

The Provisional Revolutionary Workers' and Peasants' Government of Lithuania was organized in Vilna on 8 December 1918 by the Central Committee of the Communist Party of Lithuania and Belorussia[14] and formally installed in Vilna on 16 December[15]. When the city was still occupied it was by German troops headed by the veteran communist leader Vincas Mickevicius-Kapsukas, who became the chairman of the Council of People's Commissars and Commissar for Foreign Affairs[16]. The government was recognized on 22 December 1918 by the Russian Soviet Republic.

With the collapse of Germany the Red Army entered Vilna on 5 January 1919, a move which must have further facilitated the functioning of the Bolshevik regime.

The following month, on 3 February, the Second Conference of the Communist Party of Lithuania and Belorussia, responding to a call from the First Congress of the Soviets of Belorussia, decided in favour of federation of the Lithuanian and Belorussian states. This move was endorsed by the First Congress of Soviets of Lithuania, meeting in Vilna between 18 to 23 February 1919, which also adopted a constitution based on that of the RSFSR. With this the communist experiment in establishing a Lithuanian Marxist regime ended[17]. The union was intended as a first step towards a larger federation of all the Soviet republics.

When Vilna fell to Polish forces on 21 April 1919 the Bolshevik government, caught by surprise, fled to Daugavpils, a town on the Russian side of the border with Lithuania. Although the communists still held the north-eastern part of Lithuania, the fall of Vilna signified the virtual end of communist rule in Lithuania.

1918, 22 December to 1920, January
The Latvian Soviet Republic

The Government of Soviet Latvia was created in Moscow on 17 December 1918 from among the members of the Latvian Commissariat which operated within the structure of the Commissariat of Nationality Affairs under Stalin. It was headed by Pēteris Stučka (Piotra Stuchka) and was recognized by Soviet Russia on 22 December 1918, the day on which the Red Army invaded Latvia. After the capture of Riga on 3 January 1919 the regime controlled most of Latvia. In January 1919 the General Congress of the Latvian Councils approved the constitution of the republic, which was based on that of the RSFSR and from which it departed in only a few respects. By June 1919, however, the Red Army and the Stučka government were forced by the Germans to abandon Riga. The easternmost province of Latgale remained under the Soviet Latvian government control until the first days of 1920[18].

1918, 31 December to 1919, 1 January
The Bratislava Soviet Republic

The Bratislava Soviet Republic was organized by Slovak communists, former members of the Federation of Foreign Groups in Russia, with the help of two Hungarian revolutionaries, Jeno Laszlo and Gàbor Kohn. The republic, confined to the city of Bratislava, lasted about thirty-six hours before being crushed by Czech troops[19].

1919, 1 January
The Belorussian Soviet Socialist Republic

The first attempts at the formation of a Marxist regime in Belorussia were made at the end of December 1917. In Minsk a Bolshevik Military Revolutionary Committee, which came into existence after the October revolution, established a Council of People's Commissars of the Western Region and Front and proclaimed the right of 'the toiling people of White Russia to national self-determination'[20]. For a few weeks a rudimentary Soviet government ruled in Minsk until it was overthrown by advancing German armies in February 1918.

Following the German occupation those communists who did not escape to Russia went underground. When in November 1918 the Germans started to evacuate their troops, soviets organized by the underground North-western Region Committee of the Russian Communist Party began to mushroom across the country. Consequently when the Red Army reoccupied Belorussia in December 1918 it found the country in the hands of the soviets[21].

The central government of Belorussia was created by the North-western Regional Committee of the Russian Communist Party which, acting on the instructions of Stalin[22] and of the Party Central Committee, transformed itself into the First Congress of the Communist Party of Belorussia and established on 1 January 1919 a Provisional Government of the Belorussian Socialist Soviet Republic. Its constitution was adopted by the First Belorussian Congress of Soviets of Workers', Soldiers' and Peasants' Deputies, assembled in Minsk on 4 February 1919.

However, even after its formation the Belorussian Marxist regime, like practically all others created around that time, went through a period of tribulations.

In February 1919 Belorussia and Lithuania became a federation (Litbel) which, however, collapsed in April 1919 when Polish troops invaded first Lithuania and later part of Belorussia, including Minsk itself. The country was liberated the following year by the advance of Soviet troops into Poland.

On 16 January 1921 Belorussia signed a treaty of alliance with the RSFSR which was identical in terms to those signed between the RSFSR and the Ukraine, and which laid the foundation for eventual union with the RSFSR. On 30 October 1922 Belorussia joined the USSR.

1919, 10 January to 1919, 4 February
The Bremen Soviet Republic

The republic was proclaimed on 10 January 1919 by the radical Bremen faction of the Communist Party of Germany (Spartakist League). Based on the Workers' and Soldiers' Councils, together with the Bavarian Soviet Republic it was perhaps the most successful example of the revolutionary movement which swept across Germany in the aftermath of the Russian revolution.

The republic was crushed by the Free Corps troops under General Walther von Lüttwitz after being besieged for three days[23].

1919, 21 March to 1919, 1 August
The Hungarian Soviet Republic

The Russian revolution had stirred up a wave of revolutionary enthusiasm also among the peoples of the Austro–Hungarian Empire. Their initial aim was to overthrow the Habsburg monarchy and create sovereign national states. However, in Hungary and later in Slovakia the national revolutions became inseparably linked with social revolutions organized by communist groups, whose members recently returned from Russia.

The formation of the Hungarian Soviet Republic came in the immediate aftermath of the resignation of the coalition government headed by Mihaly Karolyi. Faced with the Entente's ultimatum demanding the surrender of further Hungarian territories to Romania, he called on the Social Democrats to reach an understanding with the Communists to take over the government and to reject the ultimatum. The takeover took place peacefully and without bloodshed.

On 21 March 1919 the Hungarian Social Democratic Party and the Communist Party of Hungary[24] reached agreement to merge. The Document of Unity[25] read in part as follows:

According to the stipulations of the merger, the two parties will jointly participate in the leadership of the new party and the government. The party, in the name of the proletariat, immediately assumes complete authority. The dictatorship of the proletariat will be exercised by the councils of workers, peasants, and soldiers . . .

In order to ensure the complete authority of the proletariat and to [make a stand against] Entente imperialism, the fullest and closest military and spiritual alliance must be concluded with the Russian Soviet government[26].

'The united party's name, pending the revolutionary International's decison on the party's final name', was to be the Hungarian Socialist Party[27].

On the day of its creation the new party formed a new government, the Revolutionary Government Council[28], which derived its powers from the councils of workers, peasants and soldiers established throughout the country. The system of councils was based on the unity of legislative executive and judicial powers.

Although initially the Hungarian Soviet Republic was supported by a substantial number of the population, this began to decline, particularly after the regime attempted to solve the agrarian problem. The government having nationalised the big landed estates, instead of distributing the land to the peasants allowed it to be farmed nominally on a cooperative basis by the former owners. As a result, the peasants became alienated from the industrial working class, their output sank and the food supplies for towns became insufficient.

In addition, the Hungarian Soviet Republic was built also on the assumptions which depended completely on such external factors as military aid from Russia and world revolution, neither of which materialized during the life of Soviet Hungary[29].

The republic lasted for 133 days. Faced with diminishing mass support, Romanian military intervention, the disintegration of its Red Army and Lenin's refusal to send the Soviet Red Army, the Revolutionary Governing Council and the party executive during its joint session on 1 August decided to resign and hand over its powers to the caretaker trade-union government.

1919, 7 April to 1919, 2 May
The Bavarian Soviet Republic

Two periods should be distinguished in the short history of the Bavarian Soviet Republic. Although Bavaria was proclaimed a Soviet Republic on 7 April, the period between 7 April and 12 April is referred to by Mitchell[30] as the 'pseudo' Soviet Republic, since 'there was in reality no government at all'. The measures signed in the name of the 'Revolutionäre Zentralrat' according to him 'existed only on placards'. The second period began with the proclamation on 13 April, when the leader of the Bavarian Communist Party, Eugen Leviné, was elected the chairman of a four-man *Vollzugsrat*.

The republic was crushed by the Free Corps troops despatched to the communist-held areas by the central government in Berlin, but only after nearly two weeks of fighting. Although to all intents and purposes the republic collapsed on 27 April with the resignation of the *Vollzugsrat*, the Bavarian Red Army, led by Rudolf Engelhofer, continued to defend the city of Munich until 2 May.

1919, 16 June to 1919, 4 July
The Slovak Soviet Republic

The establishment, existence and downfall of the Slovak Soviet Republic is closely linked with the short-lived Hungarian Soviet

Republic. After the proclamation of the Hungarian republic on 21 March 1918, Béla Kun promised to implement the Leninist principle of national self-determination. Consequently, communist national committees representing almost every nationality of the former Austro–Hungarian Empire were formed in Budapest. One of them was a joint Czecho-Slovak Committee established on or about 27 March 1919[31], headed by Antonin Janoušek. Its aim was to destroy the old Imperialist–capitalist' Czechoslovakia and 'in the interest of mankind to carry out the revolution in Slovakia and Bohemia'[32].

On 6 June 1919, the Forty-Sixth Regiment of the Hungarian Red Army occupied Košice and two days later, on 8 June, Prešov. Local soviets already existed in most of the Slovak towns and villages. Some were created by former prisoners of war repatriated in early 1919 from Soviet Russia, which included scores of Slovaks who had joined the Russian Commmunist Party. Others were organized after the arrival of the Hungarian Red Army, which was enthusiastically welcomed by the local population. In this atmosphere of high revolutionary zeal which swept across Slovakia, the formation of a political infrastructure would appear to have been only a matter of time.

The Slovak Soviet Republic was proclaimed on 16 June at a mass meeting at Prešov. The proclamation read as follows:

To the proletariat of the whole world!

The victorious and unceasingly advanced revolution enriched its present achievements with a new great result. On Slovak soil, freed from imperialism, today was created an independent Slovak Soviet Republic. The first impulsive action of the proletariat, liberated from the yoke of Czech imperialism, was to realize the right of self-determination which is being exhorted by the oppressors with such a great glory; however, in reality it is being perverted by them. By sudden seizure of power the Slovak workers, soldiers and peasants continue to further the revolutionary front, started by the Russian and Hungarian Soviet Republics, and gain new territories for the great idea of Soviets in the whole world.

The newly-born Slovak Soviet Republic considers its victorious brothers, the Russian and Hungarian Soviet Republics, as natural allies and it stands under the protection of the entire international proletariat, under the protection of its united and responsible workers' international. Its first greeting belongs to the Czech proletarian brothers who are still under the yoke of imperialism.

The Slovak Soviet Republic too is built on the broadest principle of proletarian democracy; however, as far as its foundations for creative work are concerned, it turns its weapons on the dictatorship without mercy against all who threaten this real unperverted democracy, this inalienable right of self-determination. Therefore they will destroy all capitalist and imperialist organizations, remove every possibility of exploitation and will prepare a powerful, valiant future for the working class.

Intrepidly and uncompromised the Slovak proletariat is fulfilling its historical mission; it continues with the work of their forefathers in order to encurage the following generations, in order to be worthy of the name of the proletariat.

Long live the world revolution!
Long live the Communist International![33]

Following the proclamation the seat of the government of the republic, the Slovak Revolutionary Governing Council[34] headed by Antonin Janoušek, was transferred to Košice.

The disintegration of the republic began by the end of June, when Béla Kun accepted the Allies' offer under which Romanian troops holding Hungarian territory would evacuate it in exchange for the Hungarian Red Army's departure from Slovakia. The retreat began on 28 June 1919. Košice was evacuated on 30 June, and the operation was completed by 4 July.

The Slovak Revolutionary Governing Council left, together with the Hungarian Red Army and its Slovak units. While the troops of both armies continued to fight against the Romanian army, the members of the government took refuge at Miskolc, an industrial town in north-eastern Hungary. The collapse on 1 August 1919 of the Hungarian Soviet Republic also meant the final fall of the Slovak Soviet Republic.

1920, 1 February to 1924, 2 October
The Khorezm People's Soviet Republic

The Khorezm[35] People's Soviet Republic was proclaimed on 1 February 1920[36] after the Khan of Kiva[37] was deposed by a nationalist group, the Young Khivan Party[38], with support from the Red Army[39].

Initially, after the Khan's overthrow, the government of Khorezm was exercised by the Young Khivan Committee. In the spring of 1920 the Communist Party of Khorezm was organized and it soon thereafter replaced the Committee as a ruling party of the republic[40].

On 13 September 1920 the the republic entered into agreements with the RSFSR (similar to that with Bukhara), under which the Russians were granted certain economic privileges[41], such as the right to exploit natural resources, to import and export without the payment of tariffs and to use Russian currency.

The republic had no distinctive ethnographic basis, and after the formation of the USSR in 1923 moves were made to include Khorezm in the Union. In October 1923 Khorezm was transformed into a fully fledged Soviet Socialist Republic within the USSR. On 2 October 1924 the fifth Congress of Soviets of Khorezm dissolved the republic[42]. Its territory was divided and incorporated into the Tadzhik ASSR, the Uzbek SSR and the Turkmen SSR.

1920, 6 April
The Far Eastern Republic

The proclamation of the independence of the Far Eastern Republic was a culmination of several months of organized activities by local Bolshevik and nationalist groups.

News of the success of the Russian revolution was received with considerable enthusiasm in eastern Siberia. The First Congress of Workers' Organizations of the Far East was convened on 28 October 1917[43], within days of the seizure of power in Petrograd. It was soon followed by the Congress of all the Far Eastern Soviets meeting in Khabarovsk, which on 11 December 1917 established its own Council of People's Commissars[44]. By May 1918 Vladivostok came under the authority of the new government which, under the leadership of Alexander Krasnoshchekov, established its rule during the following months throughout eastern Siberia.

However, on 28 June 1918 anti-Bolshevik Czech troops seized Vladivostok, and this meant the collapse of the Council, which fled to the Zeya river. The whole of Far Eastern Siberia was subsequently occupied by American, Japanese, Czech and anti-Bolshevik Russian troops.

When in late 1919 the Red Army began its offensive against the Allies in the Far East, soviets re-emerged in various parts of the region. Among them one of the strongest was the Irkutsk soviet, headed by Krasnoshchekov. He produced the idea of establishing a 'buffer state' between Japan and Russia in eastern Siberia.

On 6 April a Constituent Assembly of representatives of all the people of the trans-Baikal territory proclaimed an independent Far Eastern Republic[45]. Krasnoshchekov became its Prime Minister and Minister of Foreign Affairs. The republic's territory constituted the former Russian possessions east of Lake Baikal and its capital was Chita. The republic was granted full recognition by the RSFSR on 16 May 1920. The elections to the Constituent Assembly in January 1921 gave the Bolsheviks and their supporters more than a two-thirds majority[46]. Although the constitution adopted on 17 April 1921[47] preserved bourgeois-democratic forms, the composition of the government reflected the composition of the Constituent Assembly.

The creation of the Far Eastern republic as a 'buffer state' against Moscow and against Bolshevism suited the Japanese, who at that time occupied Vladivostok and the maritime province. However, Japanese withdrawal from the maritime province at the end of October 1922 and the establishment of the authority of the Far Eastern Republic throughout eastern Siberia, from Baikal to the Pacific, deprived the 'buffer state' of any further meaning, even as a symbol. On 10 November 1922 the Constituent Assembly of the Far Eastern Republic voted the republic out of existence, and on 14 November proclaimed its incorporation into the RSFSR[48].

1920, 20 April
The Azerbaijani Soviet Socialist Republic

The Marxist regime in Azerbaijan was established on 20 April 1920. It followed a communist rising in Baku, during which a Military Revolutionary Committee, acting in the name of the revolutionary proletariat in the city and the toiling peasantry of Azerbaijan, appealed to Moscow to conclude 'a fraternal alliance for the common struggle against world imperialism'[49].

The following day three high-ranking members of the Russian Bolshevik Party, Ordzhonikidze (Georgian), Kirov (Russian) and Mikoyan (Armenian) arrived by train in Baku[50] to lay the foundation of Soviet power in Azerbaijan[51] and shortly afterwards the Eleventh Red Army marched into Baku.

Six months later, on 30 September 1920, a treaty of military –economic alliance together with five supplementary treaties were concluded between the Azerbaijani Socialist Soviet Republic and the RSFSR. The main treaty made it incumbent on the signatories to unify, in the shortest possible time, military command, the organs controlling the national economy and foreign trade, the supply organs, rail and water transport, postal–telegraphic administration and finance. The supplementary treaties provided the competent organs of the RSFSR in the field of finance, foreign trade and national economy, with the right to appoint plenipotentiaries to the Azerbaijan Council of People's Commissars, 'with the right of the substantive vote'[52].

The treaties between Azerbaijan and the RSFSR were the first in a series of similar treaties with other republics, which led to the creation of the Union of Soviet Socialist Republics on 30 December 1922.

1920, 20 May to 1921, October
The Soviet Socialist Republic of Gilan

The Soviet Socialist Republic of Gilan was proclaimed on 20 May 1920[53] after a meeting between Mirza Kuchik Khan, the leader of the nationalist movement of the Jangalis (inhabitants of the 'jungles' of Gilan) and General F.F. Raskolnikov, commander of a considerable Soviet force which on 18 May 1920 landed from the Caspian Sea at the port of Enzeli and occupied the capital of Gilan, Resht.

The Soviet occupation of northern Persia, which was primarily aimed at forcing British troops out of that region, gave an additional impetus to the long-established Jangalis rebellion.

The movement, which began in 1915 as a reform programme for the Iranian state, was elaborated by Mirza Kuchik Khan, Ehsanulla Khan and a number of other progressively minded middle-class Persians. The programme was directed against the corrupt ruling class and the influence of foreigners in the country's affairs. By 1917 the Jangalis were in open rebillion against both the Shah's government and the British influence in Iran. The Russian revolution added to the impetus of the movement whose programme became increasingly Islamic and progressive[54].

As early as 1919 the Bolsheviks took note of the movement. In May 1919, *Life of Nationalities* pointed out that the work of Kuchik Khan was 'closely connected with communism, although it is interpreted by the Persians in a different sense' and that it presented a 'seed which, once it is carefully and skilfully cultivated, will produce a good harvest, a revolutionary preparedness among the Persian masses'[55].

In 1918 the movement numbered approximately 6000 men[56] and established itself as a considerable political as well as resistance force. Kuchik Khan and other leaders of the movement were forewarned by a letter from a Bolshevik commander in the Caucasus about the impending invasion of Persia[57]. The letter was followed by the dispatch of a special envoy:

> During the night of May 17 . . . a Russian comrade came to the forest and revealed the fact that in a few days the Bolsheviks would strike at Enzeli[58].

Thus when the invasion took place on the following morning the identity of views and similarity of purpose between the Bolsheviks and the Jangalis appear to have been so close that the proclamation of the Soviet Socialist Republic of Gilan seems to have been almost a mere formality[59].

Following the proclamation, Kuchik Khan sent the following telegram to Lenin:

> We greet you and all your comrades at the time of your brilliant success achieved against the enemies of socialism. We, Persian revolutionaries, have for a long time cherished the same hope fighting against the evil and the hated English and Persian oppressors. Now is fulfilled the long-expected and happy act of the formation of the Persian Socialist Soviet Republic, which we proclaim before the world. We consider it to be our duty to draw your attention to the fact that there are a number of criminals on Persian territory; Persian oppressors, English traders, and diplomats supported by English troops. As long as these enemies of the Persian people are in Persia, they will prove to be an obstacle to the introduction of our just system all over the country. In the name of humanity and equality of all nations the Persian Socialist Soviet Republic asks you and all the Socialists belonging to the Third International for help in liberating us and all weak and oppressed nations from the yoke of Persian and English oppressors. Bearing in mind the establishment of brotherly union and full unanimity between us, we expect from the free Russian nation the assistance that may prove indispensable for the stabilization of the Persian Socialist Soviet Republic. Mindful that all nations liberated from the yoke of capitalism should be united into one brotherly union, we request you to include in this union the hearts of the Persian nation, liberated from a centuries-long yoke, so that our holy revolution may be fulfilled till the end.
>
> We have a firm faith that all the world will be governed by one ideal system for the Third International.
>
> Representative of the Persian Socialist Soviet Republic proclaimed in the City of Resht:
>
> Mirza Kuchik[60]

The Persian revolution did not come as a surprise; it was directed against British hegemony in south-west Asia and it coincided with the rising tide of nationalist unrest in India, Iraq, Egypt and Ireland. The republic was under constant threat from the regime in Teheran and therefore its survival depended almost entirely on the presence of Soviet troops.

In the autumn of 1920 as a result of a series of Soviet–Iranian compromises, Moscow and Teheran began to negotiate a new treaty which aimed at limiting even further British commercial and political interests in the area. The question of Gilan proved the most serious stumbling block in these negotiations and they proceeded only after the Soviet delegate declared on 22 January 1921 that Soviet troops would be withdrawn only when British troops had left Persian soil.

The treaty between the Soviet and Persian governments which was signed on 26 February 1921 did not influence the Gilan situation immediately. Neither did the withdrawal of British troops in May 1921. In June 1921 Kuchik Khan with his small army began to march on Teheran. New Soviet contingents landed at Enzeli. The Iranian Cossack Division resisted the combined forces of Kuchik and Bolsheviks and successfully checked their advance on the capital. The march was disowned by the People's Commissar for Foreign Affairs, G. Chicherin and the Soviet support for Kuchik was abandoned. Soviet troops were withdrawn on 8 September 1921. This paved the way for the final collapse of the Soviet Socialist Republic of Gilan. The Persian troops marched to Gilan, attacked Kuchik Khan and after weeks of heavy fighting defeated the Jangali forces in October 1921[61].

1920, 5 September to 1924, 20 September
The Bukhara People's Soviet Republic

The Bolshevik revolution in Russia had reverberations even in the remote Emirate of Bukhara[62]. In its aftermath a young Bukhara movement emerged and organized itself into the Young Bukharan Party. The Party consisted mainly of the young generation of enlightened merchants who drew their inspiration from the young Turks and were influenced by their idea of national renaissance. Headed by Faizulla Khodzhaev, it established close contacts with Turkestan communists[63].

In March 1918 the Young Bukharans organized a rebellion and attempted a *coup d'état* against the Emir. At the same time they requested the chairman of the Council of People's Commissars in

Tashkent to send the Red Army to their assistance. The rebellion and *coup*, however, failed and the Red Army, in spite of some local support, was forced back by the Emir's troops. On 25 March 1918 the Tashkent government concluded a treaty with the Emir, recognizing him as an 'independent Power'[64]. The Young Bukharan Party was decimated during the short-lived March uprising. Those who survived, between 150 to 200, crossed the border in Soviet Turkestan and created two political centres, one in Samarkand and another in Tashkent[65]. In the course of the months that followed, as a result of differences that developed among the members of the Young Bukharan Party, who sought refuge in Tashkent, one group formed the Bukharan Communist Party[66].

During 1919 and 1920 the Bukharan Communist Party became very active inside Bukhara and in August 1920 it organized a number of uprisings in several parts of the country. As in March 1918, the Red Army was called upon to give assistance to the newly created regiments of the Bukharan Red Army.

On 2 September 1920 Bukhara was captured by the Red Army and the Emir fled to Afghanistan. Commenting on the part played by the Soviet troops in overthrowing the Emir, a prominent Soviet historian of that period, O. Glovatsky, remarked:

> There is no need for us to keep silent . . . on the active role played by the Red Army in the struggle against the Emir. The powerful support given from outside in order to win over the Emirate in the revolution in Bukhara was inevitable, not only to fulfil the international obligations of the victorious working class towards an oppressed people who launched a struggle against their exploiters, but also to guarantee peaceful reconstruction in Turkestan and an end to counterrevolution within the Soviet land. . . . The victory of the revolution in Bukhara was a necessary and important stage in the great struggle of the proletariat and the oppressed people of the world against capitalism[67].

The formation of the Bukhara People's Soviet Republic was proclaimed on 5 September 1920[68].

The following year, on 4 March, the new regime concluded treaties of alliance and economic agreements with the RSFSR. Under these agreements Bukhara granted the Russians a number of economic privileges such as exploiting natural resources, importing and exporting without the payment of tariffs and the use of Russian currency[69]. The RSFSR in return renounced all property rights or concessions of the former Russian Empire in the territory of the republic, including the land of Russian colonists settled before the revolution in Bukhara, who could retain their land by opting for Bukharan citizenship.

In September 1923 the Bukharan Congress of Soviets passed a resolution providing for the transformation of the republic from Soviet into Soviet Socialist republic and declared its desire to be admitted to the USSR[70]. On 20 September 1924 the Fifth Bukharan Congress of Soviets decided to dissolve the republic and to approve the incorporation of its Uzbek and Turkmen populations in the proposed Uzbek and Turkmen republics, respectively.

1920, 29 November
The Soviet Socialist Republic of Armenia

The estabishment of the Marxist regime in Armenia was proclaimed on 29 November 1920 on the border between Armenia and Azerbaijan by the Revolutionary Committee of the Soviet Socialist Republic of Armenia[71]. The Committee arrived in Armenia with the units of the Eleventh Red Army, marching from Azerbaijan. The Soviet entry was apparently activated by a desire to forestall the complete collapse of the Dashnak movement of the Armenian Republic and to prevent a Turkish occupation of Erevan, at a time when Turkish armies occupied most of Armenia. According to an eminent historian of that period, Richard Pipes, the Armenian government did not consider the Soviet invasion as an unfriendly gesture[72].

Shortly after the Red Army's entry a joint Communist Dashnak government was formed in Erevan under a treaty signed between the government of the Armenian Republic and a Soviet diplomat, Legran.

According to the provisions of the treaty Armenia was an independent socialist republic (Article 1), in which all power until the convocation of the Congress of Soviets of Armenia was transferred to a Provisional Military Revolutionary Committee (Article 2). The Committee consisted of members appointed by the Communist Party of Armenia[73] and two members appointed by left Dashnak groups, with the approval of the Communist Party[74].

On 30 September 1921 Armenia signed a treaty with the RSFSR which, although confined exclusively to financial matters, nevertheless paved the way for the future union of Armenia with the USSR.

1921, 25 February
The Georgian Soviet Socialist Republic

The Marxist regime in Georgia was established with the help of the Red Army, whose presence was requested by the Georgian Revolutionary Committee. The Committee organized by the Georgian Communist Party was formed on 16 February 1921 in the village of Shulaveni, several miles inside the Georgian territory. In spite of considerable resistance by the army of the Menshevik government of Georgia, the Eleventh and Thirteenth Red Armies took control of most of the country with the capture of the capital of Tiflis, and on 25 February 1921 the Revolutionary Committee proclaimed the formation of the Georgian Soviet Socialist Republic.

Even after that the Menshevik government, which sought refuge in the coastal city of Batum, attempted to organize resistance to Soviet advances, but without success. On 18 March it capitulated to the Russians. The cease-fire agreement signed on the same day provided for a termination of hostilities, the dissolution of the Menshevik army and a full amnesty for all persons connected with the previous regime[75].

On 21 May 1921 the new Georgian regime signed a treaty of alliance with the RSFSR similar to that signed between the RSFSR and the Ukraine. The following year, on 30 December 1922, Georgia joined the USSR as part of the Transcaucasian Soviet Federated Socialist Republic.

1921, 12 August to 1944, 11 October
The People's Republic of Tannu Tuva

The October revolution also had its repercussions on the Uriankhai territory. This large but sparsely populated area to the West of Outer Mongolia had been a Russian protectorate since 1914[76]. On 8 March 1918 a congress called by Russian settlers in the Uriankhai territory elected a Regional Soviet of Workers', Peasants' and Soldiers' Deputies. A declaration adopted by this congress and addressed to the natives of the region stated *inter alia*:

> Soviet authority assures you . . . that it will not interfere in the domestic affairs of the Uriankhai natives, allowing them complete freedom of local self-determination and freedom of conscience[77].

The Russian settlers who took the decisive steps in giving the political direction to the territory also appear to have been in control three years later, when they organized the first congress of the representatives of the Uriankhais. The congress was opened on 13 August 1921 by I. G. Safianov, head of a large delegation of the Siberian Revolutionary Committee, which represented Soviet Russia. It closed on 16 August with a decision to establish an independent state, the People's Republic of Tannu Tuva, and confirmed the provisional constitution of the new republic[78].

Soviet government policy towards Tannu Tuva is contained in an official declaration issued in late September 1921. It reads in part:

At the present time when the workers and peasant masses of Russia have overthrown the despotic tsarist officials, the Russian Workers' and Peasants'Government which expresses the will of the toilers most solemnly declares that henceforth it does not consider the Tannu-Tuva [Uriankhai] region its own territory and has no design on it whatsoever[79].

Following the establishment of the People's Republic, the People's Revolutionary Party was founded on 29 October 1921[80].

Tannu Tuva remained an independent country until 1944. On 17 August of that year it applied for entry into the USSR. The request was formally made by the Small Khural of the republic at an extraordinary session on 16 August, at which the following declaration was unanimously adopted:

The Tuvan people have gone through the whole 23 year period of free revolutionary development with the great Soviet people.

The Soviet State has become mightier under the sun of the Soviet Constitution and has attained the flowering of the material and spiritual strength of large and small peoples in a unified socialist family.

To live and work in this family is the solemn desire of the whole Tuvan people. There is no other route for us than the route of the Soviet Union. Fulfilling the undeviating will and burning desire of the whole Tuvan people, the Extraordinary Seventh Session of the Small Khural of the Workers of theTuvan People's Republic resolves:

To request the Supreme Soviet of the USSR to take the People's Republic of Tannu Tuva into the composition of the USSR[81].

The request was approved by the Praesidium of the USSR Supreme Soviet on 11 October 1944. Tannu Tuva became an Autonomous Oblast within the RSFSR.

1924, 26 November
The Mongolian People's Republic

The Marxist regime in Mongolia has its origins in the national liberation movement against the Chinese militarists. Influenced by the October revolution in Russia, two independent underground revolutionary circles were formed in 1919 and 1920 in Niislel Khüree (the present Ulan Bator). On 25 June 1920 they merged into the Mongolian People's Party[82]. At the foundation conference the Party's objectives were defined as the overthrow of Chinese rule and independence for Mongolia, modernization of the country and the limitation of the powers of the Bogd (the head of the Lamaist Church) and of the princess. The conference also decided to establish contacts with the Comintern and the Soviet government in order to seek their aid for the fulfilment of these objectives. In August 1920 two emissaries of the Party met the chief of the Far Eastern Section of the Siberian Bureau of the Russian Bolshevik Party in Irkutsk and presented him with a request for 24 000 armed cavalrymen, military instructors and a loan to cover the expenditure of the Party[83]. Soviet aid was assured, and in February 1921 a small partisan army began operations[84].

After the conclusion of its First Congress[85] the Mongolian People's Party established, on 13 March 1921, a Provisional Revolutionary Government which issued an ultimatum to the Chinese military authorities to surrender. When the Chinese ignored this ultimatum the partisan army attacked and captured, on 18 March, Altan Bulag, a small town on the Soviet–Mongolian border.

Being in control of a small part of Mongolian territory and facing continuous occupation of the rest of the country, the Provisional Revolutionary Government, on 10 April 1921, officially requested the RSFSR to provide aid against foreign forces. The Russians complied, and the combined Mongolian–Soviet forces liberated Niislel Khüree on 11 July 1921.

The Provisional Government was transferred into the People's Central Government, with the Bogd as the titular head of state. The Bogd died on 20 May 1924.

On 26 November 1924 the People's Great Khural abolished the constitutional monarch, proclaimed the formation of the Mongolian People's Republic and adopted the first constitution[86].

1932, 4 June to 1932, 16 June
The Socialist Republic of Chile

The republic was proclaimed by Commodore of the Air Marmaduke Grove Vallejo, who deposed President Juan Esteban Montero and his cabinet on 4 June 1932[87]. The military *coup d'état* which overthrew a 'government of oligarchic reaction which served only the interests of foreign capitalism' had considerable popular support, particularly among the poorer section of the Chilean population, which was expressed in anti-government demonstrations and demands for the establishment of the Socialist Republic.

The republic was overthrown by a military *coup d'état* on 16 June 1932 and Grove, with his closest associates, including Eugenio Matte Hurtado who 'openly propounded Communist theories', were imprisoned on Eastern Island.

It should be added that the name Socialist Republic continued to be used by the new junta until 12 September 1932. However, the social and political reforms of the 4 June movement were abandoned and indeed reversed.

1 Cited in M. Fainsod, *How Russia is Ruled*, p. 83
2 E.H. Carr, *The Bolshevik Revolution 1917–1923*, Vol. 1, p. 120
3 Ibid., p. 129
4 Ibid.
5 Ibid., p. 133
6 Carr, op.cit. (note 2), pp. 303–304
7 Ibid., p. 306
8 Ibid., p. 401
9 See C. Jay Smith, 'Soviet Russia and the Red Revolution of 1918 in Finland' in *The Anatomy of Communist Takeovers* (ed. by Thomas T. Hammond), pp. 71–93
10 J.W. Wheeler-Bennet, *Brest-Litovsk: The Forgotten Peace, March 1918*, pp. 252–236. See also M.S. Svechnikov, *Revolyutsiya i grazhdanskaya voina v Finlyandii, 1917–1918 gg. (Vspominaniya i materialy)*
11 Georg von Rauch, in *The Baltic States: the Years of Independence, 1917–1940*, p. 34, gives an indication of this support by quoting electoral results. According to him, during the local elections conducted in September 1917 the Bolsheviks won 35 per cent of the popular vote throughout the country. The figure for the capital, Tallinn, was 31 per cent and for the second biggest city, Narva, 47 per cent
12 Ibid., p. 49
13 Ibid., p. 50

14 The Party was formed in July 1918 by a conference of communists, recently arrived from Moscow, as the Social Democratic Workers' Party of Lithuania and Belorussia. On 14 August it was renamed the Communist Party of Lithuania and Belorussia

15 V. Mickevicvius-Kapsukas, 'Borba za sovetskuyu vlast', *Proletarskaia Revolutsia*, No. 108 (1931), 81

16 Alfred E. Senn, *The Emergence of Modern Lithuania*, p. 64. For full lists of the Council of People's Commissars see ibid., pp. 239–240

17 Ibid., p. 81

18 S. Sworakowski (ed.), *World Communism: A Handbook 1918–1965*, p. 297

19 R. L. Tökés, *Béla Kun and the Hungarian Soviet Republic*, pp. 142, 254

20 Carr, op. cit. (note 2), Vol. 1, p. 313

21 Richard Pipes, *The Formation of the Soviet Union: Communism and Nationalism, 1917–1923*, p. 152

22 For a complete but somewhat exaggerated account of the foundation of the BelorussianSocialist Soviet Republic see *Istorik Marksist*, No 1, 1940, 63–78. A summary of the main facts are given by Carr, op.cit. (note 2), Vol. 1, p. 314

23 R. Fischer, *Stalin and German Communism,* pp.8, 57, 97

24 The Communist Party of Hungary was first established on 24 March 1918 in Moscow as a section of the Russian Communist Party from among Hungarian and Slovak prisoners of war in Soviet Russia, under the leadership of Béla Kun. The party's conference held in Moscow on 4 November decided on the formation of a separate communist party and the returning of prisoners of war to Hungary. Kun returned to Hungary on 17 November and embarked on talks with various left-wing groups, the conclusion of which was the formation of the Communist Party of Hungary in Budapest on 24 November 1918.

25 For the text see op.cit. (note 19).

26 Ibid.

27 The party's name was changed during its first congress (12–14 June 1919) into the Socialist–Communist Party of Hungary. The party was dissolved by the Comintern in 1921

28 The Council consisted of thirty-three people's commissars – among them seventeen socialists, fourteen communists and two non-party experts. Alexander Garbei, a Social Democratic trade-union leader, took office as President of the Republic and Béla Kun became the People's Commissar of Foreign Affairs

29 For the most comprehensive and scholarly analysis of the Hungarian Soviet Republic see Tökés. op. cit. (note 19)

30 Mitchell, *Revolution in Bavaria 1918–1919: The Eisner Regime and the Soviet Republic*. p. 305ff. This book is one of the most detailed accounts of the republic

31 While it has not been possible to determine the exact date of the establishment of this Committee, it is known that on 27 March 1919 the Committee began to publish a daily newspaper, *Cervené Noviny* (The Red Gazette) in Slovak. See P.A. Toma, 'The Slovak Soviet Republic of 1919', *The American Slavic and East European Review*, **17**, April 1958, 203–215

32 Ibid.

33 *Cervené Noviny*, 17 June 1919. See also Toma, op.cit. (note 31), pp. 208–209

34 The Council consisted of twenty People's Commissars. Among them were two close associates of Béla Kun; Ernö Pór (Commissar of Foreign Affairs) and Tibor Szamuely (Commissar for Social Production)

35 Khorezm is an ancient name for Khiva

36 The independence of Khorezm was recognized by the Turko–Afghan Treaty (Article II) signed in Moscow on 1 March 1921

37 The Khanate of Khiva was conquered by Russia in 1873 and became a vassal state, never, however, formally included in the Russian Empire

38 The Young Khivan Party was established in 1919 in Soviet Turkestan and aimed at the overthrow of the Khan and the implementation of social and political reforms. (See X. J. Eudin and R. C. North, *Soviet Russia and the East, 1920–1927, A Documentary Survey*, p. 31)
39 The Red Army entered Khivan territory in the closing stages of the civil war in response to a call for assistance in overthrowing the Khan for the Young Khivan Party
40 Eudin and North, op.cit. (note 32), p. 32
41 R. Conquest (ed.), *Soviet Nationalities Policy in Practice.* p. 41
42 E. H. Carr, *Socialism in One Country*, Vol. 2, p. 288
43 H. Norton, *The Far Eastern Republic of Siberia*, p. 53
44 Ibid., p. 54
45 Carr, op.cit. (note 2), Vol. 1
46 Norton, op.cit. (note 43), pp. 152–159
47 For English translation see ibid., pp. 282–307
48 Carr, op.cit. (note 27), Vol. 1, p. 367
49 Carr, op.cit. (note 2), Vol. 1, p. 350
50 Pipes, op.cit. (note 21), p. 227
51 Carr, op.cit. (note 2), Vol. 1
52 Conquest (ed.), op.cit. (note 41), p. 36
53 Carr, op.cit. (note 2), Vol. 3, p. 245
54 N. S. Fatemi, *Diplomatic History of Persia*, p. 217
55 'Zadachi i usloviia sotsialisticheskoi propagandy v Persii', *Zhizn Natsionalnostei*, No. 19 (27), 27 May 1919, p. 2, quoted in Eudin and North, op.cit. (note 38), p. 96
56 *Izvestia*, 10 June 1920, quoted in Fatemi, op.cit. (note 54), p. 222
57 Fatemi, op.cit. (note 54), p. 220
58 Ibid.
59 During 1920 the Soviet Government of Gilan extended its rule also to the province of Mazandaran
60 Ibid., p. 221. The Revolutionary Government formed after the proclamation consisted of the following members:
President and War Commissar: Mirza Kuchik Khan
Commissar of Finance: Mohammed Ali Pirabazari
Commissar of Trade: Abdul Kazim
Commissar of Justice: Mahmud Aga
Commissar of Postal and Telegraphic Services: Nasrullah
Commissar of Education: Hadji Jaffar
Commissar of National Economy: Ali Khumani
Commissar of Interior: Seyd Jaffar
61 The downfall of the Soviet Socialist Republic of Gilan was explained by *Novyi Vostok* in the following terms: 'The revolutionary movement in Gilan, which flourished principally on the slogan "Down with the English", went perceptibly downhill after the evacuation of Persia by the English forces. In view of the backwardness and inertia of the Persian peasantry, it found no support among the Persian peasantry; the Persian traders and bourgeoisie in general connected the improvement of their position with an opening of commercial relations with Soviet Russia, and were not inclined at the moment to take up arms against the feudal central government.' (Quoted in op.cit. (note 2), Vol. 3, p. 465
62 The Emirate of Bukhara became a tsarist vasal state in 1868
63 Eudin and North, op.cit. (note 38), p. 30
64 Carr, op.cit. (note 2), Vol. 1, p.337
65 Eudin and North, op.cit. (note 38), pp. 30–31
66 Ibid.
67 Quoted by Eudin and North, ibid.

68 As in the case of Khorezm, the independence of Bukhara was recognized by
    Turkey and Afghanistan in the Turko–Afghan Treaty (Article II), signed in
    Moscow on 1 March 1921
69 Similar agreements were signed in 1920 between the RSFSR and the indepen-
    dent Baltic states of Estonia, Latvia and Lithuania, with the important
    difference that they provided for military agreements as well
70 Carr in op.cit (note 42), Vol. 2, p. 287, quotes Baymirza Hayit, *Turkestan im
    XX Jahrhundert*, according to whom: 'The decision of the Bukharan congress of
    Soviets is said to have been accompanied by orders to remove "officials,
    merchants and priests" from posts in the government and deprive them of the
    franchise, and to confiscate the property of "capitalist classes and elements" '
71 Pipes, op.cit. (note 21), p. 232
72 Ibid.
73 The Communist Party of Armenia, whose specific policy was to overthrow the
    Dashnak government, was founded on 18–19 January 1920. In April 1920 it had
    a membership of 3000
74 For the text of the treaty see Pipes, op.cit. (note 21), pp. 232–233
75 Pipes, op.cit. (note 21), p. 239
76 The Uriankhai territory, inhabited by Turkic-speaking people, has been a
    subject of long-standing disputes between Russia and China
77 Quoted in Eudin and North, op.cit. (note 38), p. 258
78 The Constitution was finally confirmed by the Fourth Great Khural on 24
    November 1926. According to it the supreme authority of the republic was
    vested in the Great Khural and between its sessions in the Small Khural
79 Quoted in Eudin and North, op.cit. (note 38), pp. 258–259. A treaty signed in
    August 1926 between the two countries included provision for an exchange of
    diplomatic representatives, first with consular rank, made 'provisional
    representatives' in 1928 and ministers in 1929
80 The development of the sole and ruling Party of the republic appears to have
    been very slow. Although founded in October it issued its first manifesto to the
    Tuvan people only on 20 December.At its second meeting between 28 February
    and 1 March 1922 the party's organizational bureau became its Central
    Committee and the meeting is considered to be its first congress
81 Quoted after A. Rupen, 'The Absorption of Tuva', in Thomas T. Hammond
    (ed.), op.cit. (note 9), pp. 146–147
82 At its Third Congress, 4–24 August 1924, the Party changed its name into the
    Mongolian People's Revolutionary Party
83 U. Onon, 'Mongolian People's Republic' in *Marxist Governments: A World
    Survey* (ed. by B. Szajkowski), Vol. 2, p. 496
84 W.A. Brown and U. Onon, *History of the Mongolian People's Republic*, pp.
    141, 144, 147
85 The Congress was held on 1–3 March 1921 in the Russian town of Troitskosavsk
86 On 24 January 1925 the Soviet government sent a note to the MPR concerning
    the stationing of the Red Army. It read in part: 'As a result of the People's
    Government having completed the work of Revolution . . . the possibility of
    true peace and order being organized in your country, the advancing of your
    people to a democratic system, the creation of a Republic . . . We consider it is
    no longer vital that units of the Red Army be stationed on the territory of the
    MPR' (Quoted in Onon, op.cit. (note 83), p. 500). Soviet troops were
    withdrawn from Mongolia by March 1925
87 J.R. Thomas, 'the Socialist Republic of Chile', *Journal of Inter-American
    Studies*, VI, 214

Chapter 5

The extension and the dispersal of the 'socialist camp'

At the beginning of Chapter 4 a plea was made for viewing the revolutionary events of the period from 1917 to 1924 with detachment from the process in which they were overtaken and engulfed in the creation and development of the Soviet state. When we turn to the period from 1933 to 1957[1], which can be seen as a second 'wave' in the establishment of Marxist regimes, a rather different historical perspective is required. During this period the Cominterm and its successor, the Cominform, were still in existence, with all that this implies in terms of Soviet influence. What is important now is that that influence accounted directly for the establishment of a series of Communist parties in eastern Europe, whilst a rather smaller series came to power without that influence, and have, moreover, increasingly marked their distance from the Soviet Union. We are dealing, in fact, with two distinct series of revolutions, though at the time of their occurrence the authority of the Soviet Union in the communist universe led to their temporary coalescence into a single, reasonably cohesive 'socialist camp'.

1939, 30 November to 1940, late January
The Finnish Democratic Republic

When, pursuing its territorial demands[2], the Soviet Union invaded Finland on 30 November 1939 the Russians recognized a new Finnish government set up in the border town of Terijoki. The government of the Finnish Democratic Republic was composed of political refugees and was headed by Otto Kuusinen, a former leader of the Finnish Communist Party and a leading figure in the Comintern since its inception. On 2 December 1939 the USSR solemnly concluded a mutual assistance pact with the Finnish Democratic Republic and in return its government granted the Soviet territorial demands.

The Soviet attack on Finland provoked great indignation among the Western nations. The USSR was expelled from the League of

Nations on 14 December 1939 and the Western powers began to
gather an expeditionary force to go to Finland's rescue.
In late January 1940, the Soviet Union jettisoned the government of Otto Kuusinen and thus the Finnish Democratic Republic
collapsed. A peace-treaty between Finland and the USSR was
signed on 12 March 1940.

1944, 7 November to 1949, October
The Eastern Turkistan Republic

The Eastern Turkistan Republic was created in the aftermath of a
Turkic Moslem rebellion that broke out on 7 November 1944 in
north-west Sinkiang, close to the border of the Kazakh SSR. The
spontaneous outbursts of local resentment against both the provincial and the central governments was initially centred on the city of
Kuldja (I-nin)[3] and later spread to include the districts if Ili,
Tancheng and Altai[4]. From 1945 it also included the Tarim Basin
area to the south, thus uniting the Uighur, Kazakh and Kirghiz
ethnical minorities, all with a long tradition of anti-Chinese
revolts. The Republic received Soviet backing and support
throughout its existence[5].
Little is known about the political structures of the Eastern
Turkistan Republic. The earliest mention of a distinct political
organization is the creation in August 1948 of the Sinkiang
(Xiangiang) League for the Protection of Peace and Democracy.
Its aim, according to the entry on Saifudin[6] in the *Biographic
Dictionary of Chinese Communism*, was to promote the nationalist
aspirations of the ethnical minorities in north and west Sinkiang
(Xiangiang).
The Eastern Turkistan Republic ceased to exist after the
Chinese People's Liberation Army took over Sinkiang (Xian-
giang) subsequent to the proclamation of the People's Republic of
China in 1949.

1945, 20 November
The Federal People's Republic of Yugoslavia

The account of the establishment of the Marxist regime in
Yugoslavia is essentially the history of the resistance of the
Partisan army, organized around the Communist Party of
Yugoslavia[7] and led by Josip Broz Tito, to the Axis occupying
powers in the Second World War.

Hitler attacked Yugoslavia on 6 April 1941 and by 17 April the Yugoslav High Command had capitulated. The Germans immediately set about partioning the country, exploiting the lack of homogeneity of the Yugoslav state and the mutually antagonistic elements within it. Germany annexed the northern half of Slovenia and Italy received Ljubljana and the rest of Slovenia and Montenegro. Albania and parts of Macedonia were placed under Mussolini's control. Bulgaria annexed the rest of Macedonia and some of Serbia, but the largest fragment of dismembered Yugoslavia was the Independent State of Croatia, which included all of Bosnia and Herzegovina. Power was exercised in Croatia by Ante Pavelić and his Ustashi, although ultimately it rested in German and Italian hands. What was left of Serbia was kept under direct German control, but a limited government was formed by the Serbian General Nedić. At that time also the Soviet government declared officially that Yugoslavia no longer existed as a state, and that there was therefore no longer need for the Yugoslav Embassy in Moscow.

After the collapse of the Army a few scattered bands went into the hills, among them Colonel Draža Mihailović, a Serbian monarchist who organized the Chetnik's resistance groups which later fought not only the occupiers but also the Communist Partisans and Croats. Thus there were three facets of the war in Yugoslavia – the resistance to the Axis powers, the Serbo–Croat conflict and the Partisan–Chetnik conflict.

At the end of April 1941 Tito convened a meeting of the CPY's Central Committee in Zagreb. It was at that meeting that the decision on a broadly based national uprising was made. The Central Committee met again on 27 June in Belgrade. It set up the general headquarters of the National Liberation Partisan Detachments and Josip Broz Tito was appointed its commander. The decision to begin an armed rising was adopted on 4 July 1941. Fighting broke out in many parts of the country and at the beginning of September the GHQ were moved from Belgrade to one of the liberated territories controlled by the Partisans.

The Partisans eventually became the clear leader in the resistance for several reasons. They actively engaged the Axis powers. They were an all-Yugoslav organization and thus attracted growing numbers of people who hoped for national unity and who had become disenchanted with the violent feuding of the ethnic –religious groups. The leadership played down its ideological orientation. They could provide a number of well-trained leaders drawn from their party members who had been accustomed to underground work throughout the inter-war period. Important among these were their members at Belgrade University and about 200 members of the Yugoslav detachment in the Spanish Civil War who had managed to return to Yugoslavia. Finally, their behaviour towards the people was exemplary. The Chetniks were sometimes merely local warlords but the Partisans made great efforts to protect the civil population by threatening counter-reprisals on captured Axis troops, by evacuating and caring for civilians when they abandoned an area and by special efforts to prevent wounded or sick from falling into enemy hands.

Throughout the war, whenever possible the Partisans formed National Liberation Committees in the liberated areas. This enabled them to consolidate their position both militarily and politically, since the Committees had a threefold purpose: to organize supplies for the partisan units, to serve as a political and propaganda organ for these units and to create a new administrative structure.

By late 1942 the resistance movement was far enough advanced for Tito to call a session of the anti-fascist movement from all over the country. The session, which met in the town of Bihać, set up the Anti-Fascists Council of National Liberation of Yugoslavia (AVNOJ), a genuinely popular front, and issued a federalist programme, thus winning the Macedonians over to their side.

The Council was dominated by the CPY. It was the supra-regional character of Tito's organization rather than his supra-regional policies that enabled the Communists to take control. This and the eagerness of the Communists to fight were the positive reasons for the CPY gaining leadership of the resistance.

The second session of AVNOJ, which was attended by 208 delegates from all parts of Yugoslavia, was held in Jajce on 29 and 30 November 1943. It laid the foundations of the new state. The AVNOJ transformed itself into a supreme legislative body and its Praesidium became the provisional government. The session also decided to deprive the exiled government in London of the powers of government over Yugoslavia, to prohibit King Peter from returning to the country and declared that future Yugoslavia was to be a federal state.

By early 1944 the People's Liberation Army numbered 300 000[8]. Under an agreement signed by Tito and Stalin on 28 September 1944 the Red Army crossed into eastern Serbia and the Partisans and Soviet troops liberated Belgrade on 20 October 1944.

On 7 March 1945, following the recommendations of the Yalta Conference, Tito formed an all-Yugoslav government, which consisted of members of the Praesidium of the AVNOJ and representatives of the exiled government in London. The new government was recognized by the Allies as the legitimate government of Yugoslavia. The Third Sessions of AVNOJ were convened in Belgrade after the liberation of the country in August 1945. Membership of the Council was broadened to include those members of the last Parliament of pre-war Yugoslavia who had not discredited themselves during the war. In the course of its deliberations the Council was transformed into a Provisional National Assembly. Elections for the Constituent Assembly were held on 11 November 1945. The first act of the new Assembly when it met on 29 November was to abolish the monarchy and establish the Federal People's Republic of Yugoslavia.

1945, 2 September
The Democratic Republic of Vietnam

The communist movement in Vietnam and the establishment of a Marxist regime there is intrinsically linked with the long and complex process of a national liberation struggle in that country and with perhaps the most dominant figure of Vietnamese communism, Ho Chi Minh.

Ho was a founding member of the French Communist Party at the Tours Congress in December 1920. He received a brief period of training in the Communist International's school in Moscow and engaged in Comintern activities in Canton, where, in 1925, he set up the Vietnam Revolutionary Youth Association[9]. The Association trained revolutionaries who then returned to Vietnam to organize a cell structure. When Chiang Kai-shek attacked the communists in 1927 Ho returned to Moscow, but the headquarters of the Association moved to Hong Kong. The Association's conference in 1929 resulted in the fragmentation of the movement and three separate communist organizations came into existence: the Indochinese Communist Party, the Annamese Communist Party and the Indochina Communist League.

Ho emerged from obscurity and, in his capacity as a representative of the Communist International, convened a meeting of representatives of different communist groups on 3 February 1930 at Kowloon, in Hong Kong. The meeting founded the Viet Nam Communist Party and, in addition, several affiliated associations (e.g. peasants, women, youth) were established. Thus almost from its inception the Vietnamese Communist movement relied on a complex network of underground political infrastructure. On the one hand there was the highly organized and disciplined Party cells structure, on the other, the nuclei of future mass organizations.

The latter proved to be indispensable to the Party in the next forty-five years of struggle that followed its foundation.

In October 1930 the Party's name was changed into the Indochinese Communist Party, because the Comintern felt that since Vietnam, Laos and Cambodia were linked together by the French colonial administration they should be guided by a single party.

After the fall of France in July 1940 the Vichy administration allowed the Japanese progressively to occupy the whole of Indochina. In Vietnamese eyes the collaboration between France and Japan discredited both. It exposed the sham of Japanese anti-colonial propaganda and of French claims to protection. The Japanese occupation was a major turning point in the development of Vietnamese communism.

On 8 February 1941 Ho Chi Minh returned to the country to assume direct leadership of the Vietnamese revolutionary movement. In May 1941 the Indochinese Communist Party Central Committee decided that matters concerning national liberation should be dealt with within the framework of each Indochinese country and it formed the Viet Nam Independence League, the Viet Minh. Besides the Party, it included organizations of different strata of the population, associations of workers, peasants, youth, women, old folk, army men and other groups. Viet Minh thus inherited the closely knit and disciplined communist cell structure and the support of many broadly based nationalist-inspired revolutionary organizations.

The military resistance movement, under the leadership of Vo Nguyen Giap, consisted largely of the establishment of bases in the remoter parts of the country. In 1944 Ho Chi Minh joined Vo Nguyen Giap and together they established a stronghold in the province of Thai Nguyen, to the north of Hanoi. From this base the guerrillas carried out operations against the Japanese and gradually extended their control in Tongking. Thus the Indochinese Communist Party was able to build up an army of its own and to place itself in a position where it would be able to dominate the nationalist leaders when the time came.

In 1945 events began to move in Indochina. The Japanese, now facing defeat, on 9 March staged a *coup d'état* against the French. In April the ICP decided to unify all armed forces into a Vietnam Liberation Army and in June a liberated zone was created, comprising six northern provinces: Cao Bang, Bac Can, Lang Son, Thai Nguyen, Tuyen Quang and Ha Giang[10]. Revolutionary People's committees which carried out Viet Minh policies were established at all levels. The liberated zone became the principal revolutionary base for the rest of Vietnam; it was to evolve into the Democratic Republic of Vietnam. On 7 August 1945 Ho Chi

Minh formed the Vietnamese People's Liberation Committee which, under his presidency, became the government of the liberated zone.

On 14 August, earlier than it was expected, Japan unconditionally surrendered to the Allied powers, thus throwing the Western powers' plans for the reconquest of South-east Asia into confusion.

In December 1943 the French Committee of National Liberation had promised Indochina 'a new political status within the French community' and in March 1945 the French Provisional Government issued a declaration providing in general terms for a Federal Indochina with local autonomy within the French Union. France was, at the end of the war, not in a position to send troops immediately to Indochina. It was decided at the Potsdam Conference (17 July to 2 August) that Indochina would be occupied at first by British and Chinese troops, with the Chinese taking over a zone north of the 16th parallel (that is, roughly, Tonking, the northern half of Annam and northern Laos) and the British the remaining zone to the south (the southern part of Annam, Cochin-China, Cambodia and southern Laos). The premature surrender of Japan, however, ended the war long before the British troops could reach Indochina. General Gracey and his troops arrived in Saigon on 13 September to find the city under the control of Viet Minh's Committee of the South.

With the sudden Japanese surrender the Viet Minh moved into the political vacuum existing in Vietnam. By this time they had a virtually completed political infrastructure over the whole of Vietnam, though they were weak and inexperienced in the south.

On 29 August 1945 the Liberation Committee was replaced by a Provisional Government of the Democratic Republic of Vietnam, with Ho Chi Minh as President and Bao Dai (Nguyen Vinh Thuy), who had abdicated as Emperor five days previously, as Supreme Political Adviser. On 2 September President Ho Chi Minh, on behalf of the Provisional Government, read in Hanoi the Declaration of Independence, announcing the establishment of the Democratic Republic of Vietnam.

The thirty-year conflict that ensued stemmed from the efforts of external forces to reverse this verdict.

1945, 12 December to 1946, 13 December
The Autonomous Republic of Azerbaijan

The Azeris of northern Iran staged a rebellion against the central government in Tehran, which began on 15 November 1945 with the full backing of the Red Army, stationed in Iran since 25 August 1941.

The regime was based on the Democratic Party of Azerbaijan (formed on 3 September 1945) and led by Ja'far Prishehvari (former member of the Executive Committee of the Soviet Socialist Republic of Gilan, 1920–1921).

Although the separation of Azerbaijan from the rest of Iran was decided by a national congress of the Party, held at the end of November, the proclamation of the Autonomous Republic of Azerbaijan was made after the rebel forces captured the garrison in Tabriz, the capital of Azerbaijan, in December 1945.

The Soviet troops were evacuated from Iran on 6 May 1945 and the Autonomous Republic was crushed by Iranian forces on 13 December 1946[11].

1945, 15 December to 1946, 15 December
The Kurdish People's Republic

The Kurdish People's Republic was proclaimed on 15 December 1945 at Mahabad, in the aftermath of one of the sporadic Kurdish rebellions against the central government of Teheran. This national uprising received assistance from the Red Army, which had been occupying northern Iran since 25 August 1941. Soviet support was also given to the Kurdish Democratic Party, led by Qazi Muhammad, who became President of the Republic.

Although the Soviet Army withdrw from Iran on 6 May 1946, the Republic survived until 15 December 1946, when it was crushed by the troops of the Teheran regime[12].

1946, 11 January
The People's Republic of Albania

As in the case of Yugoslavia, the establishment of the Marxist regime in Albania was a direct result of the communist-led resistance movement to foreign occupation during the Second World War.

When Italy invaded Albania on 7 April 1939, two separate communist groups operated in the country, one in Korça and another in Shkodra[13]. Although both were closely linked with traditional Albanian nationalism and its aspirations, they lacked organizational and ideological cohesiveness. The revolutionary situation which arose after the Italian occupation made the unification of the Albanian Communist movement an urgent priority. The Communist Party of Yugoslavia was largely responsible for the creation of a unified communist party in Albania. On 8 November two Yugoslav emissaries, Milan Popović and Duštan Mŭgoša, convened a meeting of three communist groups: Korça, Shkodra and the Youth group, and the Communist Party of Albania (ACP) was founded. A provisional Central Committee was elected, headed by Enver Hoxha.

The Party's immediate task was to recruit new members and to consolidate its organization in preparation for a general armed liberation struggle. In late November it created the Albanian Communist Youth Organization, through which new members were drawn to join the Communist Party. It also dispatched cadres into various regions of the country to reorganize the guerrilla bands which had been in operation since the early days of the Italian invasion and to form new units in those areas where there were none[14]. By the summer of 1942 the communist-led resistance had grown in strength to the point where it was possible to create its organizational structure.

On 16 September 1942, at the invitation of the ACP, the leaders of the resistance groups operating in the country at that time met at Peza and formed the National Liberation Movement (NLM). The Conference also elected the (Provisional) National Liberation Council[15], which included both communists and non-communists, and decided to set up national liberation committees in liberated and enemy-held territories to serve as organs of future governmental authority. These decisions laid the foundations of the future government. The programme adopted by the conference called for an uncompromising struggle against the invaders and for the unification of the Albanian people 'irrespective of their religion, region or political views' into a single anti-fascist national liberation front[16].

Soon after the Peza Conference the conservative Albanian opposition to the Italians organized itself into a National Front (Balli Kombetar), a strongly nationalistic and republican movement which wanted to keep for Albania the provinces annexed to it by the Axis in 1941. The Balli Kombetar and the NLM thus became the principal contenders in the power struggle during the next two years. In many respects the contests between the two movements resembled similar struggles between Tito's Partisans and Mihailović's Chetniks.

In 1943 during the First National Conference of the Albanian Communist Party, held between 17 March and 22 March in Labinot, it was decided to form the National Liberation Army (NLA). By July, twenty partisan batallions and thirty smaller fighting units were operating under the NLA's command[17].

The greater part of southern and central Albania was liberated by the partisan units in the spring of 1944. This enabled the ACP to turn its attention to political and state affairs. Between 24 and 28 May 1944, the First Anti-Fascist National-Liberation Congress of Albania was convened in the liberated town of Permet. It elected the Anti-Fascists National Liberation Council (ANLC) as the highest legislative and executive body in Albania[18]. The Council was charged with forming the Anti-Fascist National Liberation Committee of thirteen members with the attributes of a provisional government. Enver Hoxha was chosen chairman of this committee and also appointed Supreme Commander of the NLA. This move ensured that both military and political power was in the hands of the ACP.

The Congress also took several other important decisions: Albania was to have a democratic and popular government according to the will of the Albanian people as expressed in the ANLC, the sole national authority to have arisen from the national liberation struggle; King Zog was forbidden to return to Albania; the formation of any other government in Albania or abroad was not to be recognized; and all treaties and agreements concluded by the Albanian government with other countries before 1939 were declared null and void[19].

In October 1944, after the liberation of about three-quarters of the country, the Second Anti-Fascist Congress was held (20-23 October) in the liberated city of Berat. It transformed the Anti-Fascist National Liberation Committee into the Provisional Democratic Government of Albania, with Enver Hoxha as its Prime Minister.

Tirana was liberated by the National Liberation Army on 17 November and by 29 November the last foreign troops had been driven from Albanian soil. The national liberation in which the peasantry and the urban middle classes were the main spearheads was successfully transformed by the ACP into a socialist revolution both in its character and in its objectives.

On 2 December 1945 an election for the Constituent Assembly was held on a single ballot list. The Assembly met on 10 January 1946 and on the following day formally proclaimed Albania a People's Republic.

1947, 4 December
The Bulgarian People's Republic

During the Second World War the Bulgarian Workers' Party (BWP)[20] emerged as the strongest and best-organized opposition group to Bulgaria's adherence to the Tripartite Agreement and the Nazi-backed regime. The Party controlled the partisan units which in March and April 1943 were merged into the People's Liberation Army[21]. In the summer of 1944 the Army numbered some 18 300 fighters[22]. In adition the BWP dominated the Fatherland Front, which took its organizational shape in August 1943, when the Front's National Committee was set up. It consisted of representatives of the BWP, the Bulgarian Agrarian Union (the Pladne wing), the Bulgarian Workers' Social Democratic Party (BWSDP), the Zveno (Link) political group and one independent member[23].

On 5 September 1944 the Soviet Union declared war on Bulgaria and on 8 September the Red Army entered the country from Romania. The government, headed by the Bulgarian Agrarian Union politician Konstantin Mouraviev, tried unsuccessfully to extricate itself from the war and was steadily losing control of the situation. In the ensuing confusion the Fatherland Front, on 9 September, engineered a successful uprising which overthrew the Mouraviev administration and established its own government headed by Kimon Georgiev of the Zveno group. The government consisted of four communists, four representatives of the Bulgarian Agrarian Union (BAU), four representatives of the Zveno group, two social democrats and two non-affiliated members. The Communists held the Ministries of Interior and Justice, through which opposition could be suppresed with the authority and power of the State. Both ministries were primarily responsible for the subsequent major swoop on opposition elements, in addition to former politicians, that followed[24].

Following the September uprising, the Front began the process of organizing Fatherland Committees throughout the country. They soon took over control of local adminsitration and became the nuclei of future local government. The Committees also served as an important power base for the BWP since the majority of their members were Party members[25].

In early 1945 the Communists began to exert increasing pressure on their partners in the Fatherland Front government in order to build up even further their already substantial control. This led to the withdrawal, in August 1945, of some groups from the government and the creation of several opposition parties. In view of the Communists' strong following[26] and the considerable popularity of the Fatherland Front, the Party's inability to maintain the coalition arrangements could be partially explained in terms of the lack of parliamentary tradition in Bulgaria and fear of a repetition of the inter-war suppression which they had suffered. It would also appear that the Communists were unwilling to continue the coalition because they had their own perception of the ways in which the radical change of society, to which they were committed, should be implemented.

The first post-war national elections for the Ordinary Subranie[27] took place on 18 November 1945. They were held in an atmosphere of increasing polarization, which inevitably led to accusations by the opposition parties[28] of falsification of results and the use of terror. According to official results, with 85.5 per cent of voters taking part in the elections, the Front's candidates received 88.2 per cent of the votes[29]. The new parliament contained only representatives of the government coalition.

In June 1946 a new law transferred to the cabinet as a whole the powers previously held by the War Minister, who was relieved of his functions and replaced by Georgi Damnianov, the BWP Politbureau member. In a short time 1930 officers were summarily discharged from the army and the Party gained control of the military.

For two years after the September 1944 uprising Bulgaria formally remained a monarchy. The dynasty, identified with Germany, was genuinely unpopular. Therefore the referendum for the abolition of the monarchy held on 8 September 1946 was not a controversial issue. Out of a total of 91.6 per cent of the registered voters who took part in the referendum, 92.7 per cent voted for the abolition of the monarchy[30]. A few days later, on 15 September 1946, a session of the Subranie proclaimed Bulgaria a People's Republic.

More significant were the elections for the Grand Subranie, held on 27 October 1946, which were to formulate a new Constitution for the Republic. Like the previous year's elections, they were contested by two political blocs. The Fatherland Front emerged as the winner, capturing 366 out of 465 seats[31]. However, the opposition parties this time obtained almost 30 per cent of the vote[32] and for a few months acted as an opposition force within the National Assembly. On 4 December 1947 the Bulgarian parliament accepted the new republican Constitution[33] which was closely modelled on the Soviet Constitution of 1936. It reflected the social and political changes that had taken place in Bulgaria since the formation of the first Fatherland Front government. The promulgation of the Constitution should be seen as the completion of the process of the establishment of the Marxist regime in Bulgaria[34].

1947, 30 December
The Romanian People's Republic

In Romania the beginning of the process which established the Marxist regime can be traced to the spring of 1944. By that time the representatives of the internal Romanian opposition had already been negotiating between themselves and with Western Allies on ways aiming at extricating Romania from the increasingly unpopular war being fought on Hitler's side. The joining of the Axis by Romania in November 1940 had never been popular, not only with the great majority of the country's population but even with the bulk of rightist politicians and officers. However, it was not until 26 May 1944 that a clandestine United Workers' Front was formed between the Communist Party (RCP)[35] and the Social Democratic Party. It also included a number of small organizations cooperating with the RCP: The Ploughmen's Front, the Patriotic Union, MADOSZ (the Union of the Magyar Working People), the Socialist Peasant Party, the National Lobby and the National Democratic Party[36].

In June the Front was transformed into a National Democratic Bloc (NDB) when the representatives of the two 'historic' parties, the National Peasants' and National Liberals, joined the opposition groups during their conference with the Western Allies in Cairo. The Bloc's broad platform, signed on 20 June, called among other things for a truce with the Allied powers and the United Nations; withdrawal from the Axis Agreement; liberation from German occupation; Romania to join the United Nations; the re-establishment of national independence and sovereignty; the conclusion of peace treaties; and the overthrow of the fascist government of General Antonescu.

On 23 August 1944, when the Soviet army was breaking through the Moldavian sector of the front, King Mihai and a group of officers staged a *coup d'état* against the Antonescu regime. Antonescu and his cabinet were arrested in the Royal Palace by the communist 'patriotic units'. The same evening the communist-led armed insurrection began[37]. Its initial aim was the capture of the most important strategic points in order to prevent the Germans from coordinating any strike back. Romanian forces also now joined the Allies, fighting against the Nazis. At the same time Soviet troops continued to advance on Romanian territory and entered Bucharest on 30 August 1944[38]. Fighting with the Red Army were four divisions (Todor Vladimirescu, Horia, Closca and Crisan) composed of the Romanian ex-prisoners in the USSR.

The Armistice Agreement, signed on 12 September 1944 in Moscow and the Churchill–Stalin agreement in October 1944 on 'spheres of influence'[39], gave the Soviet Union a decisive role in the shaping of the post-war government of Romania.

The beginning of the RCP bid for power was the disruption of the pre-coup NDB and the formation of the National Democratic Front (NDF), which included only parties and groups sympathetic to the Communist Party, the MADOSZ, the Patriotic Union and the trade unions. In addition an important role in the Communist advance was played by the Allied Control Commission, increasingly dominated by the Soviet representatives, which intervened on behalf of the RCP in military, administrative and political matters. Three successive, short-lived governments between August 1944 and February 1945 included representatives of the Communist Party and its supporters in increasingly important posts[40].

The process of gradual increase in influence of the RCP in Romanian politics was met with opposition by the 'historic' parties and resulted in the deepening of political instability. In January and February 1945 a rapidly escalating crisis threatened civil war. The communist demand was the formation of the National Democratic Front government.

In early 1945 splits in the two 'historic' parties and the creation of dissident Peasants' and Liberal Parties[41], which declared their willingness to join in the NDF government, helped considerably to weaken the non-communist groups. Shortly after that the Soviet Deputy Foreign Minister Andrei Vyshinsky embarked on a policy of *diktat*.

On 6 March 1945, threatened with an ultimatum delivered by Vyshinsky that Romania might cease to exist as an independent state, King Mihai entrusted Petru Groza with the formation of a government. In the new cabinet 17 out of 21 portfolios were held by the RCP and co-members of the NDF: the key ministries of the Interior, Justice and National Economy were held by Theohari Georgescu, Lucretiu Patrascanu and Gheorghe Gherghiu-Dej, respectively, all high-ranking members of the RCP[42]. The formation of the Groza government meant *de facto* the establishment of a Marxist regime in Romania[43].

The new regime was recognized by the Soviet Union but not by the Western powers, who demanded a broadening of the government. The King refused to sign Groza's decrees and spent the period until his abdication in seclusion. In early January 1945 two representatives of the 'historic' parties, the National Peasants and the Liberals, joined the government as Ministers without Portfolio. The broadening of the cabinet brought about the regime's recognition by the Western powers and consequently the disintegration of the anti-Communist opposition which counted on Western support.

On 19 November 1946, after several months of postponement, the regime decided to hold national elections. Although every democratic party was allowed to participate, essentially two camps competed for votes: the Communist-led Bloc of Democratic Parties (BDP), comprising the members of the old National Democratic Front, and the splinter Peasants' and Liberal Parties; and the independent camp comprising the National Peasants' Liberal and Independent Social Democratic Parties. The official results of the elections gave, out of a total of 414 seats, 372 to the BDP, 33 to the National Peasants' Party and three to the Liberal Party[44]. These results, in spite of the widely held belief that they had been forged, gave for many Romanians and Western observers a certain validity to the internal order of the country.

The first post-war Romanian parliament functioned only for a short time with an opposition. The National Peasants' Party was dissolved in July 1947. Later the same year the Liberal and the Independent Social Democrat parties were formally banned. Also disbanded were the splinter parties, and their members were allowed to join the RCP.

On 30 December 1947 King Mihai signed his abdication and Romania was proclaimed a People's Republic. Thus the Marxist regime became established *de jure*[45].

1948, 25 February
The Czechoslovak People's Republic

After the end of the Second World War the Czechoslovak Communist Party (CCP)[46] emerged as the strongest and the best organized among the parties that formed the National Front government on 22 March 1945. The Front served as a coalition of four independent Czech parties (Communist, Social Democratic, National Socialist and People's Party) and two Slovak parties (Communist and Democrat). The Communists held the important Ministries of Interior, Agriculture, Information and Education.

For a variety of reasons the CCP enjoyed high prestige among the population. By July 1945 the Party had almost half a million members, a figure which was more than doubled in July 1946[47]. In the first post-war parliamentary elections held on 26 May 1946 the Party won 38 per cent of the poll (40 per cent in the Czech lands and 30 per cent in Slovakia) and, together with the Social Democrats, had 153 seats out of 300 in the National Assembly[48]. The CCP became the single biggest party in the Assembly and its Secretary-General Klement Gottwald was appointed Prime Minister. In addition, the Communists continued to hold the Ministries of Interior, Finance, Agriculture and Information.

The coalition, in which the CCP held the leading role, worked well despite frictions and inter-party competition until the summer of 1947, which saw a significant deterioration of the international situation and the final break-up of the wartime Great Power Alliance. The beginning of the cold war in 1947 was one of the most important factors which led to the disintegration of the multi-party system in Czechoslovakia and the CCP's assumption of control over the government.

In July 1947 the Czechoslovak government revoked its earlier decision to take part in discussions on the Marshall Plan. The main point of interest here is that the Gottwald cabinet was forced to change its unanimous acceptance of the invitation to attend the Paris conference on direct instructions from Stalin, who interpreted the acceptance as contrary to the Treaty of Friendship, Alliance and Mutual Assistance signed between the two countries in December 1943.

The second important event of the summer of 1947 was the formation of the Cominform, which was the Soviet answer to the Marshall Plan and a conclusive act in the division of Europe. According to Zdhanov's speech delivered at its inaugural meeting: 'The world is divided into two camps: the anti-democratic imperialist camp on the one hand and the anti-imperialist, democratic camp on the other.' It is perhaps important to recall that the meeting in Szklarska Poręba was attended also by Luigi Longo and Jacques Duclos, representing the Italian and French Communist Parties. Both Parties lost their portfolios in the respective governments in the spring of 1947, an event that, in the context of the accelerating cold war, counted against the 'parliamentary road' adopted by the Czechoslovak Party.

The actual process through which the CCP acquired absolute power was a governmental crisis in February 1948[49], which is worth examining in some detail. The crisis was precipitated not by the CCP but by the non-Communist parties, who, according to Vladimir Kusin, 'chose it as a convenient pivotal point around which, they hoped, the further gradation of Communist pressure could be resisted'[50].

On 13 February 1948 a majority of the cabinet instructed the Communist Minister of the Interior, Vaclav Nosek, not to proceed with the transfer of several high-ranking police officers in Prague and their replacement with CCP members. Nosek ignored the instruction. On 21 February twelve ministers belonging to the Czech People's National Socialist and Slovak Democrat Parties resigned in protest. The other two political parties, the CCP and the Social Democratic Party, refused to resign. The Prime Minister, Klement Gottwald, proposed that as the Communists and Social Democrats jointly represented the parliamentary majority President Beneš should appoint other ministers prepared to work within the government rather than dismiss its whole membership. The Constitution permitted such a resolution of the crisis. While Beneš hesitated, considerable extra-parliamentary pressure was brought about by the Communists and their sympathizers. Delegates to the Congress of Workers' Committees held in Prague at that time passed resolutions condemning the ministers who had resigned. 'Action Committees', consisting of CCP members and their supporters, were set up in the capital and in the provinces. They practically took over the duties of the People's Committees, which had hitherto been composed of representatives of all parties. According to Pavel Tigrid, they were 'so effective that the Communists never needed to step up the pressure by staging the general strike they had been planning, let alone call upon the armed forces they had standing ready[51]. All this undoubtedly contributed to the overall pressure for the resolution of the government crisis as suggested by the Communists.

On 25 February President Beneš appointed a new government in which the key posts were held by CCP members and the Social Democratic Party. The other parties each had a representative chosen not by themselves but by the Communists.

The outcome of the February crisis is, in the literature to which we have alluded, described as a *putsch*, a *coup d'état* or a takeover. We fail to find justification for any of these descriptions.

The CCP did not infringe the law of the land and used the Constitution to their advantage. It was the opposition parties which precipitated the governmental crisis which the Communists solved, gaining advantage at the same time. If the roles had been reversed, which was the intention of the opposition, it would have been described as a governmental change or outmanoeuvering of political opponents – which is what happened to the Communist Parties of France and Italy in the Spring of 1947.

The fact that, having achieved power, the CCP never relinquished it is, as suggested earlier, mostly due to the international climate at that time rather than to the nature of the CCP, which, after all, had one of the longest and most successful traditions of parliamentary participation in Europe.

Following the governmental changes a new Constitution proclaimed Czechoslovakia a People's Republic on 9 May 1948.

1948, 9 September
The Democratic People's Republic of Korea

Throughout its existence the Korean communist movement[52] has been in the mainstream of the anti-Japanese, national liberation movement[53]. The defeat of Japan on 15 August 1945 brought to an end the Japanese colonial administration, and hope of Korean independence was expressed in the Cairo Declaration of 27 November 1943 and reiterated in the Potsdam Declaration of 20 July 1945.

Only a week before the Japanese surrender the Soviet Union declared war against Japan and began the attack on Manchuria. On 10 August the Red Army crossed the frontier in northern Korea and advanced into the country. On 13 August President Truman approved the proposal of his Joint Chiefs of Staff that, for the purpose of accepting the Japanese surrender, the 38th parallel should be the dividing line between the United States and Soviet forces in Korea[54]. Stalin requested minor changes but accepted the provision of the 38th parallel without objection.

The first American troops began landing in South Korea on 8 September and during the three weeks' interval between Japan's surrender and the arrival of the US forces an administrative machinery emerged in Korea. On 16 August the Committee for Preparation of Korean Independence (CPKI) was organized in Seoul[55] and rapidly established a network of people's committees throughout the peninsula. On 6 September the CPKI convened a meeting in Seoul of approximately one thousand delegates, representing various political groups and professions throughout the country. This assembly, two days before the Americans arrived, declared themselves the People's Republic of Korea and claimed jurisdiction over the whole nation[56].

Amidst the confusion of the post-Japanese surrender, five major forces could be identified as emerging on the political scene in North Korea: the domestic Communist group, consisting of a number of organizations that had worked underground during the

Japanese occupation; the returnees from China associated with the Yenan base of the Chinese Communist party; the returnees from the Soviet Union, some of whom were CPSU members; the Kim Il Sung group, which most probably crossed into Korea from Manchuria[57]; and the nationalist group, led by a Presbyterian deacon, Cho Man-sik.

After the establishment of the CPKI in Seoul its northern branch was formed under the leadership of Cho Man-sik. It continued to recognize the People's Republic of Korea in the South as the central body, even though the organization of people's committees had advanced much further in the north. Only when the government of the Republic was refused recognition by the Americans did its northern branch form the Five Provinces Administration Bureau (NKFPAB) on 19 October. At the same time moves were made to form a nucleus of a single Communist organization. At a meeting convened by Kim Il Sung in Pyongyang from 10 to 13 October, a Central Organizing Committee of the Communist Party of North Korea was created[58].

Although these developments undoubtedly contributed in the long run to the creation of two regimes on the Korean peninsula the institutionalization of the division of Korea was the result of the Conference of Foreign Ministers of Britain, the United States and the USSR, which took place in Moscow between 15 and 26 December 1945. The Conference decided to institute a four-power trusteeship of Korea for a period of up to five years[59]. The agreement was denounced by both Nationalists and Communists on both sides of the 38th parallel. In the North the Russians removed Cho Man-sik because of his rejection of the Moscow deal and in the South the announcement of trusteeship sparked off serious riots. The Conference had set up a joint Soviet-American commission to work out the modalities of the trusteeship. By 8 May 1946 these talks had broken down completely.

The apparent Great Power cooperation in the division of Korea also accelerated the development of separate political systems. In the North the NKFPAB was reorganized on 8 February 1946 into the Provisional People's Committee of North Korea (PPCNK) under the chairmanship of Kim Il Sung. Shortly after, the Northern leadership embarked on a programme of thorough social revolution, which included an epoch-making land reform (March 1946), labour reform (May 1946), laws giving equal rights to men and women (July 1946) and the nationalization of major industries (August 1946).

Following the breakdown of the Soviet–American talks, a major reorganization of the Communist movement took place.

The Communist Party of North Korea merged with the Yenan group (which was known at that time as the New People's Party) on 28 August 1946 and formed the Workers' Party of North Korea[60].

Later that year the PPCNK decided to conduct elections to the provincial, city and country people's committees. The list of candidates of the Democratic National United Front included members of the Workers' Party of North Korea, two non-Communist parties, the Democratic and Chongu and a large number of non-affiliated. The latter captured more than 50 per cent of the total number of places, with 32, 10 and 8 per cent going to the Workers', Democratic and Chongu parties, respectively[61].

Following the 3 November 1946 elections, delegates of the newly elected people's committees held a Congress on 17 February 1947 in Pyongyang. The Congress elected from among its attendants the North Korean People's Assembly[62] which in turn created the North Korean People's Committee, headed by Kim Il Sung, as the supreme executive organ of North Korea[63]. Many of the ministerial positions in what was *de facto* a government of North Korea were held by leaders of the Democratic and Chongu parties as well as leaders of the Yenan Communists and domestic groups within the Workers' Party of North Korea[64].

It has been suggested earlier that internal political developments in Korea on both sides of the 38th parallel were to a large extent dictated by the fluctuations in relations between the USSR and the United States. In the spring of 1947 the foreign policy of the United States decisively changed direction, adopting the principle of containment. The United States now began to develop economic commitments, defence treaties and alliances. The pronouncement of the Truman Doctrine on 12 March 1947 and later the Marshall Plan are examples of the shift in the American appraisal of the Soviet Union. The deterioration of relations between the former wartime allies had dramatic repercussions on Korea. The prolonged series of Soviet–American confrontations in the UN[65] eventually resulted in a Russian boycott of the UN Assembly resolutions on Korea and unilateral UN-observed elections in the South, conducted by the US military authorities in place of nationwide elections. The purpose in using the UN was clearly seen by most political forces in Korea to be an attempt to legitimize the decision to split the country permanently.

In an attempt to prevent the division of the country, a Joint Conference of Representatives of Political Parties and Social Organizations of North and South Korea opened in Pyongyang on 19 April 1948. It was attended by 659 representatives of both political parties and social organizations from North and South Korea[66]. The Southern delegation consisted of 240 delegates including many right-wing leaders. This conference was a crucial episode in Korean history. It showed clearly the unbreakable links between the Communist and Nationalist movements, which were able to maintain cooperation on the fundamental question almost three years after the 38th parallel division was instituted.

At the end of the conference on 30 April a joint communiqué was issued by 33 North and South Korean political parties and social organizations. It stated: (a) support for the simultaneous withdrawal of Soviet and US armies; (b) that leaders of both North and South would never permit an outbreak of civil war or any disturbance which might militate against Korean desire for unity after the withdrawal of foreign troops; (c) that, following such a withdrawal, a political conference of all Korea would be called for the purpose of establishing a provisional democratic government representing the people of all strata; (d) that the political parties and social groups signing the statement would never recognize the result of separate elections in South Korea nor a government thereby established[67].

Nevertheless, separate elections took place in the South on 10 May 1948. On 15 August the Republic of Korea was formally inaugurated in Seoul.

The course of events in South Korea brought a prompt response from the regime in the North. The establishment of the Democratic People's Republic of Korea (DPRK) was proclaimed in Pyongyang on 9 September 1948[68]. Looking at the developments in Korea in the context of Soviet–American rivalries and in the atmosphere of the steadily deteriorating international situation it is difficult to sustain the traditional argument that the Marxist regime in North Korea was simply implanted by the Russians in the shadowy presence of the Red Army.

Although the Soviet presence was undoubtedly an important factor, it was secondary to that of the division of Korea instituted by both superpowers at the expense of the Korean people. The Northern regime was not a baggage-train government but one that emerged from among various political forces, including differing Communist groups, out of the necessities resulting in the first place from the lack of American understanding of the Korean situation – shown by the non-recognition of the People's Republic. To a large extent, however, it was also a product of the cold war and the US policy of containment.

1948, 14 December
The Polish People's Republic

Although the basic framework for post-war Poland[69] was drawn at the Teheran, Yalta and Potsdam conferences, the final shape of the Marxist regime in the country was the result of a long struggle between the various groups contending for political power.

The Polish Communist Party[70] was disbanded by the Comintern, on Stalin's orders, before the war and it was not until 1942 that a new Party was set up clandestinely in occupied Warsaw. On 5 January 1942 a secret meeting, in a Warsaw flat, of about a dozen people founded the Polish Workers' Party (PWP)[71]. it carefully avoided describing itself as a 'continuator' of the Polish Communist Party but rather as a 'party of a new type'. Its first two Soviet-approved leaders, Marceli Nowotko and Paweł Finder, were killed, after which the little-known Władysław Gomułka became its Secretary-General in November 1943 at the time when radio communication with Moscow had broken down. The PWP was able to appeal to these Poles who, though not communists, were able to see that Poland was – geographically at least – an eastern European country and therefore bound to be influenced by Russia after the war. Many foresaw that the Red Army, in order to get to Berlin, would soon pass through Poland and occupy it. The consequences of this were obvious to all but the most optimistic Poles. The Party began to increase its membership. In July 1942 it had 4000 members, in January 1943, 8000, in July 1944 20 000 and a year later 150 000[72].

Meanwhile, in the Soviet Union, the first Polish Army detachments under the Red Army command were created. This Polish army consisted of ex-prisoners of war and Poles who had fled from Poland to the USSR during the Nazi invasion. Many of the top command posts were given to Soviet officers[73], while most political jobs went to Polish Communists who, on 1 March 1943, formed in Moscow the Union of Polish Patriots. This organization in Stalin's designs was to be the future Polish administration. The programme of the Union provided for a 'Democratic People's Republic', 'everlasting friendship between the people of Poland and the USSR', a uni-camera parliament and land reform[74].

The PWP on the night of 31 December 1943 formed its own nucleus of civilian administration, the National Council for the Homeland (KRN)[75]. The Council was formed without Moscow's prior approval and a few days before the Red Army crossed the pre-war Polish–Russian frontier at Volhynia, on 4 January 1944. Even at that early stage the two main tendencies of Polish communism, which have dominated the political scene ever since, the 'domestic group' and the 'Muscovites', were already competing with each other. The competition has continued to the present day.

Among the main groups represented on the Council was the PWP, the Polish Socialist Party (PSP), individual members of the Peasants' movement and some representatives of trade unions[76]. In its manifesto the Council declared itself to be 'the only democratic representation of the Polish nation and its sole spokesman'[77]. The question then arose as to which was to become the next Polish government, the KRN or the Moscow-based Union of Polish Patriots. In 1944 the issue was temporarily resolved by the cooption of the representatives of the latter group to the newly formed Polish Committee of National Liberation (PKWN).

The Red Army, together with some Polish detachments, crossed the river Bug (the present eastern border of Poland) on 18 July 1944, and on 21 July they captured the small town of Chełm near Lublin. The very day Chełm was taken the KRN formed the Polish Committee of National Liberation to govern the freed areas. In addition to the representatives of the two Communist groups mentioned earlier, the PKWN also included members of the Peasants' and Democratic Parties. On 26 July it signed an agreement with the Soviet government which defined the relationship between the Commander-in-Chief of the Soviet Armies and the new skeleton administration. The agreement left wide powers in Soviet hands as long as Polish territories remained zones of military operations and full cooperation was pledged between the new regime and the Soviet authorities[78]. In reality, however, the agreement attempted to legitimize the brutal activities of the People's Commissariat of State Security (NKGB), which followed in the steps of the Red Army. The NKGB was responsible for attacking all Polish resistance groups, especially those who had not assisted the Soviet advance, and for appointing local administrators subordinate to them in every town and village throughout Poland[79]. Its activities undoubtedly accelerated the civil war in the countryside, which continued for about four years.

On 1 January 1945 in anticipation of the capture of Warsaw by the Red Army the PKWN declared itself to be the Provisional Government of Poland and was recognized as such by the USSR on 4 January, but not by the Western powers. The Provisional Government was composed of six members of the PWP holding the Portfolios of First Vice Prime Minister (Gomułka); Public Administration (which dealt with routine bureaucratic matters concerning security); Public Security (which controlled the secret political police, the military police – who carried out operations in close cooperation with the NKGB – and the Volunteer Citizens' Militia Reserve); Education; and Industry. The Prime Ministership (Edward Osóbka-Morawski) and five ministerial posts were held by the PSP. The Peasants' Party (PP) held three Portfolios and the post of the Second Vice Prime Minister. Two ministries were held by the Democratic Party (DP) and one post – that of the Minister of Defence – was held by General Rola-Żymierski, who came from the underground movement.

The Polish question was discussed extensively at the Yalta Conference which opened on 4 February 1945. Seven out of the eight plenary meetings were devoted to the Polish situation. The main problem as far as the Western powers were concerned was that the Provisional Polish Government was only based on the Communists and their sympathizers, to the exclusion of the Polish government-in-exile in London, which was recognized by the Western Allies. At the same time Stalin was quite happy with things as they were. The compromise which eventually emerged called for the reorganization of the Provisional Government on a broader democratic basis, with the inclusion of the leaders from Poland itself and from Poles abroad. This government should then be called the Polish Provisional Government of National Unity[80].

The Prime Minister of the London government, Stanisław Mikołajczyk, also leader of the Peasants' Party, resigned and with two of his former Ministers joined the government outlined at Yalta, after protracted negotiations.

The new Government of National Unity, formed on 28 June 1945, was nominally a coalition of five parties: the Polish Workers' Party, the Polish Socialist Party, the Peasants' Party, the Democratic Party and the Labour Party. Sixteen posts were held by members of the old provisional government while five ministries were relinquished to the Poles from abroad. It was decided that Osóbka-Morawski should continue as Prime Minister, with Mikołajczyk as First Deputy Prime Minister and Minister of Agriculture and Gomułka as Second Deputy Prime Minister and Minister for the Recovered Territories. Of twenty-four ministries, only seven were directly in the hands of the PWP. The government thus formed was promptly recognized by Britain, USA and France, which withdrew its recognition from the Polish government-in-exile in London.

There is little doubt that Mikołajczyk and his Peasant movement had a considerable following in what was after all predominantly an agricultural country. The reorganized Polish People's Party

(PPP) claimed in 1946 to have 600 000 members and it was quite clearly ideologically, politically and organizationally the biggest opposition group to the Communists. In the ensuing months the PPP and Mikołajczyk personally were subjected to increasing intimidation and pressure from the security forces. The PWP was so weak in numerical and popular terms that it could never have contemplated open competition with the bourgeois parties. One of the tactics which it used against the opposition groups like the Peasants was to split their parties. Rivals who refused to support the Communists found themselves with bogus parties bearing the same name as their own and led by former colleagues who had been successfully suborned. Such was the fate of Mikołajczyk's Peasant movement.

The Potsdam Conference (17 July to 2 August 1945) stipulated that 'free and unfettered' elections should be held in Poland as soon as possible. In 1946 the PWP put forward a proposal for the postponement of the elections[81]. The delay in conducting the elections is surprisingly frankly explained in a book recently published in Warsaw. Poland wanted to escape the Hungarian experience, where the Smallholders' Party had won the elections. Victory by the opposition would have put a question mark over the fundamental reforms conducted by the government[82].

Instead it was decided to hold a referendum on reforms introduced by the provisional government. The referendum was also to test the actual strength of the opposition now gathering in increasing numbers around Mikołajczyk, and to check the efficiency of the government's electoral machine.

The referendum asked the voters three questions:

(1) Are you in favour of abolishing the Senate?
(2) Do you want the future constitution to perpetuate the economic system introduced by the land reforms and the nationalization of the basic branches of the national economy, with the preservation of statutory rights for the private sector?
(3) Do you want the western border of the Polish state to remain on the Baltic and the Odra and the Lusatian Nysa rivers?

The answer to the first question was aimed at settling the question of the nature of parliament – whether it was to conform to liberal democratic traditions (by preservation of the upper house) or, by introducing the uni-camera formula, to become what was called a 'people's parliament'. The answer to the second question was to decide whether economic and social reforms undertaken by the government were to expand even further. The third question sought to determine the nation's attitude to

Poland's post-war western border – that is, the question of reincorporating into the state the ethnically Polish territories seized by German imperialism during the past centuries. The PWP called on the voters to give 'three ayes'. The PPP as the leading party of the legal opposition sought a 'no' to the first question and 'ayes' to the remaining two. Mikołajczyk advised his supporters to reject the reform of the parliament not because he had any great belief in the Senate but simply in order to give the opposition a chance to manifest itself.

Polling took place on 20 June 1946 and the results[83] gave a backing to the reforms undertaken by the Provisional Government. The PPP challenged the results and alleged systematic falsification of the ballots on the crucial first question.

The posponed parliamentary elections took place on 19 January 1947. Prior to the elections an electoral pact was signed on 28 November 1946 between the PWP and the PPP, thus creating the Democratic Bloc. This was later joined by the Peasant Democratic Party. The elections were also contested by two opposition parties, the PPP and the Labour Party.

The official results of the elections gave the communist-led Democratic Bloc 80 per cent of the poll and 394 out of the 444 seats in the new parliament. The opposition PPP, which expected to receive 75 per cent of the votes, received only 10 per cent and 28 seats[84] and was subsequently eliminated from participating in the government.

As a result of the elections the PWP assumed a dominant position for the first time. It also meant that all practical prospects of the opposition parties came to an end.

On 6 February a new government, headed by Józef Cyrankiewicz the PSP leader, was sworn in. On 19 February a new constitution was approved, establishing the Council of State which would exercise the powers of the parliament by means of decrees when the latter was not in session.

In the parliament Mikołajczyk was publicly denounced as a foreign agent and spy, and there followed mass arrests of PSL members and a wholesale closing of its local branches. Mikołajczyk, who acted as a general focus for the opposition, fearing for his life escaped from Poland with a handful of friends. In the countryside the last remnants of the anti-communist underground were destroyed.

On 14 December the Polish Workers' Party and the Polish Socialist Party merged and created the Polish United Workers' Party (PUWP)[85]. The formation of the Party brought to an end a period of free interplay of political forces in the country and resulted in the establishment of the Marxist regime in Poland. It is important to emphasize that the Red Army played a crucial role in the process of establishing the communist regime. As the Party's First Secretary put it, 'The presence of the Soviet army paralysed our class enemies'[86].

1949, 18 August
The Hungarian People's Republic

In Hungary the organization of the new post-war political, administrative and economic order began in the footsteps of the Red Army, which in September 1944 crossed the frontier from Romania. A temporary four-party coalition government was established on 21 December 1944 in the liberated city of Debrecen, as the Soviet Army pressed westwards. The Debrecen cabinet consisted of three representatives of the newly legalized Communist Party (CPH)[87], two each from the Independent Smallholders' Party (SDP) and one Social Democratic Party (SDP) and one from the National Peasant Party (NPP), as well as a number of non-party figures from the old regime. The post of Prime Minister was held by an ex-Horthyite, General Béla Dalnoki Miklos, who had gone over to the Soviet Army. The important Portfolio of the Minister of Interior was held by an NPP member. The Communist Party held the Ministry of Agriculture. The four-party government pattern was repeated in local committees set up to run local affairs.

The coalition government remained intact until the first post-war elections. These were held on 4 November 1945 and gave the Smallholders' Party 57 per cent of the vote, with the Communists and Social Democrats each receiving 17 per cent. After the elections one of the most important problems became the allocation of portfolios. The CPH demanded the Ministry of the Interior, and when this was refused it threatened to abandon the coalition. At that point the Soviet Chairman of the Allied Control Commission, Marshal Kliment Voroshilov, intervened on the Communists' behalf and the matter was settled to the Party's advantage. It should be stressed, however, that at that time the Soviet authorities seldom intervened directly in Hungarian internal affairs.

Although the Smallholders' party received an absolute majority in the election, under the armistice agreement the government had to be a coalition and it simultaneously included the opposition. This system was institutionalized by the creation of the Left Bloc on 5 March 1946. It included the Communists, the Social Democrats and the National Peasants. The Smallholders' Party had begun to be seen by many as an opposition force. To some it served as a rallying point against the increasingly dominant role played by the CPH, whose membership grew at a fantastic rate. In October 1945 the Party had half a million members as against 2000 only eleven months earlier.

The elimination of organized opposition[88], including the KGP, was achieved by the process subsequently outlined by Mátyás Rakosi in 1952 in his 'salami-tactics' speech to the Party High School[89]. (It amounted to slicing off opponents one by one.)

The tactics used in the 'slicing off' process involved arrests of prominent members of the Smallholders' Party on charges of conspiracy or of belonging to a counterrevolutionary organization and the splitting of some opposition groups by the creation of alternative groups and the dissolution of others.

The next general elections were held on 31 August 1947, this time on a common list of candidates. The CPH now became the largest party, with 22 per cent[90]. Votes for the Smallholders dropped to 15 per cent. The new government included five members of the CPH, four each from the Smallholders' and Social Democratic Parties and two from the NPP.

By 1948 the only party of importance which had some semblance of independence was the SDP. However, the SDP and CPH signed an agreement on 10 October 1944 aimed at the fusion of the two parties at a later date[91]. This was achieved on 12 June 1948. As a result of the merger the new Hungarian Workers' Party came into being.

The establishment of the Marxist regime in Hungary was sanctioned a year later. On 15 May another general election was held for a single list of candidates of the People's Front of National Independence. The Front received 96 per cent of the votes. The newly elected Parliament on 18 August approved a new constitution which proclaimed Hungary to be a People's Republic.

An important factor in the Hungarian developments in 1947 and the establishment of the Marxist regime was the international situation. According to Eugenio Reale[92] the foundation meeting of the Cominform decided that the period of coalition in Eastern Europe was over. The Hungarian party, operating in the shadow of the Soviet troops in the country, had little choice but to follow the directives of the Cominform. This became particularly pressing in the face of the *de facto* division of Europe and the ever-increasing political, economic and military presence of the United States in Western Europe. The *cordon sanitaire* created by the Soviet Union in the face of a potential threat could only serve the purpose for which it was intended if it became politically uniform.

This was later followed by economic and military integration. The economic and military dimensions of this framework were attended to later with the creation of the Comecon (CMEA) and the Warsaw Pact.

1949, 1 October
The People's Republic of China

The impact of the Soviet Revolution reinforced by the 'Karakhan Manifesto'[93], which in the name of the new government not only renounced all tsarist rights in China but also promised the return of all concessions to China without compensation, was particularly deeply felt among sections of Chinese intelligentsia. For half a century, Chinese intellectuals had criticized their own traditional system, but their only yardstick for a solution had been the liberal ideas of the imperialist West. Now, for the first time, they had a model of non-imperialist change. In 1920 small Marxist study groups were formed[94]. In July 1921 a secret meeting of two delegates from each of the six groups in China and one delegate from a group of Chinese in Japan, together with two agents of the Communist International[95], founded the Chinese Communist Party (CCP)[96].

For the next four years the Party remained a small collection of enthusiastic but not always practical revolutionaries. The leaders were openly scornful of the narrow nationalism of the much larger Kuomintang (KMT), and instead adopted a cosmopolitan outlook which further limited their appeal within China.

In 1923 the Comintern persuaded the Communists to collaborate with the KMT against the northern warlords[97]. The form of the United Front between the two parties was complex. It allowed the Communists to retain their own organization, to join the KMT as individuals and for a certain quota to be elected to KMT committees. During the first United Front period the CCP began to transform itself into a mass-based organization. Its growth and organizational success among workers and peasants was particularly noticeable after the May Thirteenth Movement of 1925, which launched a wave of strikes and protest in the cities. The membership of the Party increased from about 1000 in May 1925 to 10 000 at the end of the year and to nearly 58 000 by April 1927[98].

In the spring of 1925, after the death of Sun Yat-sen, the leadership of the KMT passed to Chiang Kai-shek who, in the summer of 1926, launched the Northern Expedition, a military campaign to bring the warlords of the north under government control and thus unite China. The plan caught the imagination of all patriots, including many in the Communist Party like Mao Zedong. The expedition had rapid and impressive success. By the beginning of 1927 the Nationalists had captured Wuhan in central China and were approaching Nanking (Nanjing) and Shanghai in the east.

In the early spring of 1927 the Communist movement in Shanghai tried several times to rise and drive out the warlord troops to welcome the Northern Expedition. In March communist workers rose again, drove out the warlord forces and welcomed the Nationalist Army into Shanghai, which ordered the Communists to surrender their weapons. On 12 April Chiang turned on the Communists. He denounced the United Front, broke off relations with the USSR and used troops and gangs to break up the labour organizations, killing thousands of workers. Astonishingly, in spite of the Shanghai massacre, the Comintern instructed the CCP to maintain the United Front at all costs. The order was changed latet in the year and the CCP broke away from the KMT in July 1927. By then the CCP was a shattered Party with its membership reduced to 10 000[99]. Its Central Committee, directed by Comintern agents, operated underground in the cities of eastern China, trying to rebuild the proletarian base. The strategy of urban insurrection had led the CCP to a point of near-destruction.

Throughout this period the Party, and its leader Chen Tu-hsin in particular, paid very little attention to the peasantry. They still had the traditional scholar's attitude to peasants and saw them as socially inferior. The first peasant movement linked with the CCP began at Hailufeng in Kwantung (Guangdong). In 1922 P'eng P'ai[100], a student, started peasant associations which demanded and gained rent reductions and limitations of landlord powers. The associations later also spread to Hunan province and Mao Zedong helped in their foundation in 1925.

In 1927, after his experience with the peasants' associations, Mao wrote his important study 'A Report of an Investigation into the Peasant Movement in Hunan'[101]. In it he criticized those Communists and KMT leaders who deplored the rural disorder. Most importantly, however, contrary to the view of Marxists before him including Marx himself, he recognized that the peasants were capable of independent revolutionary action. Prophetically Mao reported:

> In a very short time, in China's central, southern and northern provinces, several hundred million peasants will rise like a mighty storm, like a hurricane, a force so swift and violent that

no power, however great, will be able to hold it back. They will smash all the trammels that bind them and rush forward along the road to liberation . . . Every revolutionary party and every revolutionary comrade will be put to the test, to be accepted or rejected as they decide. There are three alternatives. To march at their head and lead them? To trail behind them, gesticulating and criticizing? Or to stand in their way and oppose them? Every Chinese is free to choose, but events will force you to make the choice quickly[102].

Mao's analyses were not accepted with much enthusiasm by the urban-oriented leadership of the CCP, but after Chiang's assault on the Communists in April 1927 the real focus of the movement began to shift to the countryside. In late summer different sections of the Party organized risings against the KMT. The most important of such episodes was the so-called Autumn Harvest Uprising in Hupei and Hunan, the latter led by Mao. All the uprisings were crushed. Mao managed to rally about 1000 survivors and lead them to Chingkangshan, a mountain plateau on the Hunan –Kiangsi border. There he was joined by Zhu De (Chu Te) and his troops. Together they established a rural base for their forces, cut off from the CCP headquarters and in disagreement with many of its policies. So began what has been called the Kiangsi period (1927-1934) of the CCP, in which the significant action was the establishment of rural soviets in remote areas. The strategy of the urban insurrection was now abandoned completely and Mao and Zhu evolved techniques of peasant mobilization and built the Red Army from the disaffected, landless and semi-bandit groups of the hill area. The Army, which combined political awareness with military competence, became the key to the survival and growth of the rural revolution.

Between 1929 and 1931 several soviets in different areas of China were established. They did not merely provide military protection but also developed organs of control and local government. These were all dominated by party members in the respective soviet.

The strongest soviet of the communist base area was the one under Zhu De and Mao. It gradually expanded its area of control and in November 1931 it was transformed into the Chinese Soviet Republic, embracing a large part of Kiangsi Province with a population of some 15 million, independent not only of the government of Chiang Kai-shek but also of their own Central Committee in Shanghai. The mass support for the Kiangsi Republic clearly depended on the behaviour and policies of the Communists. Instructions for the good treatment of civilians were relentlessly and apparently effectively inculcated into the Red Army. Party leaders spent a great deal of time debating the methods of social reform most suited to rouse the support of the masses. At some times and in some areas all land was confiscated and distributed either to those able to work it or to everyone. In some cases only the land of the landlords was taken, in others rich or even middle peasants had their land expropriated.

The Kiangsi Republic was continuously harrassed by Chiang Kai-shek troops. In late 1933 Chiang launched the fifth campaign against the Republic, which by then had come under the command of the Party's Central Committee. In the latter part of 1934 the Communists abandoned their stronghold and embarked on the historic Long March[103] of more than 6800 miles. For over a year they marched and fought their way across Hunan, Kweichow (Jueizhou), Yunnan, Szechwan (Sichuan), Eastern Tibet and the fringe areas of the Gobi Desert and Kanzu until the eventually met up again in Yenan (Yanan). During the Long March Mao managed to remove some of the Russian-trained leaders, and in January 1935 he was elected chairman of the CCP.

After Japan's large-scale invasion of central China on 7 July 1937 the CCP and KMT concluded an agreement on a Second United Front. This alliance was significantly different from the first, however, being essentially an armed truce in the interests of anti-Japanese unity. The Soviet regime in Yenan was recognized as a 'special region' of the Republic of China. The Red Army was incorporated into the national forces (at least in theory) under the new name 'Eighth Route Army'. In fact, there was little cooperation between the two parties, apart from a loosely observed understanding not to make open war on each other. The Eighth Route Army, limited in strength to 45 000, fought in small units of 1000 behind the Japanese lines. It developed highly effective methods of guerrilla warfare, gradually enlarging its sphere of influence in northern and north-western provinces. As anti-Japanese sentiment swelled the CCP was able to establish a solid base of recruitment, and by 1940 the CCP increased to 800 000[104] as against 40 000 after the Long March.

In 1940 the United Front began to fall to pieces, and in early 1941 tension gave way to open hostilities as KMT troops attacked Communist soldiers. Perhaps the real significance of the Second United Front lay in the Communist revolutionary strategy, a strategy that saw the road to power as built on the broadest possible national base rather than on narrow or rigid class lines.

Between 1941 and 1945 the CCP devoted most of its attention to the consolidation of military and political organization in the

Yenan Republic. Intensified efforts were made during that period to put Mao's political and doctrinal authority directly into practice; Maoist methods for educating and disciplining party members, controlling bureaucracy, leading and working with the masses, organizing the economy and many other tasks were applied systematically and formalized as integral parts of the Party's political style[105]. The success of these efforts can be measured by the fact that by the summer of 1945 the CCP membership had grown to 1 210 000, the Red Chinese Army numbered 910 000 soldiers and the Party governed areas with a population of 95 500 000[106].

Although few contemporary observers noticed it, by 1945 the Communists had substantially won their revolution. As the war came to an end on 14 August, many smaller units of the pro-Japanese puppets went over to them. After V-E Day, Chiang, with considerable aid, managed to occupy all the major cities previously controlled by the Japanese. Despite the KMT strength, wealth and massive outside support, they were discredited in the eyes of politically aware people and this category now included tens of millions of Chinese peasants. By the middle of 1947 all attempts to patch up a truce between the two sides failed and open hostilities began. The KMT attacked and took Yenan and other centres in the north-west. The Communists made these victories meaningless by rapid and effective military moves in Manchuria and central China. At the same time they began a massive campaign of radical land distribution. This campaign destroyed the economic base of the gentry class. The methods used were to encourage peasant activists who had been leaders in the anti-Japanese war to form groups within the village or hamlet to attack the landowners. Outside cadres were used only for technical jobs such as accounting and surveying. The overall results of the campaigns were to draw millions of poor and middle peasants into political life and to associate the Communists with the economic and social improvements in village life.

By 1948 the support for the KMT was reduced to the upper levels of its party organization, its army and a few of the richer landlords. Even US support was not sufficient to back up a regime which by that time was demoralized and riddled with rivalries and corruption. In September of 1949 Chiang Kai-shek and KMT leaders fled to Taiwan after a massive offensive by the People's Liberation Army.

On 1 October 1949 Mao Zedong proclaimed the inauguration of the People's Republic of China.

1949, 7 October
The German Democratic Republic

The predominant view among Western political scientists writing on the GDR is that the Marxist regime in the Soviet-occupied zone of Germany came to power as a result of Soviet military presence[107]. Although this was undoubtedly an important factor, the assumption that the regime was merely imposed by the Soviet Union is a vast oversimplification to say the least.

The Communist Party of Germany (KPD) was decimated by the Nazis. On 27 February 1933 during the night of the Reichstag fire, Göring ordered the arrest of some 4000 KPD functionaries. The entire Party press was outlawed, the Party was deprived of its parliamentary representation and its legally operating organizations were crushed. For twelve years the KPD was to remain illegal and the slightest connection with it meant arrest, persecution, penal servitude, concentration camp, torture or death. A number of Party members, however, managed to escape to the Soviet Union, where the KPD continued to function in exile. In July 1943 they organized the National Committee for a Free Germany. In addition to the Communists the Committee was also composed of captured German soldiers. Although it had relatively little success in winning over either prisoners of war or frontline German troops, it proved to be an important training ground for many subsequent officials in the Soviet zone of Germany.

During the final stages of the Second World War the first three KPD groups returned from the Soviet Union. On 30 April 1945, the day on which Hitler committed suicide, Walter Ulbricht and a group of nine were flown to a location near Berlin. A second group, led by Anton Ackermann and Hermann Matern, arrived in Dresden. A third group, led by Gustav Sobottka, landed in Mecklenburg. They began to reconstruct the Party and organized some administrative districts, a nucleus of the future administrative structure.

The German Reich was crushed on 8 May 1945 and the arrest, on 23 May, of the remnants of the German government created a power vacuum. This led the Allies to establish the Allied Control Council (ACC) to deal with all common matters affecting the whole of Germany. Since the ACC had no executive it had to rely on the individual commanders in the four zones of occupation[108] to carry out its decisions. The Soviet Military Administration in Germany (SMAD) was established on 9 June to administer the Soviet zone.

As early as 10 June 1945 the SMAD issued its Order No. 2 permitting the formation of anti-fascist political parties and mass organizations. The KPD was the first to emerge. Its manifesto issued on 11 June stated:

> We are of the opinion that it would be wrong to force the Soviet system upon Germany, as that would not correspond to the present stage of development in Germany. Rather, we are of the opinion that the most important interests of the German nation in the present situation call for a different road, the road of establishing an anti-fascist, democratic regime, a parliamentary republic[109].

On 15 June 1945 the Central Committee of the Social Democratic Party of Germany (SPD) published its manifesto. Many of the aims set out in this document were similar to those of the KPD. It envisaged Germany not only as a democratic but also as a socialist state with a socialized economy. It favoured the organizational unity of the German working class. The similarities of their standpoints made it possible for the two parties to agree on a joint action programme on 19 June.

The Christian Democratic Union of Germany (CDU), founded on 26 June 1945, and the Liberal Democratic Party of Germany (LDPD), formed on 5 July, both called for a complete break with fascism and the development of a free market economy.

On 14 July the four parties agreed to establish a bloc of anti-fascist democratic parties. A committee composed of five representatives from each party was to pursue a common policy. Decisions of the bloc had to be unanimous. Bloc committees were founded in all cities and villages of the zone[110].

Between 17 July and 2 August 1945 the leaders of the Allied powers met in Potsdam. The Allies agreed that no German government should be formed but that some important German administrative departments, for example, for finance, transport and traffic, foreign trade and industry, should be established[111]. These departments obviously formed the nucleus of a future all-German government. It appears that at that time Soviet policy was to preserve German unity.

The political system of the Soviet zone between 1945 and 1947 displayed many characteristics of a democratic parliamentarianism resting on a plural-party system. Democratic political institutions were established on the communal level, the newly created Länder were given legislatures based on open elections, just as they were in the Western zones, and anti-Nazi politicians of almost all kinds were encouraged to take an active part in politics. Political parties

were licensed earlier than in the other zones and given considerable encouragement, funds and party newspapers.

These developments were in accordance with KPD policies.
Anton Ackermann, one of the Party's leading intellectuals, wrote
in February 1946 in the theoretical journal *Einheit*:

> The development towards socialism in Germany will doubtlessly
> carry a specific character. In other words, the strong particular-
> ities of the historical development of our people, the political
> and national individuality, the special traits of its economy and
> culture will find an unusually clear expression[112].

In early 1946 the KPD and SPD merged their organizations. It is
perhaps worth remembering that the parties had operated in the
Soviet zone and Berlin under a joint action programme since June
1945. In February 1946 a conference of thirty leading Social
Democrats and thirty leading Communists agreed on a timetable
for unity. Both leaderships were to call conferences of their
respective parties to agree to the proposal. The protagonists of
unity now became very active. In some places the rank and file of
both parties merged their local organizations without waiting for
the conferences[113].

The unification congress took place on 21 and 22 April and
created the Socialist Unity Party (SED)[114]. The delegates attend-
ing the Congress represented 620 000 Communists and 680 000
Social Democrats. Wilhelm Pieck and Otto Grotewohl, leaders of
the KPD and SPD, respectively, were elected joint chairmen of
the Party.

The hopes for a German 'third road' to socialism were short-
lived. International developments between the Great Powers, for
which Germany became the playground, led to the tightening of
Soviet control on East Germany and at the same time to the
emergence of two separate states in Germany.

In January 1947 the British and American zones were fused and
in June that year the United States launched the Marshall Plan,
from which Western Germany was to be a major beneficiary. In
the Soviet zone the Soviet Military Administration set up in June
the German Economic Commission. Its main tasks were to draw
up an economic plan for the whole zone, to supervise the delivery
of war reparation to the Soviet Union and to ensure that the needs
of the Soviet occupation forces were met. A Permanent Bureau of
the Commission was established which consisted of the
Commission's chairman, his deputy, the chairmen of the Free
German Trade Unions and the Mutual Aid Association and the
presidents of the central administration of finance, industry,

agriculture, trade and food. The Bureau, which was dominated by the SED, was *de facto* the government of the Soviet zone of occupation and was directly under the control of the Soviet Military Administration in Germany[115].

The failure of the Great Powers' Conference on Germany in London in December 1947 accelerated the political developments on both sides of Germany. In June 1948 the military governors of the Western zones announced currency reforms. The line of demarcation with the Soviet-occupied zone henceforth separated territories using different currencies, thereby virtually becoming a state border. In May 1949 representatives of political parties in the British, American and French occupation zones adopted the Constitution for the Federal Republic of Germany, which came into existence on 21 September 1949. Thus the political division of Germany was a *fait accompli*.

The proclamation of the German Democratic Republic on 7 October 1949, as a direct riposte to the formation of the Federal Republic, not only concluded the establishment of the Marxist regime in East Germany but also recognized *de facto* the social and political changes that had taken place in the zone since the end of the war. The Soviet Military Administration in Germany transferred its administrative responsibilities to the GDR's organs of government. The USSR extended diplomatic recognition to the new regime on 15 October 1949.

1 The year of the first world-wide Conference of Representatives of Communist and Workers' Parties, held in Moscow between 14 and 16 November. This conference was also the last such event before the Sino–Soviet dispute came into the open
2 The Soviet Union demanded the port of Hango at the head of the Gulf of Finland, the Karelian Isthmus and part of the area north of Lake Ladoga in order to protect Leningrad (see J. H. Hodgson, *Communism in Finland: A History and Interpretation*, pp. 176–9)
3 D. Klein and A. Clark, *Biographical Dictionary of Chinese Communism*, p. 743
4 A. S. Whiting, *Sinkiang: Pawn or Pivot?*, p. 111
5 It is interesting to note that the communist movement in Sinkiang was developed and supported not by the Communist Party of China but by the Communist Party of the Soviet Union. According to one source, 'No Local Party [CCP] members of minority nationalities were found before liberation [1949]' in Sinkiang (Whiting, op.cit. (note 4), p. 111). There were, however, members of the CPSU in that region. The most prominent among them was Saifudin, who retained his membership of the Soviet Party until 1950. In 1961 Saifudin wrote: 'Beginning in 1933, the Party sent many outstanding Party members and cadres at different times to carry out revolutionary work in Sinkiang, thus sowing the seeds of revolution on a broad front' (Klein and Clark op.cit. (note 3), p. 743). In the absence of the Chinese Party's cells this must clearly refer to the CPSU

6 Ibid., p.744
7 In the inter-war period the Party played only a marginal role in the politics of Yugoslavia. Founded on 23 April 1919, as the Socialist Workers' Party of Yugoslavia (Communist), it changed its name on 24 June 1920 to the Communist Party of Yugoslavia. In the short period of its legal existence (eighteen months) it became the third strongest party, with 59 of the 419 seats in the Constituent Assembly.

The CPY was outlawed on 30 December 1920 (and banned altogether on 1 August 1921) and forced to operate illegally until the dismemberment of Yugoslavia in the Second World War. During the long period of its underground existence the Party was almost paralysed, with its membership down from 80 000 in 1919 to about 500 in 1932 and the leadership divided into factions. In 1936, the Comintern, in a last attempt to revitalize the CYP before closing it down, appointed Josip Broz as its Secretary-General. The result of his work was unique and an outstanding success

8 I. Avakumović, *History of the Communist Party of Yugoslavia*, Vol. 1, p. 23
9 *The Outline History of the Viet Nam Workers' Party*, p. 11
10 Ibid., pp. 37–38
11 R. K. Ramazani, 'The Autonomous Republic of Azerbaijan and the Kurdish People's Republic: Their Rise and Fall', in *The Anatomy of Communist Takeovers* (ed. by Thomas T. Hammond), pp. 448–474
12 Ibid.
13 The Korça and Shkodra groups were formed in 1929 and 1934, respectively. The latter also had its members in several other towns. In 1940 the Youth group was founded as a faction of the group in Korça
14 N. C. Pano, *The People's Republic of Albania*, p. 46
15 *Istoria Albanskoi Partii Truda*, p. 137
16 Ibid.
17 Ibid., pp. 168–169
18 Ibid., p. 227
19 Cited after R. Marmullaku, *Albania and the Albanians*, p. 54
20 The Bulgarian Communist Party has its origins in the Bulgarian Social Democratic Party, formed in 1891. A split in 1903 resulted in the formation of the Workers' Social Democratic Party, which re-named itself the Bulgarian Communist Party in 1919. After the March 1920 elections it received fifty out of the 229 seats in the Subranie, thus becoming second in strength to the Bulgarian National Agrarian Union. The Party suffered badly after the unsuccessful armed uprising of September 1923 and particularly after the attempted assassination of Tsar Boris in 1925. Disbanded in 1924 it reappeared as a legal Workers' Party in 1927 and regained most of its popular support in the early 1930s. In 1932 the Party won the Sofia municipal elections. After the dissolution of all political parties in 1934 it operated illegally until 1944 as the Bulgarian Workers' party. The Party's name was changed to the Bulgarian Communist Party in December 1948
21 *A Short History of the Bulgarian Communist Party*, p. 205
22 Ibid., p. 218
23 Ibid., p. 204
24 According to official sources, 10 897 people had by March 1945 been tried as war criminals. Of these 1940 received twenty-year prison sentences and 2138 were executed. See L. Holmes, 'People's Republic of Bulgaria' in *Marxist Governments: A World Survey* (ed. by B. Szajkowski), Vol. 1, p. 141
25 The relative strength of the BWP within the Fatherland Front is illustrated by the following statistics. Of the 26 265 members of these committees, 14 120

were representatives of the BWP, 8682 represented the BAU, 854 represented the BWSP, 410 represented the Zveno group and 2179 were non-affiliated persons. Quoted after *A Short History*, op.cit. (note 21), p. 223

26 The BWP membership in 1945 was 254 000 as against 25 000 in 1944

27 To be distinguished from the Grand Subranie which, according to the 1879 Constitution, was necessary for the changes to the Constitution

28 The opposition parties were mainly splinter groups from the Front's parties, such as the opposition BAU centred on the newspaper *Narodno Zemedelsko Zname* (National Agrarian Banner) and the BWSDP (united). The old-established Democratic Party, which resumed its activities, also joined the opposition

29 *A Short History*, op.cit. (note 21), p. 219

30 Ibid., p. 241

31 Of these, 275 were taken by the BWP, 69 by the BAU, 9 by the BWSDP, 8 by the Zveno, 4 by the Radical Party and 1 by an unaffiliated deputy

32 J. F. Brown, *Bulgaria Under Communist Rule*, p. 12

33 For a survey and analysis see ibid., pp. 13–16

34 It is, however, important to summarize the subsequent development among the parties of the Fatherland Front. The Second Congress of the Front, held early in February 1948, heard a report by Georgi Dimitrov, who declared that the Front's 1942 programme was now implemented and formulated a new programme which would ensure the construction of the 'socialist social system' in Bulgaria. The Congress decided that conditions now existed for increasingly harmonious relations among its individual constituent parties on the one hand and on the other for the dissolution of some of them and the merger of others. Consequently within a few months after the Congress the BWSDP was merged with the BWP, and the Zveno group and the Radical Party were dissolved. The only remaining Fatherland Front party to exist as an independent political party was the Bulgarian Agrarian Union which became an 'organization of the poor and middle peasants and no longer a class organization of all the peasants'. See *A Short History*, op.cit. (note 21), pp. 248–249

35 The Romanian Communist Party founded on 8 May 1921, was outlawed three years later. Throughout the years of its clandestine activity it remained under strong Soviet control with its leadership constantly purged on Stalin's orders. In 1944 it had approximately 1000 members

36 'Romanian Communist Party's Decisive Role in the Historic Events of August 1944', *Lumea*, No. 34, 24–30 August 1979, p. 24. The history of this period has been rewritten several times by Romanian and Western scholars in recent years. Consequently it is difficult to find reliable sources pertaining to the activities of the various groups and parties between 1943 and 1947. The list of organizations that joined the United Workers' Front cited above comes from a recent Romanian publication. In comparison with other, older, sources, e.g. G. Ionescu, *Communism in Romania, 1944–1962*, S. Fischer-Galati, *Twentieth Century Rumania* and H. Seton-Watson, *The Eastern European Revolutions*, it includes organizations not mentioned before. But whether this new and surprisingly long list is due to a new political appraisal or new data established during further research of this period is very difficult to conclude

37 Needless to say, the history of the *coup* and the subsequent events has been reappraised several times since. For the recent Romanian version see 'August 1944 Insurrection, Political and Military Chronology', *Lumea*, No. 31, 3–9 August 1979, 21–23 and No. 32, 10–16 August 1979, 21–23

38 According to Romanian sources, when the Soviet units entered Bucharest the capital 'had already been liberated by the insurrectional forces'. See B. Teofil, *Romania: The Land and the People*, p. 55

39 The agreement was reached on 9 October 1944 during the British Prime
    Minister's visit to Moscow. The following is Churchill's account of his and
    Eden's meeting with Stalin and Molotov.
        'The moment was apt for business, so I said, "Let us settle about our affairs
    in the Balkans . . ." While this was being translated I wrote out on a half-sheet
    of paper:
        Roumania
            Russia 90%
            The others 10%
        Greece
            Great Britain 90%
            (in accord with USA)
            Russia 10%
        Yugoslavia 50–50%
        Hungary 50–50%
        Bulgaria
            Russia 75%
            The others 25%
    I pushed this across to Stalin, who had by then heard the translation. There
    was a slight pause. Then he took his blue pencil and made a large tick upon it,
    and passed it back to us. It was all settled in no more time that it takes to set
    down . . . After this there was a long silence. The pencilled paper lay in the
    centre of the table. At length I said, "Might it not be thought rather cynical if it
    seemed we had disposed of these issues, so fateful to millions of people, in
    such an off hand manner? Let us burn the paper." "No, you keep it," said
    Stalin.' (Quoted from W. S. Churchill, *The Second World War, Triumph and
    Tragedy*, Vol. 6, pp. 197–198)
40 For example, the government appointed on 4 November included not only a
    number of Communists and Social Democrats but also Petru Groza, who
    became deputy head of the government. He was the leader of the tiny
    Ploughmen's Front, who acted in the service of the RCP
41 The fragmentation of the anti-Communist political parties and the creation of
    splinter pro-Communist parties, often led by opportunist politicians with
    anti-Communist and anti-Soviet records, is referred to in the literature on the
    coming to power of the Eastern European regimes as 'salami tactics'
42 For characterization and a detailed account of the Groza government see
    Ionescu, op.cit. (note 36), pp. 107ff.
43 I. Ceterchi, O. Trasnea and C. Flad (eds), *The Political System of the Socialist
    Republic of Romania*, p. 90
44 Ibid., pp. 318–319
45 In February 1948 the Social Democratic party merged with the Romanian
    Communist Party, thus creating the ruling Romanian Workers' Party
46 The CCP was formed on 15 November 1921 and operated legally in the
    inter-war period, achieving considerable electoral successes throughout the
    1920s and 1930s. It became the third largest in a field of eight major parties
47 For membership figures see A. Pravda, 'The Czechoslovak Socialist Republic'
    in Szajkowski (ed.) op.cit. (note 24), Vol. 2, p. 273
48 It is perhaps worth recalling that the Red Army evacuated Czechoslovakia in
    December 1945, at the same time that the American forces, which had
    occupied Western Bohemia, also withdrew
49 Much has been written about the February crisis and listing the refeences here
    would have taken an unnecessarily large amount of precious space. For a
    selection of material see L. J. Cohen and J. P. Shapiro (eds), *Communist
    Systems in Comparative Perspective*, Anchor Books, New York, 1974, p. 66.

The following have been most useful: P. E. Zinner, *Communist Strategy and Tactics in Czechoslovakia*, Ch.11; P. Tigrid, 'The Prague Coup of 1948: The Elegant Takeover', in Hammond (ed.), op.cit (note 11), pp. 399–432; and V. V. Kusin, 'Czechoslovakia' in *Communist Power in Europe 1944–1949* (ed. by Martin McCauley), pp. 73–74. The account above is based in parts on Kusin's chapter

50 Kusin, op.cit. (note 49), p. 88

51 Quoted in ibid., p. 91

52 The first Korean Communist organization was created in Khabarovsk in June 1918, under the name of the Korean People's Socialist Party. Its leaders were exiled nationalists seeking active assistance from the Bolsheviks against Japanese imperialism. Many of the Koreans in Siberia – who in 1918 were estimated to number about 200 000 – fought there with the Bolsheviks against White Russians and the Allied Expeditionary Forces. In April 1919 the Party changed its name into the Korean Communist Party and moved its headquarters to Vladivostok and later to Shanghai. During the 1920s and 1930s the Party became fragmented, with groups calling themselves communist operating in Siberia, China, Manchuria (Kim Il Sung was active in this group), Korea and Japan

53 Korea was, along with Taiwan, Japan's oldest colony in Asia, seized *de facto* in 1895 and annexed formally in 1910. There had been major uprisings between 1906 and 1911, and in 1919 a nationwide revolt against Japanese rule broke out. After the 1919 uprising, the balance of power among the anti-Japanese forces gradually shifted in favour of the Communists and away from the Nationalists

54 Contrary to the widely held view that the division of Korea was another secret agreement made either at Yalta or Potsdam, the suggestion was, in fact, made by the US State–War–Navy Coordinating Committee on 11 August. When the Russians began attacking the Japanese forces in Korea on 10 August the nearest US troops were more than six hundred miles away from Korea, at Okinawa. The presence of the Red Army on Korean soil precluded the possibility that Japanese surrender in Korea could be accepted by the Americans alone. A second-best choice was that the Americans occupy as much of Korea as would be feasible. Since the United States wanted to keep the capital city of Seoul in their zone along with the port of Inchon, the line of the 38th north parallel, which lay some 45 miles north of Seoul, was thus finally selected

55 Political developments in South Korea, including the activities of the Korean Communist Party there, are beyond the scope of this study. I would therefore allude to them only insofar as they appear to have direct bearing on the establishment of the Marxist–Leninist regime in North Korea

56 On the same day a Central People's Committee was elected with 55 members and 20 candidate members. This Committee then formed the first *de facto* government of Korea. It sent a delegation to welcome General Hodge, the American commander, when he landed at Inchon on 8 September. Hodge refused to meet the delegation and declined to accept the offer of service by the People's Republic to the American occupation forces. By the end of 1945 the Republic was suppressed and its people's committees dismantled by the Americans

57 At that time Kim Il Sung apparently rejected a demand from a faction of his guerrilla organization for the establishment of 'Soviet' power in Korea in favour of an indigenous type of a Korean government of a Democratic People's Republic. See his 'On Building the Party, State and Armed Forces in

the Liberated Homeland – Speech Delivered to Military and Political Cadres 20 August 1945', Kim Il Sung, *Works*, Vol. 1, pp. 225–241

58 Kim Han Gil, *Modern History of Korea*, p-.192

59 The four trustees were the USSR, the USA, China and the UK. There are numerous accounts of the question of the trusteeship in Korea. The details of the negotiations and the text of the Moscow Agreement on Korea are to be found in Soon Sung Cho, *Korea in World Politics, 1940–1950*, pp 92–113

60 Kim Han Gil, op.cit. (note 58), pp. 214–216. A similar merger between the Communist Party of South Korea and the New People's Party took place on 23 November 1946, thus creating the Workers' Party of South Korea

61 For detailed results of these elections see ibid., pp. 226–227

62 For details on party affiliations and social status of the 237 members of the Assembly see ibid., pp. 228–229

63 For details on its composition see ibid., p. 230

64 Dae-Sook Suh, 'A Preconceived Formula for Sovietization: The Communist Takeover of North Korea', in Hammond (ed.), op.cit. (note 11), p. 486

65 For a detailed account of the Soviet–American rivalries in the UN and the creation and role of the United Nations Temporary Commission of Korea, see Soon Sung Cho, op.cit. (note 59), pp. 161–203

66 Kim Han Gil, op.cit. (note 58) p. 251

67 Ibid., p. 252, and Soon Sung Cho, op.cit. (note 59), p. 200

68 On 14 September 1948 the DPRK Supreme People's Assembly issued an appeal to the governments of theSoviet Union and the United States for the withdrawal of all foreign troops. The withdrawal of the RedArmy was completed by 24 December 1948

69 This framework is summarized by Norman Davies in the following five points: (1) Poland should be a separate sovereign state; (2) it should lie within the Soviet sphere of influence in Eastern Europe; (3) the USSR would be entitled to protect its special interest in its sphere of influence; (4) the provisional Polish frontiers, pending a peace conference, should lie on the Odra–Nysa line in the west and on the Bug river in the east; and (5) the acquiscence of the Western powers in these arrangements was conditional on the formation of a Provisional Government of National Unity from 'all democratic and anti-Nazi elements' and on the holding of 'free, unfettered elections'. See N. Davies, 'Poland' in McCauley (ed.), op.cit. (note 49), pp. 41–42

70 The Polish Communist (Workers') Party was formed on 16 December 1918 (renamed as the Polish Communist Party in March 1925). Within the twenty years of its existence it failed to become a political force of any significance. The Party refrained from participation in open political life in Poland and remained a clandestine organization. Its membership never exceeded 35 000. It regarded an independent Polish state as merely a transition to Poland's submersion in the 'international camp of social revolution where there is no problem of national borders'. During the invasion of Poland by the Red Army in the summer of 1920 the Communists supported the invading army. The Party's attitudes to the question of independence in a country which had only recently regained its statehood was perhaps the major factor contributing to the Communists being hated in Poland. As a result, the Communist Party of Poland was caught in a vicious descending spiral. The less support Polish Communists had at home, the more they leaned on the Soviet Union; yet the more heavily they relied on assistance from Russia, the less popularity they had in Poland. In March 1938 the Executive Committee of the Comintern dissolved the Party on the charge that it was thoroughly infiltrated by agents of the Polish Secret police and counter-intelligence. Almost all its leaders

residing in Russia were arrested and were either executed or deported to forced labour camps in Siberia

71 An account of the meeting can be found in M. Malinowski *et. al.*, *Polski Ruch Robotniczyw Okresie Wojny i Okupacji Hitlerowskiej* (The Polish Workers' Movement During the War and the Nazi Occupation), p. 155

72 W. Góra, *P.P.R. W Walce o Niepodległosć i Władzę Ludu* (The Polish Workers' Party in the struggle for Independence and People Power), p. 165

73 A typical example is General Konstantin Rokossovsky who, between 1949 and 1956, was the Polish Minister of Defence

74 M. K. Dziewanowski, *The Communist Party of Poland: An Outline of History*, p. 167

75 A graphic description of the foundation meeting can be found in N. Bethell, *Gomułka: His Poland and his Communism*, p. 71

76 N. Kołomejczyk and B. Syzdek, *Polska w latach 1944–1949* (Poland during the years of 1944–1949), p. 9

77 Dziewanowski, op.cit. (note 74), pp. 171–174

78 Kołomejczyk and Szdek, op.cit. (note 76), p. 17

79 Davis, op.cit. (note 69), p. 42

80 Churchill, op.cit. (note 39), p. 338

81 Kołomejezyk and Syzdek, op.cit. (note 76), p. 153

82 Ibid.

83 The votes were cast as follows:
First question: YES 7 844 522 (62.2%); NO 3 686 029 (31.8%)
Second question: YES 8 896 103 (77.3%); NO 2 634 446 (22.7%)
Third question: YES 10 534 967 (91.4%); NO 995 854 (8.6%)

84 Kołomejczyk and Syzdek, op. cit. (note 76), p. 172

85 For an account of the unification congress see Dziewanowski, op.cit. (note 74), pp. 208–222. Soon after the foundation of the PUWP the Peasant Party merged with the remnants of the Polish Peasant Party, thus creating the United Peasant Party

86 B. Bierut, *O Partii* (On the Party), p. 207

87 After the collapse of the Hungarian Soviet Republic in 1919 most of the Party leaders fled abroad and those who remained in the country went underground. The Comintern dissolved the Party in 1921 and permitted its reorganization only in 1925. Earlier that year the Communists had succeeded in forming a legal left party, the Hungarian Socialist Workers' Party. During the inter-war period, at a time when communism made considerable progress in other European countries, the Party in Hungary remained isolated both from the industrial proletariat and the peasantry. The Party intermediary levels were disbanded again by the Comintern, and its headquarters transferred to Prague in 1936. The organized communist activities thus ceased in Hungary until late 1939. When the Second World War broke out the Communists made repeated attempts to unite diverse socialist and anti-fascist elements. These efforts were interrupted, however, by the dissolution of the Communist International. In 1943, misinterpreting the dissolution of the Comintern, the Communist Party of Hungary dissolved itself as well. It was not reconstituted until September 1944. In November that year it had 2000 members

88 For a detailed description see H. Seton-Watson, *The Eastern European Revolution*, pp. 193–202

89 G. Schöpflin, 'Hungary', in McCauley (ed.), op.cit. (note 49), p. 98

90 According to Schöpflin the result was achieved 'by substantial fraud', ibid., p. 101

91 E. Ferenc, *Information Hungary*, p. 294

92 E. Reale, 'The Founding of the Cominform' in M. Drachkovitch and B. Lazitch (eds), *The Comintern – Historical Highlights*. Quoted by Schöpflin, op.cit. (note 89), p. 109

93 Leo Karakhan, who signed this proclamation on 25 July 1918, was a deputy Commissar for Foreign Affairs

94 In addition to six groups formed in Chinese cities there were also one each in Japan, Moscow, Berlin and Paris

95 In the spring of 1920 the Comintern's Far Eastern Secretariat dispatched G. N. Voitinskii and Maring (Sneevliet) to organize the first Communist cells in Peking and Shanghai

96 For a detailed study of the pre-1949 history of the CCP see J. Chen, *Mao and the Chinese Revolution*. Many key documents of the 1921–1949 period are translated and analysed in C. Brand, B. Schwartz and J. K. Fairbank, *A Documentary History of Chinese Communism*

97 The first United Front was based on a declaration signed on 1 January 1923 by Sun Yat-sen and Adolf Joffe, the Soviet envoy to China

98 Chen, op.cit. (note 96), pp. 11,116

99 J. W. Lewis (ed.), *Major Doctrines of Communist China*, p. 112

100 See Eto Chinkichi's articles on P'eng in *China Quarterly*, No. 8, 1961, 161–83, and No. 9, 1962, 149–81

101 Mao Zedong, *Selected Works*, Vol. 1, pp. 23–59

102 Ibid., pp. 23–24

103 For a graphic account see D. Wilson, *The Long March*

104 Lewis (ed.), op.cit. (note 99), p. 112

105 For an analysis of the CCP policies during that period see M. Selden, *The Yenan Way in Revolutionary China*

106 R. J. Townsend, *Political Participation in Communist China*, pp. 43–51

107 See, for example, D. Childs, *East Germany*; Arnold J. Heidenheimer, *The Governments of Germany*; Wolfgang Leonhard, *Child of the Revolution*

108 Germany was to be divided into three zones. The French zone was negotiated separately after tripartite agreements at Yalta that France should have one. (The original agreement was USSR 40 per cent, USA and Britain 60 per cent)

109 C. Stern, 'History and Politics of the SED 1945–1965' in W. E. Griffith (ed.), *Communism in Europe*, Vol. II, p. 64

110 Martin McCauley, 'East Germany' in McCauley (ed.), op.cit. (note 49), p. 61

111 Ibid., p. 59

112 Quoted by H. Wassmund, 'German Democratic Republic' in Szajkowski (ed.), op.cit. (note 24), Vol. 2, p. 346

113 Childs, op.cit. (note 107), p. 23

114 McCauley (op.cit. (note 49) p. 63) states that the proposal for amalgamation came from the SPD and was made first in June 1945. It should be noted that in the other countries of Eastern Europe where mergers took place they were instigated by the respective Communist Party

115 McCauley, op.cit. (note 49), p. 67

Chapter 6

Communism and national liberation

It is with the Cuban revolution of 1959 that the link between communism and movements of national liberation, which had hitherto been latent, became clearly apparent. Furthermore, with the exception of Afghanistan in 1979, none of the Marxist regimes which have been established since 1959 can be attributed to a direct Soviet presence. The period thus contrasts with the second period (1938-1957) in that, in the latter period, the majority of newly established Marxist regimes owed much to Soviet intervention. It contrasts with the period 1917-1924 in a rather different way, whilst at the same time it shows an important similarity with that earlier period. It was argued at the beginning of Chapter 4 that the dissolution of the tsarist empire and the Bolshevik success in Petrograd brought into being a whole series of national Marxist governments, which thereafter either collapsed or came to be engulfed in the Soviet Union. What we have seen since 1959 is the creation – and the constant and extended creation – of viable and autonomous nationalist movements which derive their ideology and claim to derive their policies from the tenets of Marxism, but whose close relationship with the Soviet Union is based upon something other than *force majeure*.

1959, 2 January
The Republic of Cuba

Three quite distinctive phases should be distinguished in the process that brought about the establishment of the Marxist regime in Cuba. The first phase is essentially a nationalist revolution, and dates from the assault on Fort Moncada on 26 July 1953 to the actual seizure of power by the *fidelistas* on 2 January 1959. This period undoubtedly was the most crucial. It saw the successful establishment of Fidel Castro and his July 26 Movement in control of the new Cuban regime. What followed subsequently was a result of the achievement of Castro's goal set out back in 1953: the overthrow of the brutal and corrupt regime of Fulgencio Batista[1].

The second phase was centred on the radical reorganization of the island's social and economic structure which began with the unexpectedly radical Agranian Reform Law of 17 May 1959[2].

The focal point of the third phase was the building of a new Communist Party, starting with the dissolution on 13 March 1961 of political parties and groups and culminating with the formation on 3 October 1965 of the Communist Party of Cuba[3].

Although a detailed analysis of these phases is beyond the scope of the present study, a summary is in order to illustrate the complexity of the factors involved.

In 1953 a few weeks after the *coup d'état* which brought the dictator Fulgencio Batista back to power, Fidel Castro, who had recently graduated as a doctor of law at Havana University, petitioned the Urgency Court of Havana with a brief, claiming that Batista had violated six articles of the Code of Social Defence for which the prescribed sentence was 108 years. He asked the Court to declare the regime illegal, or else to dissolve itself as ineffectual. When, not surprisingly, his petition was rejected he attempted to overthrow Batista by force. On 26 July 1953 Castro led 200 of his followers, mainly students, in an assault on Fort Moncada, Cuba's second largest military fortress. The attack failed and most of the insurrectionists were slaughtered in cold blood after capture – an action which caused a national outcry, and which marked the beginning of Castro's career as a popular hero. Castro himself was brought to trial on 16 October 1953, when he delivered his famous 'History Will Absolve Me' speech[4]. In the speech Castro cited Milton, Locke, Rousseau and the American Declaration of Independence as precedents for the right to rebel against tyranny, but mentioned no socialist thinkers and disclaimed any connection with the Communist Party[5] (which had, in any case, denounced the Moncada attack as 'putschist', 'adventurist' and 'guided by mistaken bourgeois conception'). He also included a programme of five revolutionary laws, which provided for the re-establishment of the 1940 Constitution; for the ownership of land by tenants with less than 165 acres (with compensation paid to former owners by the state); for the distribution of 30 per cent of 'big business profits among employees; for the right of tenant farmers to 55 per cent of the return on the sale of sugar; and for the confiscation of the property of corrupt politicians. In all, this document was far more radical than any of the programmes advanced by Castro during the subsequent guerrilla period, and in fact it disappeared from view until after the seizure of power.

Castro was sentenced to 15 years in prison and sent to the Isle of Pines, where he formed the 'July 26 Movement'. Unexpectedly released when, in May 1955, to counter popular discontent Batista declared an amnesty, he returned to Havana to be welcomed by a huge crowd: the July 26 Movement was already becoming a legend. In July Castro left for Mexico, where he organized a small expeditionary force.

On 15 November 1956 the yacht *Granma* set sail for Cuba with Castro's invasion army of eighty-two men. The intention was to establish an urban base in Oriente Province from which to strike at Havana while simultaneous uprisings and general strikes were staged in other parts of the country. The plan failed disastrously, however: the old yacht, desperately overloaded, arrived three days late and was stranded on an unknown part of the coast. Abandoning their heavy equipment, Castro's men waded ashore, and took to the Sierra, harassed all the way by Batista's airforce. Only twenty-two survived, ten of whom were captured, while the other twelve, including Fidel Castro, his brother Raul and Che Guevara, hid out among the highest peaks of the Sierra Maestra.

From this precarious foothold Castro began to reconstruct his movement. A small executive committee was set up, headed by Frank Pais, who had been organizing the July 26 Movement in Oriente during Castro's exile, and who had led the abortive uprising in its capital on 30 November. The formation of workers' actions began: the urban-based 'Resistencia Civica' was founded in February 1957. In March 1958, when Castro issued his famous 'Manifesto of the Sierra' declaring all-out war on Batista, he still believed that the rural struggle was of secondary importance. He was forced to change his mind, however, after the total failure of the general strike on 9 April which his manifesto had tried to promote. Abandoning his hopes for mass risings, he had to change his tactics to full-scale guerrilla war. This unleashed a wave of counter-terror from Batista, a wave of torturing and murders which caused the mass revolution from Batista's side of the sections of the middle class which had still supported him and dealt a fatal blow to the morale of the army.

The failure of the general strike was at least partly due to the lack of support from the PSP, who again branded Castro as 'adventurist' at the time of the *Granma* landing and who was still advocating a policy of peaceful mass action and a democratic front. When the tide obviously began to swing in Castro's favour in mid-1958 they modified their attitudes. However, the united opposition front, which was set up in Caracas on 20 July 1958, did not include the PSP. But in the same month Carlos Rodriguez, the PSP leader, visited Castro in the Sierra and the fact that some sort of pact had been made between them was confirmed by the setting-up of a united trade union front, including the PSP, in October.

The failure of the general strike had encouraged Batista to launch a general offensive against the rebels in May. Twelve thousand heavily equipped troops were sent to Oriente, but by the end of July they were already losing the positions they had gained at the beginning of the offensive. By the end of December the morale and discipline of Batista's army collapsed completely, and the dictator escaped by plane on the morning of 1 January 1959. On 2 January Fidel Castro accepted the unconditional surrender of the armed forces at Fort Moncada.

What occurred during the different stages of the guerrilla war, which was an important factor in the establishment of the Marxist –Leninist regime in Cuba, is perhaps best summarized by Che Guevara in his book *Guerrilla Warfare*.

At the outset there is a more or less homogenous group with some arms, that devotes itself almost exclusively to hiding in the wildest and most inaccessible places, making little contact with the peasants. It strikes a fortunate blow and its fame grows. A few peasants, dispossessed of their land or engaged in a struggle to conserve it, and young idealists of other classes, join the nucleus; it acquires greater audacity and starts to operate in inhabited places, making more contact with some column or other and destroys its vanguard . . . later it sets up temporary camps for several days; it abandons these upon receiving news of the approach of the enemy army . . . The numbers in the guerrilla band increase as work among the masses operates to make of each peasant an enthusiast for the war of liberation. Finally an inaccessible place is chosen, a settled life is initiated, and the first small industries begin to be established: a shoe factory, a cigar and cigarette factory, a clothing factory, an arms factory, bakery, hospitals, possibly a radio transmitter, a printing press, etc . . . the number of men fighting with the guerrilla band increases. A moment arrives when its radius of action will not have increased in the same proportion as its personnel; at that moment a force of appropriate size is separated, a column or a platoon, perhaps, and this goes to another place of combat . . . The original nucleus also continues to grow . . . there will also exist an enemy territory, unfavourable to guerrilla warfare. These small groups begin to penetrate, assaulting roads, destroying, planting mines, sowing disquiet . . . so opens the final stage, which is suburban guerrilla warfare.

Sabotage increases considerably in the whole zone. Life is paralyzed; the zone is conquered . . . The enemy falls when the process of partial victories becomes transformed into final victories, that is to say, when the enemy is brought to accept battle in conditions imposed by the guerrilla: there he is annihilated . . .[6]

Although the guerrilla war was a significant factor in the *fidelistas* victory, perhaps the decisive confrontation in Cuba was not between two military forces[7] but between two personalities: the island was no exception to the general Latin American cult of personality. The 'caudillo', the dictator, the strong president, have always dominated Latin American politics and have always commanded greater loyalty and obedience than any party or ideology. And by 1959 there was only one leader in Cuba: Batista was universally detested, his state-power isolated and his last support – the army – rapidly disintegrating. Castro, on the other hand, was at the height of his popularity and, because of the almost entirely nationalist nature of his appeal, he was able to command the support not only of the peasantry but also of the urban proletariat. Even the Catholic Church and many large industrialists supported Castro. However, the crucial support was that of the middle classes; it was their desertion of Batista that finished the war. Fidel Castro appeared as a revolutionary, not in a Marxist–Leninist sense but in an older, romantic, Latin American sense. Of course, Castro's seizure of power was not a mere administrative reshuffle but the administration of a long guerrilla war with peasant support[8]. Nevertheless, the precedents in terms of appeal and tactics are local and Latin American heroes like Bolivar and Marti rather than Lenin or Mao.

The second and third phases of the process of establishing the Marxist regime in Cuba are subsequent to the seizure of power by the new revolutionary regime and span a period during which the building of the regime's infrastructure was completed, thus in a sense finalizing the establishment process. Through lack of space it is not possible to chart these two phases in detail. Nevertheless, some account is clearly necessary to give if only a somewhat limited description of the entire process. Therefore what follows is a summary of the crucial events of these two phases.

On 17 May 1959 the Land Reform law was passed, establishing the National Institute of Agrarian Reform (INRA). An upper limit of land ownership of 30 caballerias (about 400 hectares) was established. Expropriated land was turned over to peasant cooperatives. The bill clearly marked the beginning of the social revolution. By the end of the year INRA had created 485 'agrarian cooperatives' and over 400 'People's Stores' in the countryside, while additionally extending its activities into mining and industry[9].

In July the crucial conciliation took place between Castro and the PSP. Meanwhile, relations with the United States began to deteriorate. Castro had financed an abortive invasion of Santo Domingo in June, and the influence of Che Guevara's 'internationalism' was becoming more apparent. Prevented by US diplomatic pressure from buying arms in Western Europe Castro began turning towards the socialist countries.

In February 1960 Anastas Mikoyan visited Havana to sign a trade and credit agreement. On 19 April Soviet oil began to arrive in Cuba and, when the American-owned oil companies refused to refine it, Castro confiscated the Texaco refinery on 29 June and those of Shell and Standard Oil two days later. On 6 July the United States reduced the Cuban sugar quota for 1960 by 700 000 tonnes; three days later Khrushchev offered to purchase that amount.

Between 6 August and 24 October Cuba nationalized virtually all wholly or partially American-owned properties and most large Cuban-owned businesses[10]. On 19 October the United States announced a total trade embargo on Cuba. By this time diplomatic and trade relations had been established with most of the socialist countries, including China.

Castro now saw that he would have to move firmly towards the socialist bloc politically if he was to survive his economic isolation from the United States and the threat of military intervention. On 16 April 1961, the day after the air attacks in preparation for the Bay of Pigs invasion on 17 April, Castro officially declared the 'socialist' nature of his revolution.

The PSP found itself in a dilemma. According to its ideology, the proletariat is to play a leading role in the period of the construction of socialism. In Cuba, however, the Communists were still not represented in the government mass organizations and the armed forces. Fortunately, however, Castro, in order to carry out the radicalization process, needed the PSP's organizational machinery. In July 1961 a new Integrated Revolutionary Organization (ORI) was set up, incorporating the PSP, the July 26 Movement and Revolutionary Directorate of March 13. In November the PSP was officially dissolved.

On 2 December 1961 Fidel Castro announced that he was now a confirmed Marxist–Leninist. However, he confessed to having read only Marx's *The Communist Manifesto* and Lenin's *State and Revolution* in their entirety and only part of Marx's *Das Kapital*. Thus it was not doctrine but the struggle with imperialism, he explained, that had led him and his followers to become 'sentimental Marxists, emotional Marxists' and to 'discover all the truths which the Marxist doctrine contained'[11].

Explanations for the radical transformations during the second phase outlined above should not be sought only in an area of foreign policy. The argument that it was the stupidity of the American administration and the 'economic war' which forced Castro to turn to the Soviet bloc for aid and subsequently to accept the donor's ideology can hardly be the full answer. This explanation tends to overlook the fact that the nationalization of American companies in the 'economic war' was only the first stage in a much more comprehensive nationalization plan, which had clearly been worked out in advance, and the fact that the crucial alliance with the PSP had already been formed by then.

The more important explanation has much more to do with the inner dynamics of 'fidelismo'. Castro wanted to maintain the mass support of the people, and, sincerely, to improve their social conditions. He discovered that he was unable to execute the necessary revolutionary change with the bureaucratic machinery of the bourgeois–democratic state, and needed an efficient, nationwide, financially incorruptible executive organization to carry through his programmes. The PSP was the only such organization: indeed, it was the only organized political party that had survived the Batista regime.

Building a new Communist Party, which occurred during the third phase, proved to be a difficult undertaking in Cuba. After the formation of ORI it became dominated by former PSP members at the exclusion of members of other organizations, since only the PSP had the apparatus and expertise to build a new party. On 26 March 1962 Castro expelled the 'old Communists' and dissolved ORI itself in February 1963.

In the second attempt to form the Party a new recruiting method was used. Members were chosen by coworkers in factories, cooperatives, offices, etc. as candiates for membership and then ratified by the Party's final recruitment bodies. The new party was initially called the United Party of the Socialist Revolution. On 3 October 1965 it was transformed into the Communist Party of Cuba. Throughout the 1960s the Party remained extremely weak. Operating without either programme or statutes[12] rather than directing the political process, it was essentially an organizational extension of Fidel Castro's personal authority, which had been perhaps the single most valuable political resource in Cuba's revolution.

1963, 16 August
The Republic of the Congo

Although the proclamation of adherence to Marxism followed directly after the Congolese Revolution of August 1963, the roots of the new, radical option for the republic can be traced to the activities and political affiliations of some of the labour unions and youth organizations which dominated Congo's politics even before its independence on 15 August 1960.

The oldest of the unions was the *Confédération Générale Africaine du Travail* (CGAT), formed in 1956, which, like its metropolitan parent organization, the *Confédération Générale du Travail* (CGT), had close links with the French Communist Party and the World Federation of Trade Unions (WFTU). The CGAT continued to receive funds as well as directives from CGT even after independence, and its leaders were trained at the Marxist Labour Union School at Gif-sur-Yvette in France. By 1960 the Union's membership comprised 33 per cent of all unionized Congolese workers[13] and its influence on Congolese politics was increasing up until May 1960, when its leaders were arrested after their attempt to organize a revolutionary party.

Parallel to the CGAT was its youth branch, the *Union de la jeunesse Congolaise* (UJC). This Marxist organization of young Congolese – mainly Lari of the Brazzaville area – had particularly close ties with the French Communist Party and the Budapest-based World Federation of Democratic Youth. It became a dynamic movement, articulating the views and interests of the mass of unemployed urban youth.

Both organizations were the main force of the Congolese Revolution which, in many ways, was the culmination of a process of ethnic strife between the peoples from the southern part of the country and those from the northern regions; urbanization of a large number of traditionally village-based population[14] and radicalization of the urban population, which included large numbers of unemployed[15].

Early in August 1963 the two Marxist organizations, together with the *Confédération Africaine des Travailleurs Croyants* (CATC) and the *Confédération des Syndicats Libres* (CCSL), presented the autocratic and arch-reactionary President Fulbert Youlou with demands for a drastic reform of the government, the election of a new legislature and the dismissal of incompetent and corrupt ministers. Youlou responded by banning all public meetings, which in turn was met by a call for a general strike on 13

August. The President promptly retaliated by arresting several people, including the CGAT leader, Julien Boukambou.

On the morning of 13 August some 3000 people tried to hold a meeting in the capital in defiance of Youlou's order[16]. They refused to obey the gendarmes' order to disperse, and in the ensuing clash three persons died and 12 were wounded. The crowd then stormed the prison, released those arrested and from there went on to burn the houses of some unpopular ministers. That evening, Youlou proclaimed a state of emergency in the three southern provinces of the country, forbade the assembling of more than five persons and instituted a curfew in Brazzaville.

On 14 August, as the demonstrations gathered momentum, it became clear to Youlou that he could not count on the support of the army. He then asked General de Gaulle for French troops to be flown in. In the meantime, realizing the seriousness of the situation, he promised half-measures such as the formation of a new government and the dismissal of some ministers.

On 15 August, the third day of the revolution, the crowds, which by now had grown to some 7000, stormed the presidential palace[17]. At 11 a.m. the French troops withdrew, and two hours later Foulbert Youlou resigned in favour of the Congolese army[18] which handed over authority to a *Conseil National de la Révolution* (CNR), headed by a former President of the National Assembly, Alphonse Massamba-Debat. He was presented by the CGAT and other organizations which had initiated the revolution with a list of potential cabinet ministers who were said to enjoy the confidence of the working class.

In his first policy statement, on 16 August, Massamba-Debat declared Congo's adherence to Marxism as a doctrine guiding the state and its institutions. In the following months a Marxist –Leninist party, the *Mouvement National de la Révolution* (MNR), was organized by Massamba-Debat, together with a single radical youth organization, the *Jeunesse du Mouvement National de la Révolution* (JMNR) and a single labour organization, the *Confédération Syndicale Congolaise* (CSC).

A new constitution was approved in a national refendum held on 8 December 1963. At the same time a fifty-five-member National Assembly was elected from a list containing the names of only MNR candidates. It subsequently elected Massamba-Debat to a five-year term as president.

The holding of the MNR inaugural Congress in July 1964 completed the building of the infrastructure of the Marxist regime in the Republic of the Congo[19].

1967, 30 November
The People's Republic of South Yemen

Two clearly identifiable stages in the establishment of the Marxist regime in South Yemen should be distinguished. The first extends over the period from the formation of the National Liberation Front in 1963 and the nationalist struggle of independence to the formal declaration of independence on 30 November 1967. The second stage encompasses the process of the creation of the vanguard party, which culminated with the formation of the Yemeni Socialist Party on 11 October 1978.

The National Liberation Front (NLF) was formed in 1963. Although its aim was to overthrow the British-created Federation of Saudi Arabia[20] and the British presence in South Yemen, the NLF should also be seen in the larger context of Arab nationalism in the Middle East in the late 1950s and early 1960s, exemplified by the nationalization of the Suez Canal, the formation of the United Arab Republic and the Iraqi revolution. However, the most direct appeal and influence on Arab nationalism at that time was Nasserism. Nasser armed and trained the NLF cadres. On 14 October 1963, in the Radfan mountains of Aden, the Front opened the armed struggle with Britain.

According to a recent analysis[21], at the time of its foundation the NLF had two wings: the liberal–democratic, under Qahtan al-Shaabi, and the Marxist wing, under Abdul Fattah Ismail. It is difficult to ascertain how far this analysis reflects the realities of the situation at that time or how far it is a contemporary attempt to explain the subsequent confrontations within the Front. Nevertheless, it is worth noting that the Front also received military and political support from both China and the Soviet Union and that its first congress, which was convened in June 1965, adopted a Marxist platform. This antagonized the Egyptians, who began supporting a rival group, the Front for the Liberation of Occupied South Yemen (FLOSY). Subsequent attempts to reconcile the two groups ended in failure and led to periods of fighting between the two Fronts.

While the NLF's military operations were becoming increasingly successful, Britain attempted several solutions to the problem of the future of the Federation of South Arabia – always, however, without the Front's participation.

A conference of all the major political parties that was convened in London in September 1965 broke up without a lasting agreement, showing that there was no political common ground left in South Yemen and in the following year Britain proposed that a new Federated Republic of South Arabia should become independent in February 1968. The NLF responded by demanding the evacuation of British forces from South Yemen, the liquidation of the colonialist presence and the rule of the reactionary sultans, and the surrender of authority to the National Liberation Front. When these were refused the Front stepped up its military campaigns.

Within a period of a few weeks in August and September 1967 the South Arabian Federal Government ceased to exist and its authority completely disintegrated before the advancing forces of the NLF. The latter's swift advance was due not least to the alignment on its side of a large measure of support amongst the local tribes, against their traditional rulers, and also to the Front's great internal discipline and unity at that time.

On 5 September the British High Commissioner announced the recognition of the nationalist forces as 'representatives of the people' and Britain's readiness to enter into immediate discussions with them on the formation of a government.

By mid-September the NLF was in full control of the whole of the Federation except Aden itself, which was completely surrounded by the Front's controlled territory. While consolidating its military gains the Front also entered into what turned out to be abortive negotiations with FLOSY in an attempt to reach agreement on a government in which both organizations would be represented. On 6 November 1967, however, after bitter internecine fighting in Aden between supporters of the two groups, the High Command of the South Arabian Armed Forces announced its recognition of the NLF as the only organization representing the people of South Arabia, pledging its full support for the NLF and calling upon Britain to negotiate the transfer of power to the Front immediately. Thus the Front could claim full political control of South Yemen, exercising *de facto* sovereignty outside British-manned enclaves.

Negotiations between Britain and the NLF for the transfer of power opened in Geneva on 21 November 1967, while Britain continued the evacuation of its forces which had begun earlier in August. On 27 November, after the British troops had made over large areas of Aden to the armed forces of the Federation, the NLF proclaimed the creation of the People's Republic of South Yemen. At the Geneva talks an agreement was reached with Britain on 28 November over the cession of Aden and its associated territories. The last British troops in Aden were withdrawn on 28 November and at midnight Qahtan al-Shaabi, the Secretary-General of the NLF, was appointed the first President of the People's Republic.

The National Liberation Front had thus attained part of its objective, the liberation of the country from foreign occupation. However, the revolution, which began as a patriotic nationalist movement with the primary goal of attaining political independence, acquired another goal at the time of the NLF's first congress, the construction of a socialist society under the vanguard Leninist Party.

The first move in this direction was the dismantling of a faction group within the NLF's leadership led by Qahtan al-Shaabi. The showdown took place at the third annual conference of the National Front (its middle name 'Liberation' was dropped after independence) at Zinjibar in March 1968, where a moderate land reform programme[22] was approved against a background of dissension from the Left. The Left in turn put forward resolutions calling for the appointment of political commissars, on the Soviet Red Army model, to all army units for the strengthening of the NLF militia and for the creation of 'popular guards', as well as popularly elected soviets in each governorate which would in turn elect a supreme council in charge of the affairs of the new Republic. These proposals were rejected by the Right, and on 20 March the Army forced several radical ministers to resign their posts. However, the radicals controlled the eastern governorates and went ahead with these proposals, ignoring the protests of the centrally appointed governors. After fifteen months of internal struggle al-Shaabi was forced by the radicals to resign on 22 June 1969. His resignation marked the victory of the left forces within the NF and it is referred to as the '22 June corrective step'.

The first constitution of the Republic, promulgated on 30 November 1970, defined the leading role of the Front in the country:

> . . . The National Front organization, on the basis of scientific socialism, leads political activity of the public and public organizations in order to develop the society in a manner which achieves national democratic revolution following a non-capitalist course. (Article 7)[23]

The next step in the creation of a single vanguard party was the unification, in October 1975, of the National Front, the People's Democratic Union (a Marxist party) and the People's Vanguard Party (a former Ba'ath Party) into the Unified Political Organization – The National Front (UPONF). The new organization was the 'political framework for the transitional stage' in the 'creation of a vanguard party which adheres to the principles of scientific socialism and believes in the leading role of the working class' in the country[24]. Thus the aim of the Unified Political Organization was the transformation of itself into a vanguard Marxist–Leninist party.

The second stage in the establishment of the Marxist–Leninist regime in South Yemen was concluded on 11 October 1978, when the UPONF transformed itself into the Yemeni Socialist Party. According to the Party's General Secretary, Abdul Fattah Ismail:

> The Yemeni Socialist Party is the vanguard of the Yemeni working class aligned with the peasants and other working segments of the population and revolutionary intellectuals. It is the living expression of this class consciousness – a consciousness of its real interests, future and historic role. The aim of the Party is to transform the society in a revolutionary manner to consolidate the achievements of the national democratic revolution and the transition to socialism. [This transition] is guided by . . . the theory of scientific socialism which takes into account local conditions of growth and the development of the national democratic revolution in our country[25].

1970, 20 October
The Somali Democratic Republic

The foundation for the subsequent Marxist regime in Somali was the bloodless *coup d'état* staged by army officers led by Major Mohamed Siad Barre on 21 October 1969[26]. In its aftermath, in an attempt to reverse the previous government's pro-Western leaning the military leaders began to form closer political contacts with the socialist countries of Europe and Asia.

It should be pointed out that, in the absence of any communist organization in Somalia at that time, the decisive factor in forging new political alliances must have been the fact that the Somali army was for years trained and equipped by the Soviet Union. The close military contact between Somalia and the Soviet Union began in the early 1960s just after independence. The critical issue for Somalia at that time was, and has remained since, the unity of the Somali nation. When in July 1980 the former British Somaliland and Italian Somaliland united to form the independent republic, three remaining branches for the nation were left outside the ultimate goal of Somali statehood. The first was the Somali community in the French territory of Djibouti; the second the Ogaden and other Somali clans in the Harar Province of Ethiopia; and the third the Somali tribesmen living in northern Kenya. Somalia decided that its interests demanded a 20 000-strong army and, since the United States was already a large arms supplier to Ethiopia, Somalia turned to the USSR, which in 1962 granted it loans worth $32 million to develop the Somali army. During the 1960s about 300 Soviet advisers undertook to train the army and some 500 Somali pilots, officers and technicians were trained in the Soviet Union[27].

When the army seized power the Soviet Union had been its established and trusted ally to whom it could turn for political guidance but who was also in a position to exert great influence. After the initial post-*coup* period[28] enthusiasm began to wane, and the leaders were under increasing pressure to produce a coherent and explicit ideology which would both legitimize and consolidate the new regime.

Apart from the reasons suggested above, another very important factor in the choice of ideological orientation of the Somali Revolution was the exceedingly egalitarian nature of the traditional Somali society, which Lewis called 'Pastoral Democracy'. Although an emergent social stratification based on urban–rural, regional and linguistic differentials was recognizable in the late 1960s, the traditional Somali society had a considerable symbolic appeal, and this appears to have been used by the military regime. In this context it was perhaps understandable that the idealistic young intellectuals associated with the regime should look to the Soviet Union for prototypes in both ideology and structures.

In a speech commemorating the first anniversary of the revolution the President of the ruling Supreme Revolutionary Council (SRC) announced the country's adherence to scientific socialism:

> In our Revolution we believe that we have broken the chain of a consumer economy based on imports, and we are free to decide our destiny. And in order to realise the interests of the Somali people, their achievement of a better life, the full development of their potentialities and the fulfilment of their aspirations, we solemnly declare Somalia to be a Socialist State . . .
>
> We do not want to delude ourselves by accepting some formula or a set of untenable concoctions in the belief that these will solve our problems. What we propose is very simple, the adoption of the most scientific method that will enable us to realistically face the conditions of economic underdevelopment in our society[29].

For six years after the acceptance of Marxism–Leninism Somalia was ruled by the military Supreme Revolutionary Council. The intention to organize a single political party, the 'vanguard of the revolution', was first announced in 1971. At that time a Public

Relations Office (PRO) was created and given the task of disseminating the resolutions and decisions of the SRC and of spreading the ideology of scientific socialism among the population. In 1972 the PRO became the Political Office of the SRC, creating a network of revolutionary centres in residential areas all over the country. It also carried out its tasks of political education at workplaces in administration offices, educational institutions, factories, etc. The Political Office was also responsible for the publication of revolutionary literature and for sending cadres for training to socialist countries, mainly the Soviet Union and the GDR. Its operations were supported by the Ministry of Information and National Guidance, the Ministry of Education and that of Higher Education and Culture. Thus, with the backing of the personnel and financial resources of the state apparatus, preparations were made in the regional and district capitals and in some towns and cities for the creation of future party structure.

The period between 1972 and 1976, in Somali writings, is referred to as the proto-party stage of the Somali Revolution[30].

On 11 July 1974 Somalia signed the Treaty of Friendship and Cooperation with the Soviet Union. It appears now that after the signing of the Treaty the Somali regime have come under considerable pressure to adopt a civilian party structure based on the Soviet model.

The Somali Revolutionary Socialist Party, with General Mohamed Siad Barre as Secretary-General, was launched at its foundation congress on July 1976[31]. In spite of the formation of the SRSP it seems that its grass-roots structure was far from complete. According to the Party's official organ, *Halgan*: 'Since the Party was established from above the next step was that the members of the Central Committee were sent to the Regions and Districts in August 1976' in order to 'select the revolutionaries who had themselves qualified to become members of the Party', and to build up Party membership in the Regions and Districts to the extent that it would be possible to establish 'Party organizations at these levels'[32].

1973, 24 September
The Republic of Guinea-Bissau

The announcement, on 24 September 1973, by the Partido Africano de Independencia de Guine e Cabo Verde (PAIGC) of the independence of Guinea-Bissau should be seen as perhaps the most significant step in the establishment of the Marxist regime there. Its structures, however, did not fully crystallize until November 1977.

At the time of its foundation, by six people, on 19 September 1956 in Bissau[33] the basic strategy of the PAIGC was to unite the few intellectuals and urban workers in order to make demands on the Portuguese authorities through a series of strikes and demonstrations. Until 1959 the PAIGC remained a mere handful. But after an incident on 3 August 1959 in the Pidjiguti dock area in Bissau, when a strike of longshoremen was brutally suppressed with at least fifty killed, the PAIGC leadership decided to reverse its tactics. It concluded that the Portuguese were not about to grant independence to their African colonies and that the tactics of strikes, demonstrations and petitions would not be sufficient to gain national liberation. The small party decided on a protracted armed struggle and to abandon its urban base. Instead it began to concentrate its attention on the *mato* (rural forested area) where people living in formal separation from colonial life resisted the Portuguese presence.

As early as 1962 the PAIGC initiated raids into the south of the country across from Guinea-Conakry, where it established its temporary headquarters. In January 1963 open warfare was launched and within months the guerrillas were able to set up a series of camps based on the *mato*. These grew into liberated areas. By 1964 the politico–military struggle was sufficiently advanced to call the first national congress of the Party. Between 13 and 17 February of that year some 200 military and political leaders met in the southern forest and agreed on the PAIGC's new political structure, based on the principles of democratic centralism, the creation of the People's Revolutionary Armed Forces, administrative zones and the nuclei of local government[34]. As the PAIGC's success continued to grow by 1968 the insurrectionary army and its supporting peasant militias controlled half of the rural areas. With the successes came increased international recognition and military and financial help as well as diplomatic backing from the USSR, Cuba, China and the countries of Eastern Europe[35].

As the liberated areas continued to grow in size a network of representative committees was created together with a system of elementary schools, bush clinics and revolutionary courts[36]. These realities of an independent state were emerging from 'the grass roots' while the bulk of the youth were volunteers in the military, social or political organizations of the PAIGC. Already in the making were the embryos of further youth, women's and trade union organizations[37] which took effective shape after independence.

In the liberated areas during 1972 a general election by secret ballot and manhood suffrage was held[38] in which some 54 400 out of 58 000 eligible voters elected 15 regional councils. These in turn elected 80 members of the National Assembly, which was augmented by the appointment of 40 PAIGC representatives. On 24 September the National Assembly, meeting in the provisional capital of Medina de Boe, proclaimed *de jure* the independence of Guinea-Bissau[39].

During the struggle for national liberation the PAIGC was more or less a mass movement open to all anti-colonialists prepared to support the struggle. There was never any functioning system of membership cards or systematic files of registered numbers. The background of the organization, i.e. all members with special responsibilities and tasks from the local committees up, were, however, referred to as 'the party within the party'. This open political movement with its core of committed and trained cadres also provided the administrative and judicial structure of a new polity emerging in the liberated areas. It was, in other words, both a party and a state at the same time.

After independence the need emerged for a separation of functions between the party and the state, and a discussion began as to whether the new party should be an open mass organization or some kind of vanguard party for the most dedicated and politically conscious, 'the best children of the people'[40].

The issue was resolved at the Third Congress of the PAIGC, meeting in Bissau between 15 and 20 November 1977. The 305 delegates decided in favour of the vanguard party controlling the state. The Congress confirmed the principle of democratic centralism for the PAIGC and the governmental structures, and restated socialist class analysis, thus reaffirming the ideological stance acquired during the national liberation war.

The acceptance of Marxism by PAIGC as its guiding ideology came with the experience of intensified struggle for national liberation. As Amilcar Cabral explained to a meeting at London University in October 1971:

> Moving from the realities of one's own country towards the creation of an ideology for one's struggle doesn't imply that one has pretensions to be Marx or Lenin or any other great ideologist, but is simply a necessary part of the struggle. I confess that we didn't know these theorists terribly well when we began. We didn't know them as half as well as we do now!

We needed to know them, as I've said, in order to judge in what measure we could borrow from their experience to help our situation – but not necessarily to apply the ideology blindly just because it's very good ideology . . . Is Marxism a religion? I am a freedom fighter in my country. You must judge from what I do in practice. If you decide it's Marxism, tell anyone it is Marxism. If you decide it's not Marxism, tell them it is not Marxism. But the labels are your affair: we don't like those kind of labels. People here are very preoccupied with the questions: are you Marxist or not Marxist? Are you Leninist or not Leninist? Just ask me please, whether we are doing well in the field. Are we really liberating our people, the human beings in our country, from all forms of oppression? Ask me simply this and draw your own conclusions . . . Our society is developing in the same way as other societies in the world, according to the historical process; but we must understand clearly what stage our society has reached. Marx, when he created Marxism, was not a member of tribal society. I think there is no necessity for us to be more Marxist than Marx or more Leninist that Lenin in the application of their theories[41].

1974, 30 November
The Republic of Dahomey

In the absence of any communist organization in Dahomey[42] radical politics in the country were introduced via the trade unions and the highly politicized student unions. The largest and most influential of the trade unions was the Union Générale des Travailleurs du Dahomey (UGTD)[43]. Set up by law as a unified trade union in 1961, it became progressively more radical under the leadership of its Marxist Secretary-General Theophile Paoletti. The UGTD had close links with its French counterpart the Confédération Générale du Travail (CGT) and through it with the French Communist Party. It was also linked with the communist-backed World Federation of Trade Unions. The union was directly responsible, through its strike actions, for the collapse of the Dahomean governments in 1963 and 1967 and the subsequent *coups* that followed. Among the youth and student organizations a very substantial influence on the politics of Dahomey was exercised by the ultra-left Union Générale des Etudiants et Elèves Dahoméens (UGEED), some of whose leaders had held office in militant student organizations in France. Throughout the 1960s and early 1970s both groups became involved in periodic confrontations with the respective Dahomean governments, confrontations which acquired a distinctly Marxist rhetoric[44].

The firm foundation for the establishment of the Marxist regime in Dahomey was laid by the military *coup d'état*[45] on 26 October 1972. Staged by para-commandos led by Lieutenant-Colonel Matheiu Kerekou, it was the sixth *coup* since the country's independence on 1 August 1960. Neither the *coup* leader nor members of his entirely military government were known Marxists, and nothing in their personal backgrounds could suggest that the 1972 *coup* was different from the previous military takeovers. The new leaders were almost unknown[46].

The previous six *coups* must have almost exhausted the reservoir of civilian and military leaders that had, perhaps for too long, dominated Dahomean politics. The new and unknown elite, in order to remain in power, had to stabilize the political scene. But in order to solidify the latter it had to legitimize itself. Partly due to the absence of viable options and partly because of its appeal to the radical union of students and youth groups, the natural choice was Marxism–Leninism. Not only was it a hitherto untried option but also one on the basis of which the new regime could seek support from the radical section of the population, which was otherwise divided along traditional tribal lines.

Dahomey's adherence to Marxism was announced by Kerekou in a speech on 30 November 1947[47] commemorating the second anniversary of the *coup* – henceforth referred to as the Revolution. In his speech he also spelled out the major principles of Beninois socialism: economic independence through the nationalization of most of the means of production; transformation of society via various structures and reforms into a model socialist alliance of farmers and workers; and a realignment of Dahomey's foreign policy towards the 'progressive bloc'[48].

In the aftermath of Kerekou's speech some nationalization took place but major attention was given to construction of a new infrastructure. Revolutionary Councils were established and Political Commissars appointed at each level of administration, i.e. regional, district, etc., and Revolutionary Committees were set up in villages, townships and urban communities. In addition, an attempt was made to organize Committees for the Defence of the Revolution in places of work. These various structures were aimed at the politicization and mobilization of the population in support of the military regime and its policies.

The final stage in the establishment of the Marxist regime was the creation, on 17 May 1976, of a vanguard party, the People's Revolutionary Party of Benin (PRPB)[49].

1975, 17 April
The Royal Government of National Union of Kampuchea

The capture of Phnom Penh by the People's Armed Forces for the National Liberation of Kampuchea[50] (PAFNLK) on 17 April 1975 not only ended five years of national liberation war and US intervention but also contributed to the overall defeat of the United States in Indochina and in Vietnam in particular. The liberation of Phnom Penh also laid the foundation of the Marxist regime, which fully emerged only a year later on the first anniversary of liberation.

The duality of the Royal Government of National Union (RGNU) which took over on 17 April is striking. It was royal in name since it was headed by Prince Norodom Sihanouk and included his supporters. But in fact the Marxists were the dominant group in the government, which carried out their policies almost entirely. The common ground for both groups was the desire to drive the American and the American-sponsored government out of the country. Therefore it would be incorrect to ignore the RGNU altogether and suggest a later date for the *de facto* coming to power of the Communist regime in Kampuchea. The RGNU was an essential and decisive milestone in that process.

Although the origins of the Communist movement in Kampuchea, as in the rest of the region, are in the Indochinese Communist Party[51], the forces which attained victory in 1975 were based on the more recent Communist Party of Kampuchea (CPK)[52].

The Communist Party of Kampuchea was formally established at its foundation Congress in September 1960[53] by a group of Marxist nationalists. Many of them had been educated in France, where they joined the large anti-colonial movement and left-wing student groups associated with the French Communist Party. In 1961 the CPK formed a guerrilla force in the countryside which became very successful over the years, establishing large liberated zones where the first experimental policies of the Party were executed[54]. These forces were the basis of the liberation armed forces when the Party entered the anti-US, national liberation war phase after the parliamentary–military *coup d'état*, which was CIA-backed, against the regime headed by Prince Norodom Sihanouk[55].

Following the *coup* an alliance was formed between the Prince and the Party's armed wing, the Khmer Rouge[56]. At a National Congress held in Peking on 3-4 March 1970 the National United

Front of Kampuchea (NUFK) was established, and on 5 May the Royal Government of National Union (RENU) was formed, with Sihanouk as Head of State. Out of twenty-one RGNU ministers, ten remained in Peking while the majority operated inside Kampuchea. The latter included Khieu Samphan, Acting Premier, Defence Minister and Commander-in-Chief of the PAFNKL; Hon Yuon, Minister of Interior, Communal Reforms and Cooperatives; and Hu Nim, Minister of Information and Propaganda. Thus the Party was in a strong and commanding political, military and social position not only inside Cambodia but also as far as the RGNU was concerned. While Prince Sihanouk retained his symbolic appeal as a unifying force for an overwhelming majority of the population and became a roving ambassador for Kampuchea, gaining the support of the international community, the CPK was directing the fight inside the country and continuing to carry out its programme of social reforms. By 1975 the PAFNLK controlled 90 per cent of the country and 80 per cent of the population. When the war ended the CPK's dominant position was such that it could not be challenged by its partners within the NUFK alliance.

Although a Special (Second) National Congress which met in Phnom Penh on 25–27 April 1975, under the chairmanship of Khieu Samphan, decided that Prince Sihanouk should remain Head of State, the Prince stayed in Peking until September, and when he eventually returned his role was entirely ceremonial.

Meanwhile the new regime was now in the hands of the still clandestine CPK, which embarked on a series of radical social and economic reforms. The evacuation of almost the entire population of Phnom Penh was partially explained by the following reasons. There was famine in the city, which had swollen from 200 000 to 3 million due to the influx of refugees. The channels of transportation, which had been destroyed, did not allow for rapid re-supply, and in any event the previously liberated zones were not capable of providing sufficient food for that mass of population. The rainy season was on its way and everybody had to produce. In addition, there was also the problem of security. A mass of underfed and in some cases hostile people, many of whom were former soldiers, could have destabilized the regime. To prevent this almost everybody had to march to the outskirts of the city, where they were allocated rural communes to which they were then transported. Thus the new regime tried to find solutions to two of its biggest problems, lack of food and internal security in the war-ravaged country.

Other reforms included the immediate nationalization of land, facilitated to some extent by Khmer traditions which had never been destroyed by the tendency towards private land-ownership. Money and the salary system were abolished. The ownership of property other than personal and everyday goods was also abolished. Administrative distribution and barter replaced trade.

The framework of the infrastructure of the Marxist regime in Kampuchea was formalized at the third Congress of the NUPK, meeting in Phnom Penh on 14 December 1975, which approved the country's new Constitution[57]. The new document formally replaced the Royal Constitution of Prince Sihanouk. It described Kampuchea as 'an independent, unified, peaceful, neutral, non-aligned, sovereign and democratic State . . . a State of the people, workers, peasants and all other Kampuchean working people'. Its official name was Democratic Kampuchea. The means of production were the collective property of the state and only personal property remained in private hands. The constitution made no reference to monarchy or Marxism, since it was promulgated before the Party emerged from secrecy. It also established the State Praesidium, consisting of a President and two Vice-Presidents elected for five years, who would represent the state inside and outside the country.

After the elections to the People's Representative Assembly on 20 March 1976 Prince Sihanouk resigned as Head of State and the Royal Government of National Union was replaced by a new cabinet headed by Pol Pot, in which all the portfolios were held by the Khmer Rouge. The dismantling of the RGNU and the Sihanoucist group of ministers marked the final step in the process of establishing the first Marxist regime in Kampuchea.

1975, 25 June
The People's Republic of Mozambique

The establishment of the Marxist regime in Mozambique was the culmination of ten years of guerrilla struggle waged by the Front for the Liberation of Mozambique (FRELIMO) and three years of post-colonial rule.

FRELIMO's path to Marxism was an evolutionary one. The Front was formed at Dar es Salaam on 25 June 1962 by the merging of three pre-existing and competing exile nationalist organizations – the National Democratic Union of Mozambique (UDENAMO), the Mozambique African National Union (MANU) and the African Union for Mozambican Independence (UNAMI) – and the incorporation of a number of independent Mozambican nationalists. There was at this time no clear political line within FRELIMO, which, with each of its constituent organizations, was perhaps as much an ethnic as a nationalist union[58].

Marxist influence in Mozambique at that time was practically non-existent. With no industrial workforce to speak of, Mozambique, like the other countries of Africa, did not meet the classic Marxian preconditions for revolution. But it had other potential ingredients for revolution which were recognized by FRELIMO – hard colonial rule, an impoverished rural population and no legal or open channel for political opposition.

A few of FRELIMO's leaders encountered Marxist ideas through underground contacts with the Portuguese Communist Party while studying in Portugal. Among them were Eduardo Mondlane, later President of FRELIMO, Marcelino dos Santos (economist and later Planning Minister) and Oscar Monteiro (the Front's Organizing Secretary).

FRELIMO's First Congress was held in September 1962 and soon afterwards the Front started preparations for war, with a list of aims to secure independence rather than with an integrated blueprint for reconstructing Mozambican society. According to dos Santos:

> It is true FRELIMO as such had no clear ideological line apart from primary nationalism. But the very fact that the leadership was heterogeneous meant that different types of ideologies were represented in it from the start . . . But the tasks facing us in those early days demanded that we create a collective which would accommodate all those who were prepared to work together to get the basic struggle off the ground. So the nature of the political, social and economic realities of the situation, as it then was, demanded a pragmatic attitude. But the struggle grew and new situations emerged and in the process political consciousness and political awareness were increasing and developing even though in some ways our approach still remains pragmatic[59].

After his visit to China in 1963, a year before the launching of the guerrilla war, the Front's leader Eduardo Mondlane gave a clear indication of the direction of the Mozambican revolution when he said[60]: 'I am convinced that the historical struggle of the Chinese peoples has great relevance to the present struggle of the peoples of Africa.'

When on 25 September 1964 the guerrilla war began, FRELIMO's strategy was modelled on Mao's people's insurgency, influenced not only by similarities between Mozambique and China's rugged terrain and economic and political circumstances but also by the success of the Chinese Communists' example and increasing Chinese aid. It is, of course, almost impossible to determine the correlation between the growth of military and economic aid and the development of a Marxist orientation by the movement. Undoubtedly, however, the Chinese, Soviet and Eastern European supplies of military equipment, foodstuffs and vehicles must have been an important factor in the radicalization of the movement[61].

In the initial stages of the liberation war FRELIMO avoided built-up populated areas as the guerrillas attempted to consolidate their position in the back country while inflicting a few casualties and reducing their own. During the first half of 1965 the guerrillas, preceded by political cadres, established their first stronghold in the highlands of the Niassa district. Later liberated areas were established also in the remoter sections of the Tete and Cabo Delgano districts. In their base areas FRELIMO established the nuclei of the infrastructure for future independent Mozambique; village political committees, judicial structures, as well as crop-growing schemes, People's Shops, rudimentary education programmes and health services[62].

By the Second Congress of FRELIMO, which was held between 20 and 25 July 1968 in a liberated zone, the Front had adopted the standard Communist Party procedures such as cell structures, democratic centralism and self-criticism sessions. The Congress adopted new statutes which required members to be politically conscious and a new programme which set the seal on the ideological path along which FRELIMO was moving. According to this programme the Front's struggle was:

> . . . part of the World's movement for the emancipation of the peoples, which aims at the total liquidation of colonialism and imperialism and at the construction of a new society free from exploitation of man by man[63].

Over the next six years the Front extended its guerrilla activities into the central areas of the country. The extension of the guerrilla warfare contributed considerably to the deterioration of Portugal's military standing not only in Mozambique but also in the other colonial wars in Angola and Guinea-Bissau. On 25 April 1974 army units in Portugal, led by field-grade officers deeply disenchanted with the unwinnable African wars and imbued with a revolutionary doctrine gained from their guerrilla opponents, overthrew the authoritarian Caetano regime. In June the new Portuguese government entered into negotiations with FRELIMO on the transfer of power, which resulted in the agreement signed on 7 September 1974 in Lusaka.

The agreement called for independence on 25 June 1975 (the thirteenth anniversary of the founding of FRELIMO), a multiracial society, a transitional government with a prime minister, six of the nine ministers appointed by FRELIMO, acceptance by the nationalists of financial obligations incurred by Portugal if deemed in the country's interest and a cease-fire. Thus with the installation of the transitional government on 20 September the national liberation was won. The final phase of FRELIMO's transition to power was peaceful, with independence achieved, as planned, on 25 June 1975.

When FRELIMO was founded its objective had been to overthrow Portuguese colonialism. As the liberation struggle advanced, its policies became increasingly radical, particularly after the Front's Second Congress and the experience gained in the liberated zones, where it had been possible to experiment and adopt a new type of social relations. In January 1974 the Front's School began its work, synthesizing and drawing theoretical conclusions from the experience of the liberated zones and providing a theoretical base for cadres and militants[64]. The Front's political evolution continued after Mozambique's independence until the Third Congress of FRELIMO held in Maputo from 3 February to 7 February 1977.

The Congress[65] decided on FRELIMO's adoption of socialism as its goal and of Marxism as its official ideology. FRELIMO ceased to be defined as a national liberation movement and became a Marxist–Leninist vanguard party. According to President Samora Machel,

> Within the framework of the construction of the new society the Third Congress was of fundamental historical importance. Here we drew up the essential strategy for our struggle in the phase of the construction of People's Democracy. Here we created the Party of the working class, the Vanguard Party and highest form of organization of the working classes, the Marxist–Leninist Party. Here we defined our line of action in all fields: in the building of The People's Democratic State, in the organization of collective life, in the construction of our developed and independent economy at the service of the broad masses in defence of our country and our Revolution[66].

The transformation of FRELIMO from a nationalist movement into a vanguard party concluded the process of the establishment of the Marxist regime in Mozambique.

1975, 5 July
The Republic of Cape Verde

The Marxist regime in the Cape Verde islands was established as a result of the victory of Partido Africano da Independencia da Guine e Cabo Verde (PAIGC) in Guinea-Bissau[67]. Ever since its foundation the programme of PAIGC stipulated: (1) immediate achievement, by all necessary means, of the total and unconditional national independence of the people of Guinea and the Cape Verde Islands; (2) the taking over of power in the Cape Verde Islands by the people of Cape Verde[68].

Unlike in Guinea-Bissau, no armed struggle took place on the islands. Between 1956 and 1974 the PAIGC remained a clandestine organization with many of its members imprisoned at Tarrafal on Santiago Island. Others who managed to get to the mainland fought in Guinea-Bissau as the first stage in securing the independence of their own country.

After the 25 April 1974 coup in Portugal, which overthrew the fascist regime, the PAIGC clandestine network in Cape Verde came into the open. From July that year veterans of the armed struggle on the mainland began to filter home again, sent by the PAIGC leadership to direct and help the work of reinforcing and extending PAIGC influence in the islands[69]. The Secretary-General of the PAIGC and future President of Cape Verde, Aristedes Pereira, and the future Prime Minister, Pedro Pires, returned to the islands as soon as the full independence of Guinea-Bissau was assured in September 1974.

Later that year on 30 December 1974 an agreement was signed between Pedro Pires, representing the PAIGC, and Portugal, under which Portugal formally transferred power in the Cape Verde to a transitional government which ruled the country until independence. It consisted of five ministers, two Portuguese and three from PAIGC. On 30 June 1975 in accordance with the agreement, the government held elections to the People's Assembly in which the PAIGC was the sole contesting party. Some 85 per cent of the voters went to the polls, and of these, 92.17 per cent voted for the candidates of the PAIGC. The first meeting of the National Assembly took place on 4 July. The following day the Assembly proclaimed the independence of Cape Verde and elected the Secretary-General of the PAIGC, Aristides Pereira, President of the Cape Verde Republic. In a unique experiment the PAIGC was in power in two different sovereign states: in Guinea-Bissau from 24 September 1973 and in Cape Verde from 5 July 1975. The experiment came to an abrupt end on 14 November

1980 when a military *coup d'état*, organized by the Minister of Defence and former guerrilla leader Joao Bernardo Vieira, deposed President Luis Cabral and broke all relations with its Cape Verdian counterpart. On 20 January the split was institutionalized with the formation of the Partido Africano de Independencia de Cabo Verde (PAICV) in Praia[70].

1975, 11 November
The People's Republic of Angola

The Angolan Communist movement, which dates back to the late 1940s, had been nurtured by the metropolitan Portuguese Communist Party (PCP). Already by 1948 three secret Communist organizations existed in Angola: the Angolan Federal Committee of the PCP, the Youth Commission for the Struggle Against Colonial Imperialism in Angola and Black Angola. In 1952 these groups joined in a Council for Liberation of Angola and in October 1955 the Angolan Communist Party was established. The Party was one of the groups who on 10 December 1956 founded the Popular Movement for the Liberation of Angola (MPLA)[71]. The movement's manifesto[72] issued on the same day outlined the immediate and long-term aspirations of the MPLA. In the short run the movement focused its attention on the need for the consolidation of the common front of all anti-imperialist forces in Angola. Also in the interests of the masses of peasants and workers it called for an alliance with the 'progressive forces' of the world. The programme also included long-term pledges to install democratic government and economic justice, to nationalize 'land belonging to the enemy of the nationalist movement', to carry out educational reforms including the prohibition of 'colonial and imperialistic culture and education' and to bar the establishment of foreign military bases on Angolan soil. However, it also pledged to protect private enterprise and 'foreign economic activities which were useful' to the society.

The Angolan war of national liberation began in 1961 with the attack on 4 February by MPLA militants on the colonial prison, the secret police (PIDE) post and the radio station in Luanda. One group was destroyed in the Portuguese counter-attack, but others were able to escape into hiding and then to the bush north of Luanda, where they continued the armed struggle. A separate revolt broke out later that year in the northern coffee plantations among the Bakongo people. A tripartite rivalry complicated the politics of Angola's war for independence. The Marxist-oriented and *mestiço*-led MPLA drew mass support from about a million and a half Moundu living in the area surrounding the capital. After the failure of its 1961 Luanda attacks the MPLA launched campaigns in 1966 on northern and eastern Angola along with fruitless operations in Cabinda, the oil-rich enclave surrounded by Zaire and the Congo. Firefights in the bush and assassinations in towns characterized relations between the MPLA and the National Front for the Liberation of Angola (FNLA), whose primary constituency was the one million Bakongo in the north-eastern corner of Angola. The third group, the National Union for the Total Independence of Angola (UNITA), was based on the two million Ovimbundu in the Central Highalnds area. The FNLA and UNITA opened their military operations in 1966.

Thus each of the liberation movements had its primary constituency among one of the three major ethno-linguistic groups of the country. Nationalist sentiments existed along ethnic lines and there was a lack of a larger 'Angolan' identity. The Portuguese fostered the development of the separate ethnic bastions. However, this policy backfired when in the aftermath of the 25 April 1974 *coup* in Portugal they sought to establish a transitional government comprised of the representatives of the three liberation movements to carry out orderly decolonization. Formed on the basis of the 15 January 1975 agreement signed in Alvor, the coalition government began to disintegrate soon after its inauguration on 31 January, torn apart by the mutual distrust and suspicion of its participants.

At this juncture foreign involvement in Angolan affairs also increased[73]. In late January the United States gave a covert grant of $300 000 to the FNLA, the movement most committed to a military strategy[74]. In response, the Soviet Union, who had long suspected that the United States would try to assert is influence over Angola when Portugal was finally forced out, increased arms deliveries to the MPLA. In March Soviet arms began to be sent

> . . . by air to Brazzaville, by truck to Cabinda, by rail to Pointe Noire, and by small craft down the Angolan coast. In April, chartered aircraft flew perhaps a hundred tons of arms into Southern Angola, and large shipments, including heavy mortars and armored vehicles, began to come in on Yugoslav, Greek, and, finally, Soviet ships[75].

This massive Soviet military aid undoubtedly played an important role in the subsequent political and military victory of the MPLA.

However, perhaps one of the most important factors in the MPLA's successes was the use of Cuban troops. It also allowed the Soviet Union to avoid the potentially volatile issue of sending 'white' troops to Africa while at the same time it gave Castro a chance to demonstrate his commitment to international socialist solidarity[76].

With the final collapse of the transitional government in August 1975 and an escalating civil war between the three nationalist movements, the Portuguese High Commissioner in Angola folded the Portuguese flag on 10 November and stole out of besieged Luanda, leaving the Angolans to fight it out. The MPLA, in control of the capital, proclaimed an independent People's Republic of Angola (PRA) on 11 November, and obtained prompt diplomatic recognition from the Soviet Union, Yugoslavia and other socialist states. UNITA and the FNLA proclaimed their own governments in territories controlled by them and secured recognition from some African countries.

After the proclamation of the PRA, Soviet, Cuban and Eastern European military and economic support increased even further, securing the eventual complete political and military victory for the MPLA. Afterwards the broad anti-colonialist anti-imperialist front which had always operated within the framework of socialist objectives began to transform itself into a Marxist–Leninist Party. A Party school, with the purpose of training militants in Marxist –Leninist theory, was established in October 1976. In the provinces special courses were held for the most senior political, military and civil leaders. The training was thought to be necessary because

> . . . thousands of members of the MPLA have not had an equal opportunity of contact with historical materialism and dialectical materialism.

Their adherence to scientific socialism was 'empirical' and relied on the trust and guidance of the MPLA[77]. After a massive campaign of political mobilization and the creation of primary party structures the MPLA held its First Congress from 4 to 10 December 1977.

On 10 December 1977, the twenty-first anniversary of the MPLA's foundation, the First Congress closed with the foundation of the MPLA–Workers' Party, a vanguard party guided by Marxism–Leninism, thus completing the establishment process of the present Angolan regime.

1975, 2 December
The Lao People's Democratic Republic

The Communist movement in Laos was until 1945 an integral part of the Indochinese Communist Party (ICP) and since its dissolution closely linked with the Vietnamese Communist movement[78]. The Vietnamese Party gave continuous support and assistance to the Laotian national liberation movement against French colonialism in the inter-war period, Japanese occupation during the Second World War and the reintroduction of French power after October 1945[79], and was instrumental in setting up and aiding the nationalist communist guerrilla forces in Laos.

It is not our intention to analyse here the very complex post-Second World War political history of Laos. Although undoubtedly the foundations for the subsequent emergence of the Marxist regime were laid during the period between 1945 and 1973, space does not permit discussion of such milestones in this process as the formation of the Pathet Lao (Lao Nation) guerrilla forces and the establishment, in April 1953, of its first territorial base in Houa Phan province; the Geneva Agreement of 20 July 1954; the foundation on 22 March 1955 of a separate Laotian Communist party, the Lao People's Party[80]; the formation of the Lao Patriotic Front (NLH – Neo Lo Haksat) on 6 January 1956 when conditions were propitious for a switch from a primarily military to a primarily political strategy; the *coup d'état* of 9 August 1960 and its aftermath; the Geneva Agreement of 1962; and several coalition governments[81].

Instead we shall concentrate here on the period since the signing, on 21 February 1973, of a fourteen-article Agreement on the Restoration of Peace and Reconciliation in Laos (The Vientiane Agreement)[82]. The Agreement provided for a cease-fire between the Royal Lao Army and the military arm of the NLH, the Lao People's Liberation Army, better known as the Pathet Lao. It also recognized the existence of two zones and two separate administrations, and established the Provisional Government of National Union (PGNU) in which half of the Cabinet posts were held by the representatives of the NLH. Another institution established by the Agreement was the National Consultative Political Council (NPCC) under the chairmanship of Prince Souphanouvong, the leader of the Patriotic Front. The NPCC was a coequal body with the Provisional Government of National Union.

The Vientiane Agreement had left the Pathet Lao in control of a zone established by years of warfare and which consisted of four-fifths of the Laotian territory. Although the rightist faction of the coalition government controlled the remaining part of Laos which included the more populous villages and towns along the Mekon river, it possessed its greatest asset – the continued American aid supplied through the US Agency for International Development (AID). After the surrender of Phnom Penh and Saigon to their respective Communist forces and the removal of the United States' support and presence in Vietnam and Kampuchea, large-scale demonstrations took place at the beginning of May in several cities in Laos, demanding the closing of all the offices of AID and the dismissal of prominent right-wing ministers. This resulted in the termination of the aid programme at the end of May and the resignation of several anti-communist ministers and generals.

With the departure of the leading generals and several mutinies in the Royal Army wich took place in May and June, the Royal forces 'merged' with the Lao People's Liberation Army through a combination of insurrections, invitations to merge with neighbouring Pathet Lao units, requests for LPLA advisers and orders from the Minister of Defence forbidding resistance. This peaceful seizure of military power, coinciding with the seizure of administrative power, spread from district to district throughout the summer and culminated in the triumphal parade of the Pathet Lao in 'liberated' Vientiane on 23 August 1975.

Starting on 5 November, elections for people's councils were organized throughout the country (i.e. in both zones) on the lowest (canton) level and proceeded in a number of rounds to higher levels. As a result, a wholly new administrative system for the country was established. This was followed by a national Congress of People's Representatives consisting of 264 delegates elected by the new people's councils.

The Congress, which met in Vientiane between 1 and 2 December, accepted the 'voluntary' abdication of King Savang Vatthana[83]; dissolved the PGNU and NPCC; and declared Laos a People's Democratic Republic. It also appointed 'Mr' Souphanouvong as the Repulic's first President and a new government headed by the Lao People's Revolutionary Party General Secretary, Kaysone Phomvihane.

It is perhaps worth noting that although the process of the establishment of the marxist regime in Laos was forged in three decades of revolutionary struggle, its final phase, exemplified by the country's fundamental political transformation, was achieved with great rapidity and an almost complete absence of coercion.

1976, 20 April
Socialist Ethiopia

The establishment process of the Marxist regime in Ethiopia is still in progress[84] and several attempts to create a vanguard party for the Ethiopian revolution have ended in failure. Therefore the date of 20 April is a tentative one and it is not intended to imply that the Ethiopian regime has assumed its final shape. It is, however, a significant date in the diary of the revolution, since on 20 April the Programme of the National Democratic Revolution was announced and also the Proclamation establishing the Provisional Office for Mass Organization Affairs (POMOA) was issued.

The Ethiopian revolution erupted on 18 February 1974 with a taxi strike in Addis Ababa, protesting at a 50 per cent increase in the price of petrol. During the following months a mounting wave of strikes, boycotts and demonstrations hit the urban sector with increasing force, loosening the already greatly eroded foundations of the regime of Haile Selassie. The movement involved several social groups, including students, teachers, workers, civil servants, traders, Muslims and even a section of the Christian clergy. At the same time, peasant uprisings took place in the provinces. A parallel series of mutinies occurred in the army. The initiative was taken by non-commissioned officers and soldiers, who arrested all officers and took command of their units. These soldiers were recruited primarily from the peasant class, while the majority of the junior officers shared the social origins and the political aspirations of the educated petty bourgeoisie. Consequently, these officers proved highly sympathetic to the rebellious mood of the soldiers. Untouched by the miasma of corruption that had enveloped the senior officer corps, the junior officers retained the trust of the soldiers and were able to participate from the outset in the gradually forming military movement against the imperial regime. Eventually they assumed a guiding role and emerged ultimately as the dominant element in the Coordinating Committee of the Armed Forces Police and Territorial Army which assumed command of the military establishment in the spring of 1974. The Dergue (Amharic for Committee) was composed of representatives elected by the various units of the armed forces. Its initial membership comprised 120 persons, ranging in rank from plain soldier to major.

As the popular movement gained strength its demands became explicitly political, ranging from the dismissal and punishment of corrupt officials to a call for a constitutional government and land reform.

The more the demands of the civilians and military were met by the Emperor, the more demands were generated. Haile Selassie tried in vain to control the situation through the use of his personal authority and the efforts of his military and civilian supporters. When the Dergue realized that the Emperor was dragging his feet it moved swiftly to arrest a host of ministers, local governors, imperial advisers and members of his family. Finally on 12 September 1974, Haile Selassie was deposed himself and placed in detention. The Dergue renamed itself the Provisional Military Administrative Council (PMAC) and took over the control of the governmental apparatus.

The old state thus disintegrated rapidly. In the absence of a political party or organized civilian revolutionary movement the only institution which amidst the revolution, economic disaster, famine and confusion survived intact was the army. It was commonly assumed that without the participation or at least the consent of the soldiers it would have been impossible to carry out a political revolution. This assumption was logical enough, given the fact that an army whose mission was to defend the regime could not be expected to remain neutral. The expectation was that the soldiers, of course, would help to topple the regime, which they did, but in the power vacuum that this created they found themselves also replacing it.

Subsequently the PMAC, which had engineered the liquidation of the old regime's leadership cadre, turned to socialism for a variety of reasons, pragmatic as well as ideological[85]. The first clear espousal of socialism came in December 1974 after Mengistu Haile Mariam assumed the leadership of the PMAC. It would appear that the Dergue was in great need to legitimize itself, particularly in the minds of university and high-school students whom it proposed to send on a *zemecha* campaign to the rural communities to explain the revolution and the 20 December declaration on 'Ethiopia Tikdem' (Ethiopia First)[86].

The first socialist statement was very general in its foundations. It said:

> In short: 'Ethiopia Tikdem' means Hibrettesebawinet (Ethiopian socialism): and Hibrettesebawinet means equality; self-reliance; the dignity of labour; the supremacy of common good; and the indivisibility of Ethiopian unity. That is our philosophy. And those are the principles upon which the foundations of the new Ethiopia will rest[87].

While this explanation of Ethiopian socialism may appear vague, it was in fact addressing itself to an important problem in traditional Ethiopian social relations[88]. The notion of equality was as revolutionary in deeply class- and status-conscious Ethiopia as it had been in eighteenth- and nineteenth-century Europe. Self-reliance was also a singular innovation in a society where begging was pervasive and carried little stigma and where the patron–client relationship was central to social relations. The dignity of labour was foreign to a long tradition of disdaining manual activity. The unification of the empire had been a problem throughout its long history, and the threat of the Eritrean secessionist movement made it central to the contemporary situation. Perhaps the most important new idea of Ethiopian socialism was that the common good was to take precedence over the individual, ethnic or regional interest. The Declaration made it clear:

> If our basic objective is to give shape and direction to the present movement, to achieve desired change by mobilising the support so prevalent in our nation today the existence of an Ethiopian socialist political party which brings together progressive elements in the nation and which has the capacity to attract and accommodate the entire people is absolutely indispensable[89].

The 'Ethiopia Tikdem' proclamation was followed on 3 February by the 'Declaration on the Economic Policy of Socialist Ethiopia'[90], which nationalized all major industrial and commercial companies and took majority control in remaining ones. In so doing the government seized control of practically every important company in the country. In March of the same year a sweeping land reform was proclaimed. All agricultural land was nationalized, possession was limited to a maximum of ten hectares, the rent or sale of land was outlawed and both tenancy and landlordism were eliminated. Subsequently, also, urban land and extra housing were nationalized and ownership was limited to one housing unit per family. Associations were formed in both urban and rural areas to implement the reforms and to administer local affairs. The PMAC also recorded official recognition of Islam, and proclaimed the equality of all national groups and cultures within Ethiopia.

The course of the Ethiopian revolution was also greatly influenced by external factors connected with the Somali attack on the Ogaden. The revolutionary upheaval in Ethiopia and the disorder and confusion which it generated proved irresistable to the Somalis, who began attacking Ogaden (which it claimed as part of Somalia) in 1975, under the name of the Western Somali Liberation Front. At that time the Ethiopian forces were totally dependent upon American arms and the United States was unwilling to be involved, at least openly, in the escalating war in the Horn of Africa. Furthermore, there was no ready alternative supplier for Ethiopian arms since the Soviet Union was backing Ethiopia's principal enemy, Somalia. The Ethiopian attitude towards the United States became increasingly ambivalent. A continuing Alliance with Washington hardly fitted in with the increasingly radical policies of the PMAC, which began in early 1976 sounding out the Soviets on the possibility of obtaining arms. The Soviet Union presented the PMAC with a stark choice: in order to get Soviet arms and backing it would have to commit itself to a clean break with the United States. Between 1975 and 1977 there was a rapid deterioration in Ethiopian–American relations, marked by increased Soviet and Cuban military assistance. And when, on 13 November 1977, Somalia expelled the 6000 Russians in the country, withdrew all their military facilities and abrogated the 1974 Soviet–Somali Treaty of Friendship and Cooperation[91], the Russian personnel flew from Mogadishu, with a stop-over in Aden, directly to Addis Ababa.

On 21 April 1976 the military regime released the Programme of the National Democratic Revolution, which represented a major offensive to set in motion processes that would result in the emergence of a viable political leadership for the revolution[92]. The essence of the programme was not the creation of the political movement itself but the specification of guidelines within which the movement was to develop. The programme set as its objectives the 'total eradication of feudalism, bureaucratic capitalism and imperialism from Ethiopia . . .; to build a new People's Ethiopia and lay a firm foundation for the transition to socialism'. It also maintained that the 'historical rights . . . of every nationality would be given equal respect'.

Perhaps the most important feature of the Programme was the process proposed for creating the revolutionary political movement. The armed forces were assigned a dual role in this process:

(1) To guard the revolution against domestic and foreign enemies; and

(2) To act as a catalyst in the process of generating social and economic change in line with the planned reforms[93].

The Programme also created the Provisional Office of Mass Organizational Affairs (POMOA)[94] as a forum for the coming together of various clandestine organizations and for the purpose of dissemination of Marxism–Leninism. In addition, in May of the same year, the Yekatit '66 Political School was established for the training of cadres of the future working-class vanguard party.

Five organizations which until then had operated clandestinely decided to establish a common front within POMOA with a view to forming eventually a vanguard Marxist–Leninist Party. These were the All-Ethiopian Socialist Movement (MEISONE), the Revolutionary Struggle of the Oppressed Ethiopians (ECHAT), the Marxist–Leninist Revolutionary Organization (MALERID), the Revolutionary Flame (SEDED) and the Labour League (LEAGUE).

These five organizations all claimed to be socialist and Marxist –Leninist in orientation. The main difference among them appeared to be their attitude towards military rule and the personalities who led them. Of the five, only the Revolutionary Flame and the Labour League were pro-military in the sense of accepting the necessity of military rule. In Feburary the five groups had signed a joint communiqué in which they pledged eventually to form a united front that would provide the leadership for a vanguard party. Although shortly afterwards the Union of Ethiopian Marxist–Leninist Organization (EMALEDH) was established, within a few months MEISONE and SECED were fighting each other for control of positions not only within EMALEDH but also in local, regional and central administration.

After the expulsion of MEISONE and ECHAT the union of Ethiopian Marxist–Leninist Organization reached the conclusion that the workers' party could not be established by mechanical formation or by simply moulding different organizations together on the basis of a quota awarded to each of them, and that the right step would be to bring together individual communists[95].

Thus Ethiopia embarked on a second attempt to create a Marxist–Leninist Party through the Commission for Organizing the Party of the Working People of Ethiopia (COPWE), established on 18 December 1979, by the PMAC and accountable to it. The purpose of COPWE, which operates under the chairmanship of Mengistu Haile Mariam (also chairman of the PMAC), is the

dissemination and propaganda of the philosophy of Marxism –Leninism among government and mass organizations, cooperatives and the broad masses generally, and to organize a sole, strong party of the working people based on the teachings of Marxism–Leninism, whose historical mission shall be to liquidate from the land of Ethiopia feudalism, imperialism and bureaucratic capitalism and to establish the new people's democratic republic of Ethiopia and to guide the people to achieve socialism and subsequently communism[96].

The proclamation[97] prohibited the existence of any political organization or group other than COPWE and compelled individuals and institutions to cooperate in all its activities. The membership of COPWE is open to individuals who accept the Programme of the National Democratic Revolution of Ethiopia and the Commission's rules and regulations.

Six months after the formation of COPWE its First Congress[98], which was held between 16 and 20 June 1980, officially inaugurated its activities by issuing membership cards (card number one was presented to Mengistu) and electing its Central and Executive Committees, Regional Committees and other organs. Although it is difficult to judge whether the second attempt to create a Marxist–Leninist Party will be successful, one thing appears to be quite clear. Looking at the composition of COPWE organs, the PMAC is in control of political developments in Ethiopia as firmly in 1981 as it was in 1974. Seven years of experiments with Marxism–Leninism appear not to have changed the role of the military in the Ethiopian society nor their perception of Marxism.

1976, 2 July
The Socialist Republic of Vietnam

The proclamation of the Socialist Republic of Vietnam was the result of the ending of thirty years of war of national liberation and the unification of Vietnam. The war ended on 30 April 1975, with the surrender of the South Vietnamese troops[99] and the fall of Saigon[100]. What needed to be created subsequently was a unified political, social and economic structure for the northern and southern zones of Vietnam.

On 15 November delegations from the two zones, each consisting of 25 members, met in Saigon[101] and on 21 November decided to call general elections to a single Vietnamese National Assembly. As a result of the elections, which were held on 25 April 1976, a National Assembly of 492 deputies, 249 representing the North and 243 the South, was elected[102].

The Assembly on 2 July proclaimed Vietnam an independent, unified country under the official name of the Socialist Republic of Vietnam.

Later that year, from 14 to 20 December, the long-delayed[103] Party Congress was held to celebrate victory and reunification.

The Congress changed the Party's name from the Vietnamese Workers' Party to the Vietnam Communist Party (VCP).

The changes in the names of both the country and the party were intended to emphasize that, having accomplished the unification of the country, all energies would be devoted towards building socialism.

1978, 27 April (7 Sowr)
The Democratic Republic of Afghanistan[104]

The first organizational structure for the Afghan Communist movement was the People's Democratic Party of Afghanistan (PDPA)[105]. Founded at its First (and so far only) Congress on 1 January 1965 in the home of Noor Mohammad Taraki, who became its Secretary-General, the PDPA split into two groups in June 1967, the *Khalq* (The People, led by Noor Taraki) and the *Parcham* (The Flag, led by Babrak Karmal). The groups differed on at least two issues. The first concerned the construction of the Party and its role in Afghan society. While the *Khalq* wanted to build a working-class party with strict Leninist discipline, the *Parcham* insisted on a broad national democratic front in which other left-wing and liberal groups could participate. Another dividing issue was Pushtunistan, which was closely linked with the different ethnic composition and policies of the two groups. While the membership of the *Parcham* consisted almost exclusively of Kabul Pushtuns with a relatively well-off social background, the *Khalq* by contrast included not only Ghilzai Pushtuns but also members of other ethnic groups. The *Khalq*'s approach to the nationalities question was based on trying to achieve a workable autonomy for all ethnic minorities, including the Pushtuns of Pakistan. The *Parcham* urged self-determination as the first step towards amalgamation with Afghanistan. In addition there were bitter personal differences within the PDPA, particularly between Taraki and Karmal.

On the international level the *Khalq* had close relationships with the Communist Party of India and, although there appear not to have been official contacts between the PDPA and the CPSU, Taraki received a Soviet literary prize for one of his books.

After the split into two groups the main area for the *Parcham*'s activities became the military. The task of political and ideological education among the armed forces was made easier by the fact that most of the officers came from peasant or working-class families. At the same time, the *Parcham* formed a tenuous alliance with Mohammad Daud Khan, first cousin and brother-in-law of the King, who subsequently seized power on 17 July 1973. The *Khalq*, on the other hand, refused to work among the military on the grounds that it contradicted Leninist principles of party work.

For almost a year after Daud's coup, the *Parcham* was represented on the Revolutionary Committee and had four ministers in the government, but after its members were moved away from power the group abandoned its attempts to influence the Daud regime.

The *Khalq* and *Parcham* were reunited in July 1977 to oppose the Daud regime. Less that a year later on 27 April 1978 (7 Sowr, 1357) the People's Democratic party of Afghanistan staged a successful *coup* with the backing of the army, which was its strongest base[106].

The event which most directly precipitated the *coup* against Mohammad Daud was the killing on 17 April 1978 of Mir Akbar Khyber, a university professor and former editor of the *Parcham* newspaper, who was to a great extent responsible for the reunification of the two factions. He was popular with both factions of the party, and his killing was seen by the party as an attempt to eliminate its leadership. Massive demonstrations at the Khyber funeral on 19 April, led by Taraki, at which over 15 000 people took part, alarmed the government, which began arresting leading members of the PDPA[107]. Taraki, Karmal and five other members of the PDPA's leadership were arrested in the early hours of 26 April. Hafizullah Amin, the person in charge of military affairs, was arrested at 11 a.m. on 26 April. However, prior to that, he was able to give his instructions to PDPA personnel in the army.

The revolution began at 9 a.m. on 27 April 1978. As crowds gathered in the central park in protest against the imprisonment of PDPA leaders, Mig-21s attacked Daud's palace. Fifty out of the army's total of 70 tanks moved into the city at the same time.

The tanks reached the prison where seven of the PDPA leaders were held at 5 p.m. They were taken aboard the tanks to Radio Afghanistan, which served as the revolutionary headquarters. They took immediate control on behalf of the civilian wing of the party – a condition laid down by Taraki for the whole operation. The first communiqué was broadcast at 7 p.m. and the next day a Revolutionary Council and Cabinet were announced.

The establishment of the Marxist regime in Afghanistan was perhaps one of the most rapid and unexpected in the history of the Communist movement.

1979, 7 January
The People's Republic of Kampuchea

The second Marxist regime in Kampuchea was established as the result of war between Democratic Kampuchea and the Socialist Republic of Vietnam. Military clashes between Kampuchean and Vietnamese armies, which began shortly after the capture of Saigon in 1975, escalated into a full-scale military conflict, with each side blaming the other for its initiation[108].

On 2 December 1978 a group of Kampuchean intellectuals, soldiers, peasants and Buddhist monks and nuns opposed to the internal policies of the Pol Pot regime and the escalating conflict with Vietnam met on the Vietnamese side of the border between the two countries and formed the National United Front for the Salvation of Kampuchea (NUFSK)[109]. The Front's explicitly declared aim was the overthrow of the established regime of Democratic Kampuchea.

Within a month a military offensive spearheaded by regular troops of the Vietnamese People's Liberation Army (although this has always been denied by Vietnam) reached Phnom Penh. While the government of Democratic Kampuchea fled to the *maquis* to fight the invading armies, a new Marxist regime consisting of the high-ranking officers of the NUFSK was established on 7 January 1979. The country was renamed the People's Republic of Kampuchea (PRK) on the same day. It received full political and military backing from the SRV and diplomatic recognition from the Soviet Union and other members of the Comecon (with the exception of Romania). However, it was some two and a half years later before the full state and party structures were created.

Between 26 and 29 May 1981 the Congress of the new Marxist –Leninist party, the Kampuchean People's Revolutionary Party[110] (KPRP), was held in Phnom Penh. The party, which was described by its secretary-general Pen Sovan as the legitimate heir to all the genuine revolutionary movements in Kampuchea since the fifteenth century, now assumes the direct leadership of the new regime.

Party-building efforts in May were followed in June by the unveiling of a new structure. Following the holding of general elections in June 1981, the first session of the New National Assembly ratified on 24 June the Constitution of the PRK. The document, stressing the role played by Vietnam in the establishment of the present Phnom Penh regime, expresses gratitude for the 'sincere assistance of the Vietnamese army and the Lao people' and refers also to the strengthening of 'bond of solidarity, friendship and cooperation with Vietnam, Laos and other fraternal socialist countries[111]. The emphases on the special relationship with Vietnam 'without which the Kampuchean revolution would have collapsed in defeat' have also been underlined during the KPRP congress. The National Assembly also created a new government which replaced the Kampuchean People's Revolutionary Council.

The creation of the party and government structures at the central level by the new Marxist regime in Kampuchea should be seen as the final stage in the process of its establishment[112].

1979, 13 March
The People's Revolutionary Government of Grenada

The People's Revolutionary Government of Grenada was established on 13 March 1979 by the New Jewel Movement[113] after it overthrew the dictatorial regime of Eric Gairy.

At 4.15 that morning forty-six armed men belonging to the People's Revolutionary Army stormed the True Blue Military headquarters of the Grenada Defence Force, south of St George's, with Molotov cocktails and hand-grenades. The unprepared soldiers were overpowered and disarmed in half an hour. The rebels broke into the armoury, seized more weapons and set fire to the barracks. They then moved on to the radio station at Morne Rouse, which was captured without a fight[114]. By 6 a.m. all but two of the members of the Gairy government, surprised in their houses, were in custody[115]. At the same time in Grenville, the island's second town, local members of the New Jewel Movement captured the local police station[116].

At 10.30 a.m. Maurice Bishop went on the air to announce the formation of a provisional revolutionary government under his leadership. The last stronghold of opposition, the main police headquarters in St George's, surrendered just before 4 p.m.[117]. The revolutionary seizure of power was accomplished in twelve hours.

The Grenadian revolution is descended from the Black Power movement of 1968-1970 which echoed through the Caribbean and reached its height in the 1970 Army revolt in Trinidad. The Trinidad uprising was a hopeless ragbag of uncoordinated intellectuals and ideologies, unready for the practicalities of revolution. But out of that debacle came a clutch of more serious radical groups, including the New Jewel Movement.

The NJM did not initially present itself as a Marxist party, although it did so increasingly over time. Its manifesto, issued in

1973, called for the nationalization of banks and insurance companies and for a system of democracy based on people's assemblies, adult citizens and workers' assemblies of all those who earned their living[118].

The NJM, which maintained that the struggle 'must aim at destroying the whole class relationship in our society'[119] from the very early stages of its existence was organized into cell groups in various villages[120].

After the demonstration on 21 January 1974, during which one person was killed and scores of protestors severely beaten by the police, the NJM strengthened its organizational structures and its ties with the various sectors of the population, particularly the workers, while forging an alliance with the different opposition forces[121].

In anticipation of the 1976 elections the NJM, along with the Grenada National Party and the United People's Party, formed a 'people's alliance'. In the elections held on 7 December 1976 the alliance received 48.5 per cent of the votes and Maurice Bishop became the leader of the parliamentary opposition[122].

However, the parliamentary road did not prove to be particularly successful. For six years the NJM used all forms of struggle, including strikes, peaceful mass demonstrations, elections and eventually parliament. Given the mounting repression and political persecution and the impossibility of making change peacefully, the organization resorted to armed struggle. The NJM began to develop a clandestine wing trained in armed insurrection. This group was later to become the nucleus of the People's Revolutionary Army of Grenada, which spearheaded the overthrow of the dictatorship[123].

The ideological content and inspiration for the Grenadian Revolution has quite clearly come from Cuba. As Maurice Bishop stated on the first anniversary of his government coming to power, 'the greatest debt of gratitude owed to the Cubans is that if there had been no Cuban Revolution in 1959 there could have been no Grenadian Revolution in 1979'[124].

At the same time the ideology of the Grenadian Revolution echoes the anti-dogmatism of Amilcar Cabral. This was succinctly put by Grenada's Deputy Prime Minister Bernard Coard, who, when asked how could the objective of building socialism with such a small population and little or no working class be realized in Grenada, replied:

> I think that one has to have a very clear objective and a realistic appraisal of what is possible, and over what period of time and in what way. I think that the first thing that has to be said is that

we do not subscribe to nor do we take a dogmatic approach to this question. We have to try to develop a socialist society, a society of genuine equality, a society that genuinely serves the interests of the broad masses of the country, based on our objective conditions – our size, the kind of natural resources we have, the kind of skill levels we have to deal with, the type of organizational capacity we have at any given moment[125].

1 For an account of this phase see L. Huberman and P. M. Sweezy, *Cuba: Anatomy of a Revolution*
2 For an informative first-hand account of this period see E. Boorstein, *The Economic Transformation of Cuba* and J. O'Connor, *The Origins of Socialism in Cuba*; also A. Suarez, *Cuba: Castroism and Communism 1959–1966*
3 On this period the most useful is Suarez, ibid.
4 For text see Fidel Castro and Régis Debray, *On Trial*, pp. 9–67
5 The Communist Party of Cuba (PCC), founded in August 1925, grew rapidly and by 1930 had become one of the largest and most influential Marxist –Leninist parties in Latin America. The PCC was legalized in 1938 after it entered into an alliance with the military government of Fulgencio Batista. The alliance with the Communists enabled Batista to make the transition from a virtual military dictator to a constitutionally elected president in 1940. The same year the Party changed its name into the Revolutionary Union Communist Party. During the Second World War the Communists became the first in Latin America to receive ministerial posts in the government. In the presidential elections of 1944 the Communists, who by now had renamed themselves the Popular Socialist Party (PSP) and were rising towards their peak membership figures (37 000 in 1946), again supported Batista, who lost this time to Grau San Martin of the Antenticos Party. In 1947, the Antenticos launched a campaign of repression against the PSP. The campaigning, which coincided with the outbreak of the cold war on the international arena, drove the Party underground, where it remained until 1959. At the time of Batista's second *coup* in 1952 the PSP opposed his suspension of the Constitution but, having lost its influence over the labour unions, it became isolated and numerically rather insignificant
6 C. Guevara, *Guerrilla Warfare*, p. 74. Che Guevara appears to be the only Cuban leader to have published reminiscences of guerrilla war. It should be pointed out that though the book from which the above quoted passage is taken is the most reliable source available so far, between the end of the war and writing it, Guevra had read works on guerrilla warfare including those of Mao and Giap. His work is explicitly intended not as an objective account of the past, but as an encouraging manual for the future. See also his memories of the war in J. Gerassi (ed.) *Venceremos! The Speeches and Writings of Che Guevara*, Ch. 2, pp. 57–139
7 It is important to recollect the size of some of the guerrilla forces. In March 1958, when Castro was claiming that the peasants 'make our victory certain', he still only had 160 men. By Guevara's own testimony the biggest single rebel operation of the war was mounted by 220 men in all. See T. Draper, *Castroism: Theory and Practice*, p. 13

8 Although the guerrillas clearly could not have succeeded without support from the peasantry, the extent and nature of that support is rather controversial and obscure. What is clear, however, is that the force which won power was not a genuine peasant revolutionry movement such as, for example, that led by Zapata in Mexico in 1910

9 E. Gonzales, *Cuba Under Castro: The Limits of Charisma*, p. 118

10 For details see ibid.

11 Quoted after ibid, p. 146

12 The First Congress of the Cuban Communist Party took place ten years later, 17–22 December 1975

13 V. Thompson and R. Adloff, *Historical Dictionary of the People's Republic of the Congo*, p. 74

14 No detailed data on population movements prior to 1974 is available. It is estimated, however, that in 1945 the urban population of the country represented 10 per cent of the total population. See *Area Handbook for the People's Republic of the Congo*, p. 50. According to the 1974 Census, 33 per cent of the 1.3 million population lived in towns and cities and roughly 60 per cent of the population was below the age of 16. See *West Africa*, 12 August 1974

15 In 1965 approximately 8 per cent of the potential labour force was unemployed, including a large proportion of unskilled urban migrants. See *Area Handbook*, op.cit. (note 14), p. 193

16 The account of these events is based on detailed search of newspaper and press agencies' reports. It also draws on R. Gauze, *The Politics of Congo-Brazzaville*, pp. 152–153

17 M. Ngouabi, 'Scientific Socialism in Africa', *World Marxist Review*, May 1975, p. 41

18 Apparently two army majors, David Mountsaka and Felix Mouzabakany, had convinced Youlou of the necessity to resign

19 In January 1966 the institutionalization of the MNR as the Congo's single party confirmed legally its ascendancy over the government

20 By 1965 the Federation comprised 17 emirates, principalities, sheikdoms and the Crown Colony of the town of Aden

21 See the article by V. Naumkin published in January 1978 in the Soviet journal *International Affairs*, 'Southern Yemen: The Road to Progress'

22 According to a recent official Yemeni publication the first agrarian reform of 25 March 1968 was 'promulgated under the government headed by Qahtan al-Shaabi. This law, however, did not correspond to the aspirations of the masses of the poor peasantry . . . This measure failed for the following reasons: (1) The size of the maximum permitted individual holding – 25 feddas of irrigated and 50 of non-irrigated land – enabled those affected by the law to evade its provisions and to keep considerable areas of land. (2) The law did not stipulate the way in which lands confiscated from the Sultans and emirs should be worked or make any definite regulations for the organization of agriculture. (3) The law permitted individual freehold ownership of land and thus consolidated the fragmentation of agricultural holdings, preventing the development of agricultural cooperation and any moves towards setting up cooperative projects' (*Economic Achievements of Democratic Yemen*, p. 10). See also M. H. Ali, 'Land Reforms in Southern Yemen', *World Marxist Review*, **15**, No. 2 (February), 1972, 29

23 Constitution of the People's Democratic Republic of Yemen, in A. P. Blaustein and G. H. Flanz (eds), *Constitutions of the Countries of the World*, Vol. 10, pp. 3–4

24 The Political Report: presented by Comrade Abdel Fattah Ismail, Secretary-
    General of the Unified Political Organization, The United Front to the
    Unification Congress, 11 to 13 October 1975, p. 78
25 T. Y. Ismael, 'People's Democratic Republic of Yemen' in *Marxist Govern-
    ments: A World Survey* (ed. by B. Szajkowski), Vol. 3, p. 775
26 For a discussion of the precipitatory factors behind the *coup* and its account,
    see I. M. Lewis, 'The Politics of the 1960 Somali Coup', *Journal of Modern
    African Studies*, **10**, No. 3, 383–408
27 *Area Handbook for Somalia*, pp. 323–325
28 The *coup* retrospectively came to be called the 'revolution'
29 M. Siad Barre, 'A Second Revolution'. Speech delivered on 21 October 1970
    in M. Siad Barre, *My Country and My People*, Vol. 2, p. 4. The nature and
    importance of Somalia's acceptance of scientific socialism has been empha-
    sized unequivocally in the introduction to the third volume of President Siad's
    speeches, written by the Vice-President of the Somali Revolutionary Council,
    Colonel Ismail Ali Abokor. 'In the last four years, i.e. since the advent of our
    blessed Revolution of 21 October 1969, the President of the Supreme
    Revolutionary Council Jaalle (Comrade) Maj. General Mohamed Siad Barre
    has been instilling into the psyche of Somali society the principles of the
    Revolution within the context of a harmonious marriage between religion and
    scientific socialism. This is indeed an original departure from the more
    generally accepted view that theological difference has no place in the ungodly
    world of scientific socialism. This contention owes two main sources to its
    currency: firstly, the originators of the ideology of scientific socialism – the
    great Karl Marx and Frederick Engels – denigrated religion because the
    Church, a wealthy parasite feeding on the fears and ignorance of the working
    masses, sided with the capitalists in the historical confrontation between
    entrenched capitalist monopolies and the budding ideology of scientific
    socialism. This apparent incompatibility has become even more accepted when
    the founder of the first socialist state, Comrade Vladimir Illyich Lenin of the
    Soviet Union, abolished religion thus bringing the theoretical prophecy of
    Marx and Engels into practical reality. Secondly, the capitalists further
    promoted and propagated this Marxist–Leninist stand in order to alienate
    socialism from the God-fearing masses of the world.
       'The capitalist strategy confused the broad masses especially of the so-called
    third world, and hoodwinked genuine socialist revolutions into accepting
    pseudo-socialism like 'liberal socialism', 'pragmatic socialism' and such like,
    implying the existence of diverse brands of socialism tailor-made for different
    peoples at various stages of development, thus deflating these genuine
    revolutions and compromising them into some form of 'accommodation' with
    the capitalist mode of production in order to abate the wrath of the capitalist
    monopolies.
       'Strangely enough no modern Moslem state had adopted scientific socialism
    before the Somali Democratic Republic. Indeed nobody before Jaalle
    Mohamed Siad Barre was through the haze of socialist literature to realise that
    the apparent incompatibility between religion and scientific socialism is not
    fundamental. Just as it took V. I. Lenin to realise that a high level of industrial
    development was not necessarily a pre-requisite to the inception of a true
    socialist revolution as stipulated by Marx and Engels, just in the same way it
    took Jaalle Siad to postulate that the classless nature of Islam and the
    egalitarianism of its principle absolutely refute its incompatibility with the
    tenets of scientific socialism.'
30 *Halgan*, No. 1, October 1976, 19

31 The Foundation Congress met between 26 June and 1 July 1976. It was attended by 3000 delegates – workers, peasants, herders, members of the armed forces, progressive petty-bourgeois traders and intellectuals, members of youth and women organizations drawn from 82 districts in 16 regions of the country. (See *Halgan*, No. 1, October 1976, 13)

32 *Halgan*, No. 9, July 1977, 19. The newly organized committees consisted of eight or nine members including a three-man executive, which in turn consisted of the committee's secretary and two assistants. The first assistant dealt with Party affairs while the second one was responsible for administering government business. The structure of the Regional Committees was similar.

33 For a comprehensive and penetrating account of the foundation of the PAIGC see Basil Davidson, *The Liberation of Guinea: Aspects of an African Revolution*

34 Ibid., pp. 79–85

35 Ibid., pp. 88–89

36 For a detailed analysis of these structures see Lars Rudebeck, 'Political Mobilisation in Guinea-Bissau' in Sam C. Sarkesian, *Revolutionary Guerrilla Warfare*, Precedent Publishing, Chicago, 1975, pp. 432–451

37 Basid Davidson, 'Republics of Guinea-Bissau and Cape Verde' in Szajkowski (ed.), op.cit. (note 25), Vol. 2, p. 370

38 Ibid.

39 The independence of Guinea-Bissau was officially recognized by Portugal on 10 September 1974

40 Davidson, op.cit. (note 37), p. 372

41 Amilcar Cabral, *Our People are Our Mountains*, pp. 21–22

42 An attempt to organize a Marxist–Leninist party in the country was made in 1959 with the formation of the Parti de la Révolution Socialiste du Benin (PRSB). Co-founded by Lois Benanzin, a Marxist instructor in Guinea and a Dahomean trade union leader, Theophîle Paoletti, the PRSB was linked to the Marxist–Leninist Parti Africain d'Indépéndence in Dakar, Senegal. It attracted only a few intellectuals and students. The PRSB collapsed stillborn when it could not gather more than 50 members

43 The UGTD membership in 1961 was 10 000, approximately 48 per cent of the total union membership in the country

44 For example, in December 1971 the UGEED had called for the transformation of Dahomey into a 'vast battleground'

45 For a detailed account of the *coup* see 'Dahomey, Kerekou's coup', *West Africa* (6 November 1972), 1479 and 1481

46 Only four members of the new government, out of twelve, had briefly held office in the previous military governments

47 *Africa Research Bulletin*, Political Series, January 1975, and *Africa Research Bulletin*, Economic Series, December 1974

48 S. Decalo, 'People's Republic of Benin', in Szajkowski (ed.), op.cit. (note 25), Vol. 1, p. 93

49 Although the creation of the PRPB was announced on 30 November 1975, the official date of its setting up was its first Extraordinary Congress held in Cotonou on 15–17 May 1976. It is worth noting that on 30 November 1975 the country's name was changed into the People's Republic of Benin

50 'Kampuchea' is the Khmer language name for the country of the Khmer people. The French 'Camboge' and the English 'Cambodia' are colonial derivations. The Khmer Rouge always used the national name and after 1975 it also acquired common usage in English

51 See the section on the Democratic Republic of Vietnam, pp. 47–49

52 Very little is known about the Party and its history, and what information is available is often contradictory. In view of the subsequent overthrow of the Pol Pot regime in January 1979 details about the CPK would probably never be known. For an outline of the Party's history and discussion of its policies and activities see Pol Pot, *The Grand Victories of the Revolution of Kampuchea Under the Correct and Clearsighted Leadership of the Communist Party of Kampuchea*; T. M. Carney, *Communist Party Power in Kampuchea (Cambodia): Documents and Discussion*, Cornell University Southeast Asia Program Data Paper, No. 106; and K. M. Quinn, 'Political Change in Wartime: The Khmer Krahom Revolution in Southern Cambodia, 1970–1974', *Naval War College Review* (1976), 3–31

53 The existence of the CPK was a closely guarded secret for security reasons. The first official mention of the existence of the Communist Party of Kampuchea was by radio, Phnom Penh home service, on 25 September 1977, while reporting that a government and Communist Party delegation, led by Pol Pot as Party Secretary, would pay an official visit to China from 28 September. On 27 September Pol Pot delivered his famous speech on the occasion of the solemn proclamation of the official existence of the CPK. See Pol Pot, op.cit. (note 52)

54 See *Documents in Communist Affairs – 1979* (ed. by B. Szajkowski), 'Interview with Comrade Pol Pot, Secretary of the Central Committee of the Communist Party of Kampuchea, Prime Minister of the Government of Democratic Kampucha with Delegation of Yugoslav Journalists', pp. 174–185

55 See N. Sihanouk, *My War with the CIA: The Memoirs of Prince Norodom Sihanouk*

56 Since the Party's existence was not known at the time the popular assumption had been that the Khmer Rouge were a Chinese-backed communist guerrilla group

57 The Constitution came into force on 5 January 1976. For text see *Constitution du Kampuchea Democratique*, Mission du Kampuchea Democratique, Paris, 1976

58 For an account see E. Mondlane, *The Struggle for Mozambique*

59 'FRELIMO Faces the Future', *African Communist*, No. 55 (1973), 47

60 E. Mondlane, *Mozambique Revolution*, Dar es Salaam, No. 1 (December 1963), 2

61 For discussion of the various factors determining Soviet and Eastern European aid to African countries and the nature of their penetration see A. A. Brayton, 'Soviet Involvement in Africa' in *Journal of Modern African Studies*, **17**, No. 2 (1979), 253–269

62 T. H. Henriksen, *Mozambique: A History*, pp. 202–203

63 *FRELIMO, Estatutos e programa*, p. 195

64 *Central Committee Report to the Third Congress of FRELIMO*, p. 34

65 The Congress was attended by 379 Mozambican delegates and 39 delegates from abroad. For the text of the Central Committee's report see ibid.; see also Spectator, 'Building the Party in Mozambique', *The African Communist*, No. 79 (1979), 45–63

66 S. Machel, 'Consolidating People's Power in Mozambique', *The African Communist*, No. 72 (1978), 39

67 See section on Guinea-Bissau, pp. 101–104

68 The PAIGC Programme is in Amilcar Cabral, *Revolution in Guinea, An African People's Struggle*, pp. 136–140

69 Basil Davidson, 'Cape Verde: Liberation and Progress', *People's Power*, No. 17, Spring 1981, 5–15

70 For documentary material on the formation of the PAICV see *Communist Affairs*, **1**, No. 1, 1982, pp. 55–60. See also Barry Munslow, 'The Coup in Guinea Bissau and the Cape Verdian Response', ibid., pp. 55–60. A useful chronology of the coup is given in *People's Power*, No. 17, Spring 1981, 16–22

71 For a detailed account of this complicated period see J. Marcum, *The Angolan Revolution*, Vol. 1

72 For an English translation of the manifesto see T. Okuma, *Angola in Ferment*, pp. 112–118

73 For a detailed discussion of external assistance to the nationalist movements during the various stages of the independence war see Marcum, op.cit. (note 71), Vol. 2, pp. 14–20, 221–240, 264–275

74 Ibid., p. 257

75 Ibid., p. 259

76 See Castro's speech on the anniversary of the Antonio Maceos' Baragua Protest, Szakowski (ed.) op.cit. (note 25), pp. 45–50. For details of Cuban military involvement on behalf of the MPLA see Marcum, op.cit. (note 71), Vol. 2, pp. 273–274 and E. Gonzalez, 'Cuban Foreign Policy', *Problems of Communism*, Nov-Dec. 1977, 1–15

77 M. Wolfers, 'People's Republic of Angola' in Szajkowski (ed.), op.cit. (note 25), Vol. 1, p. 73

78 Kaysone Phomvihane, 'The Victory of Creative Marxism–Leninism in Laos'. See also the section on the Democratic Republic of Vietnam, pp. 47–49

79 On 12 October 1945 in the wake of the Japanese surrender in Asia, a Lao Itsala (Lao Independence) government unilaterally declared the independence of the country. The French, however, succeeded in restoring their authority by 24 April 1946

80 At its Second Congress in February the Lao People's Party was renamed the Lao People's Revolutionary Party (LPRP). The Party, like the Communit Party of Kampuchea, operated clandestinely until it assumed power

81 For details on this see J. J. Zasloff, *The Pathet Lao: Leadership and Organization*; Phoumi Vongvichit, *Laos and the Victorious Struggle of the Lao People Against US Neo-colonialism*; N. Adams and A. W. McCoy, *Laos: War and Revolution*; Manich Jumsai, *A New History of Laos*; and J. J. Zasloff and M. Brown (eds), *Communism and Indochina*

82 For text see *The Paris Agreements on Vietnam and the Agreement on Laos*, pp. 11–14

83 The letter of abdication signed by the King on 29 November 1975 in the Royal capital of Luang Prabang read: 'Considering the change in the politics of Laos, the function and title of the King in the monarchy as defined by the constitution cannot get along with the people's democratic system; it may even be an obstacle to the progress of the nation. To help the country to advance favourably and national unity to become stronger, I hereby voluntarily and proudly declare my abdication as King of Laos. It is of my complete free will, with absolute selflessness, and with perfect peace of mind, that I renounce the throne. I now leave it to the people of Laos to shape the destiny of our country. This will affirm the right of the whole people to be their own masters. And as an ordinary citizen of Laos, I wish my beloved people, unity, independence, happiness and prosperity.' (Foreign Broadcast Information Service, 3 December 1975)

84 In view of this the following analysis is somewhat longer than in the previous studies

85 It is worth noting that in 1974 the industrial proletariat in Ethiopia consisted of about 240 000 workers in the processing industries, in textiles, leather, shoes

and food, in communications and in transportation. Although there existed a trade union organization – the Confederation of Ethiopian Labour Unions (CBCU) – it operated under the Emperor's auspices. Marxist ideas began penetrating sections of Ethiopian society, particularly university students, as a result of educational facilities. Strict censorship applied to books and magazines, but did not, however, extend to the Haile Selassie I University, where the collection of Marxist books was in great demand. Among African leaders, the university students were particularly attracted to the writings and practices of Julius Nyerere. In Ethiopia, however, there was neither a classical Marxist–Leninist Party nor a civilian revolutionary movement. There was not even any secret military group like Nasser's Free Officers in Egypt. There is no evidence to suggest that the Ethiopians in 1974 were inspired to mount the revolution by specific socialist movements or organizations from abroad. The PMAC's first pronouncements gave little indication that militant socialism would soon become the masthead of the revolution

86 *Declaration of the Provisional Military Government of Ethiopia*, Addis Ababa, 20 December 1974
87 Ibid., p. 8
88 M. Ottaway and D. Ottaway, *Ethiopia: Empire in Revolution*, p. 63
89 *Declaration of the Provisional Military Government of Ethiopia*, op.cit. (note 86), p. 9
90 Provisional Military Government, *Declaration of Economic Policy of Socialist Ethiopia*, Addis Ababa, 7 February 1975
91 See B. Szajkowski (ed.), *Documents in Communist Affairs – 1977*, pp. 206–219
92 *Programme of the National Democratic Revolution of Ethiopia*
93 Section 2, paragraph 7, of the Programme reads in part: 'The role of Ethiopia's armed forces and police is to safeguard Ethiopia's territorial integrity, unity and peace. They will be given all the necessary socialist education that will enable them to fulfil these tasks and protect the welfare of Ethiopia's broad masses. Steps will be taken that during peace time, side by side, with the masses they take active part in production and development areas . . .'
94 See *The Roles of POMOA and the Yekatit '66 Political School in the Ethiopian Revolution*, Propaganda and Information Committee, Fourth Anniversary of the Ethiopian Revolution, Addis Ababa, September 1978
95 *Enashenifalen*, No. 1, November 1979, 23
96 *Ethiopian Herald*, 19 December 1979
97 For text see ibid.
98 For text of Mengistu speech see *Ethiopian Herald*, 17 June 1980
99 At 10.15 a.m. on 30 April General Duong Van Minh, who was sworn in as President of South Vietnam only two days earlier, broadcast the surrender statement: 'Our political line is one of reconciliation. I believe deeply in reconciliation among Vietnamese to avoid unnecessary bloodshed. For this reason I ask the soldiers of the Republic of Vietnam to cease fighting, remain calm and stay where they are. I ask the brother soldiers of the Provisional Revolutionary Government of South Vietnam to cease hostilities. We are waiting here to meet the Provisional Revolutionary Government of South Vietnam to discuss the formal handing over of power in an orderly manner, so as to avoid useless shedding of our people's blood'
100 The Vietnamese People's Army began entering the city soon after noon. A tank flying the North Vietnamese flag crushed the gates to the Presidential Palace, where President Minh surrendered to a North Vietnamese officer
101 The South Vietnamese delegation included representatives of the Provisional Revolutionary Government; the National Liberation Front; the Vietnam

Alliance of National Democratic and Peace Forces; the trade unions; the Catholic, Buddhist, Cao Dai and Hoa Hoa churches; and the Montagnards and the Khmer community. The North Vietnamese delegation was elected by the Standing Committee of the DRV's National Assembly

102 In both zones the number of candidates exceeded the number of seats, 308 being nominated for 249 seats in the North and 297 for the 243 seats in the South

103 The last (third) Congress was held in September 1960

104 The following is drawn from the author's article 'People's Afghanistan' in B. Szajkowski (ed.) *Documents in Communist Affairs – 1980*, pp. xv–xxxv

105 Little is known abut the early left-wing or communist activities in Afghanistan. In contrast to all the other Asian countries bordering the Soviet Union (China, Korea, Mongolia, Persia and Turkey) no Communist Party was founded in the early years after the Russian revolution. In the 1920s Afghan socialists travelled to and from the USSR, but as individuals. The lack of Bolshevik interest in founding a distinct communist party is perhaps best explained by the fact that the Russians wanted to consolidate their relations with the reform-minded and anti-British King Amanullah, who headed the only state in the world at that time willing to cooperate with the Bolsheviks. The external influence, therefore, did not come from the CPSU but in the late 1940s from the Communist Party of India, whose influence appears to have facilitated the creation of communist and left-wing groups such as the Wikh-i-Zalmayan (Awakened Youth), whose main recruits were intellectuals and army officers. The first public acknowledgement of the existence in the country of organized left-wing groups occurred during the 'Liberal Parliament' (1949–1952), which included 50 (out of 120) left-wing members, most of them linked with Wikh-i-Zalmayan

106 See interview with Hafizullah Amin in Szajkowski (ed.), op.cit. (note 91), p. 168

107 A detailed account of the 27 April Revolution is given in 'Interview with Hafizullah Amin', op.cit. (note 91), pp. 168–169. See also Alexander Ignatov, 'Three months of the Revolution', *New Times*, **35**, August 1978, 29

108 For Kampuchean and Vietnamese accounts of the conflict and its background see Szajkowski (ed.), op.cit. (note 91), pp. 174–224

109 See the author's 'People's Republic of Kampuchea' in Szajkowski (ed.), op.cit. (note 25), Vol. 2, pp. 437–442. The name of the NUFSK was changed in June 1981 to the Kampuchean Front for National Construction

110 The new party's name appears to have been selected to suggest kinship with the Cambodian party formed in 1951, the Khmer People's Revolutionary Party. The May KPRP congress was designated the 'fourth', the first said to have been held in 1951, the second in 1960, and the third – a 'secret' congress – in January 1979, following the present regime's assumption of power in Phnom Penh. Efforts have also been made to dissociate the KPRP from the rival Communist Party of Kampuchea of the ousted Pol Pot. The congress resolution says the new party was 'appropriately' named both to 'underline and reassert the continuity' of the 'best traditions' and to distinguish it from 'the reactionary Pol Pot party'.

There was some confusion about the name of the new party during the pre-congress period. In April 1981 the Phnom Penh media departed from their usual practice of referring simply to 'the party' in reporting a reference to 'the Kampuchean Workers Party'. Later that month Phnom Penh radio mentioned a 'Revolutionary Party'.

For background and analysis of the formulation of the PRP see Michael

Williams 'Kampuchean People's Revolutionary Party', *Communist Affairs* No. 2, March 1982, pp. 96–100

111 For the text of the draft of the Constitution of the People's Republic of Kampuchea see *Saporanem Kampuchea Bulletin*, 10 March 1981

112 However, it has been acknowledged by the KPRP and the official media in Phnom Penh that the critical shortage of cadres, both civilian and military, continues to hamper the government's attempts to consolidate administrative control over the country. The final congress resolution, for example, spoke of only 'initial' achievements in building party structures. It is believed that at the time of the PRP in May 1981 only seven of Kampuchea's nineteen provinces had party structures

113 The New Jewel Movement is a successor to two radical organizations that had emerged in Grenada in the early 1970s. The first of these organizations, JEWEL (Joint Endeavour for Welfare, Education and Liberation of the People), was formed in March 1972. It was based in the south-eastern part of the country in Vincennes, St David's parish, and comprised a few teachers, an ex-policeman, a few peasants and a number of youths. The group, which was led by Unison Whiteman and Teddy Victor, had a farming cooperative as well as a news sheet which they started. It directly challenged Gairy's proclaimed power base, the agricultural workers, by giving concrete pointers to an alternative way forward for the countryside. The other organization, MAP (Movement for Assemblies of the People), was formed in September 1972 in the capital of St George's. It was composed of a mixture of professional people, mostly graduates, including a number of lawyers. Among them were Maurice Bishop and Kendrick Radix. Bishop had just returned from Britain, where he had been involved in political work among London's black community. Members of this group moved about the country in connection with their work in the courts, coming into contact with people of all walks of life, which exposed them to the poverty and harsh realities of life for most Grenadians.

What they all had in common was that they were young. They had come out of a Black Power tradition of the late 1960s and early 1970s. Many had lived in Britain, the United States and Canada and had studied and worked in those countries. They sought radical restructuring of the very mechanism of Grenadian society.

On 11 March 1973 MAP and the JEWEL formed a new organization, the New Jewel Movement. Maurice bishop and Unison Whiteman were elected joint coordinating secretaries of the new political organization.

114 Ernest Harsch, 'How the Gairy Regime was Overthrown', *Intercontinental Press*, December 3, 1979, 1187

115 *Grenada: Let those who Labour Hold the Reins*, Interview with Bernard Coard of the Revolutionary Grenada by Chris Searle, p. 1

116 Ibid.

117 Ernest Harsch, op.cit. (note 115), p. 1187

118 Ibid.

119 Ibid.

120 Francis J. Bain, *Beyond the Ballot Box*, p. 43

121 Arnold Hutchinson, 'The Long Road to Freedom', p. 15

122 Ibid.

123 Ibid.

124 Maurice Bishop. *Forward Ever! Against Imperialism and Towards Genuine National Independence and People's Power*, p. 4

125 *Grenada: Let Those who Labour Hold the Reins*, p. 11

Chapter 7

The historical pattern

The previous chapters have examined the main features in the establishment of each of the fifty-three regimes (see *Table 1*). Rather than looking for the typology of ways in which they came to power it would be more useful to survey the whole historical nexus of the *overall* establishment process. An approach which concentrates on the timing and geographical context, as well as on the causes which led to the emergence of those regimes, appears to be more fruitful than mere emphasis on the techniques of coming to power.

The total process of the establishment of Marxist regimes, which now spans a period of more than six decades, should be viewed as a series of related events that take their source in the Bolshevik revolution of 1917.

Perhaps the most stimulating description of the entire sequence is that of a *spiral* within which these events took place. Such a spiral is a continuous curve moving around a fixed point in the

Table 1

1	1917, 25 October	The Military Revolutionary Committee of Petrograd Soviet of Workers' and Soldiers' Deputies
2	1917, 25 December	Ukrainian Soviet Republic
3	1918, 28 January to 1918, 5 May	Finnish Socialist Republic of Workers
4	1918, 29 November to 1919, February	Estonian Workers' Commune
5	1918, 16 December to 1919, 21 April	Provisional Revolutionary Workers' and Peasants' Government of Lithuania
6	1918, 22 December to 1920, January	Latvian Soviet Republic
7	1918, 31 December to 1919, 1 January	Bratislava Soviet Republic
8	1919, 1 January	Belorussian Soviet Socialist Republic
9	1919, 10 January to 1919, 4 February	Bremen Soviet Republic
10	1919, 21 March to 1919, 1 August	Hungarian Soviet Republic
11	1919, 7 April to 1919, 2 May	Bavarian Soviet Republic
12	1919, 16 June to 1919, 7 July	Slovak Soviet Republic

13	1920, 1 February to 1924, 2 October	Khorezm People's Soviet Republic
14	1920, 6 April to 1922, 14 November	Far Eastern Republic
15	1920, 20 April	Azerbaijani Soviet Socialist Republic
16	1920, 20 May to 1921, October	Soviet Socialist Republic of Gilan
17	1920, 5 September to 1924, 20 September	Bukhara People's Soviet Republic
18	1920, 29 November	Soviet Socialist Republic of Armenia
19	1921, 25 February	Georgian Soviet Socialist Republic
20	1921, 16 August to 1944, 11 October	People's Republic of Tannu Tuva
21	1924, 26 November	Mongolian People's Republic
22	1932, 4 June to 1932, 16 June	Socialist Republic of Chile
23	1939, 30 November to 1940, January	Finnish Democratic Republic
24	1944, 7 November to 1949, October	Eastern Turkistan Republic
25	1945, 29 November	Federal Republic of Yugoslavia
26	1945, 2 September	Democratic Republic of Vietnam
27	1945, 12 December to 1946, 13 December	Autonomous Republic of Azerbaijan
28	1945, 15 December to 1946, 15 December	Kurdish People's Republic
29	1946, 11 January	People's Republic of Albania
30	1947, 4 December	Bulgarian People's Republic
31	1947, 30 December	Romanian People's Republic
32	1948, 25 February	Czechoslovak People's Republic
33	1948, 9 September	Democratic People's Republic of Korea
34	1948, 14 December	Polish People's Republic
35	1949, 18 August	Hungarian People's Republic
36	1949, 1 October	People's Republic of China
37	1949, 7 October	German Democratic Republic
38	1959, 2 January	Republic of Cuba
39	1963, 15 August	The Republic of the Congo
40	1967, 30 November	People's Republic of South Yemen
41	1970, 20 October	Somali Democratic Republic
42	1973, 24 September	Republic of Guinea-Bissau
43	1974, 30 November	Republic of Dahomey
44	1975, 17 April	Royal Government of National Union of Kampuchea
45	1975, 25 June	People's Republic of Mozambique
46	1975, 5 July	Republic of Cape Verde
47	1975, 11 November	People's Republic of Angola
48	1975, 2 December	Lao People's Democratic Republic
49	1976, 20 April	Socialist Ethiopia
50	1976, 2 July	Socialist Republic of Vietnam
51	1978, 27 April	Democratic Republic of Afghanistan
52	1979, 7 January	People's Republic of Kampuchea
53	1979, 13 March	People's Revolutionary Government of Grenada

same plane, namely the Russian revolution of 1917, while steadily increasing its distance from this fixed point. The fifty-three regimes thus constitute points along which the curve can be drawn (*Table 2* illustrates this point). In popular language, of course, the term 'spiral' immediately calls to mind a three-dimensional development which goes up or down, implying progress or decline. However, a spiral can be conceived of mathematically as two-dimensional, and this is the image which will be adopted for the purpose of this study.

Table 2

	Russia	Western Europe	Eastern Europe	Asia	Latin America	Africa
1917	*					
1917-1924		**	***	***		
		*	**	***		
			**	**		
				**		
1932-1939		*			*	
1944-1949			***	**		
			**	**		
			**	**		
		*				
1959-1970					*	**
						*
1973-1979				**	*	***
				**		**
				*		*

The emergence of Marxist regimes have followed major wars, disintegration of the Russian, British, French and Portuguese empires and other significant events that have shaken the power and legitimacy of long-established political systems. Although these events generally accelerated the forces of political changes, it was conscious political decisions and actions which channelled these forces and determined the particular scope and nature of these transformations. The First World War speeded up change in Russian society, but it was the determined action of the Bolsheviks which launched Russia on its particular path of development. In the same way the Second World War opened the way for the

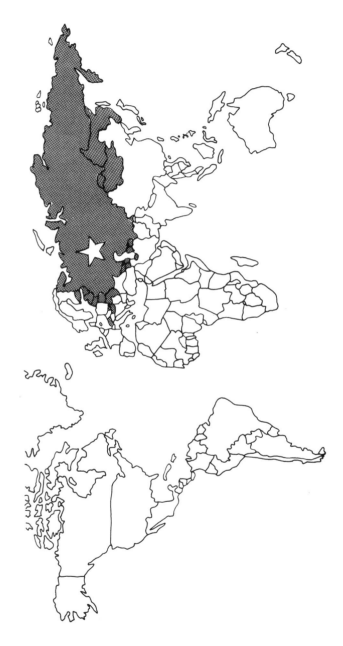

Figure 1 First period: 1917–1924

transformation of a number of societies in Eastern Europe by altering the social structure and radicalizing political opinion. Similar radical changes took place as a result of the de-colonialization of parts of Asia, the Gulf area, the whole of the African continent and the nationalist and anti-imperialist upheavals in Cuba and Grenada.

It should be remembered that the socio–political systems which emerged in these enormously varied regions were not, however, an inevitable consequence of these changes but a result of a conscious effort by ideologically committed groups to seize political power and implement their particular programme.

As indicated in the previous chapters, it is possible to identify three clearly distinguishable periods in the historical pattern of the establishment of Marxist regimes. The first period between 1917 and 1924 is centred on the Bolshevik Revolution and the subsequent disintegration of the tsarist empire (see *Figure 1*). Other factors which are most directly connected with the establishment of the Marxist regimes, particularly in Europe, are the end of the First World War, the disintegration of the Austro–Hungarian empire and the formation and activities of the Third International.

The Russian revolution and the Bolshevik regime's policies towards the national minorities had a dramatic impact on the peoples of the former Russian empire. The Declaration of the Rights of the Peoples of Russia, issued on 15 November 1917, which proclaimed the right to 'free self-determination up to secession and formation of an independent state'[1] not only met the national aspirations of non-Russian peoples of the former empire but also gave support and encouragement to the various communist groups on the peripheries of Russia, in the Ukraine, Finland, Latvia, Estonia, Lithuania and Belorussia (among others), which subsequently asserted their autonomy and independence from Petrograd.

National self-determination was given further impetus after the adoption of the Second Congress of the Communist International (19 July 1920) of Lenin's theses on national and colonial questions, and the Manifesto to the Peoples of the East, issued later that year by the Baku Congress of the Peoples of the East. Both stressed that it was the duty of the Communist International to give active support to the revolutionary liberation movements in the colonies and the backward countries[2]. Azerbaijan, Armenia, Khorezm, Gilan, Bukhara, Tannu Tuva and Mongolia were established as a result of a 'meeting' of the aspirations and policies of the indigenous communist and nationalist movements and Comintern's support for both.

The creation of these Marxist regimes was most directly due to the intermingling of two major factors, the fast-growing indigenous nationalist and anti-imperialist (anti-Russian, British, Chinese and Turkish) movements and the indigenous communist groups in these countries[3]. After the Bolsheviks' proclamation of 15 November 1917 and the renunciation of the imperialist policies of the Tsars, the nationalists regarded the Soviets as a natural ally in the struggle for the fulfilment of their aspirations, and looked to the new regime for help and assistance. The revolutionary upheaval had telescoped in some cases into a period of a few months (or two or three years in others) an ideological and social evolution which under more normal circumstances might have taken an entire generation. The support for the nationalists from local communist groups are subsequently backed up by that from the Comintern and Bolshevik Russia.

The Russian revolution had also stirred up a wave of revolutionary enthusiasm among the peoples of the Austro–Hungarian empire. But, as in Germany, the revolutions in Hungary and Slovakia were not touched off by Bolshevik initiative; they developed after Austria's defeat had become certain. The initial aims of their revolution were nationalist: the overthrow of the Habsburg monarchy and the creation of sovereign states. But as the Hungarian and Slovak prisoners of war, many of whom had taken part in the October revolution and had joined the Bolshevik Party, began returning from Russia, national revolutions turned into socialist workers' revolutions. The popular appeal of the Bolshevik principle of national self-determination was undoubtedly both an important factor in the change of direction and an inspiration for mass action.

The short-lived Bratislava Soviet Republic was their first revolutionary attempt. The second was the Hungarian Soviet Republic led by Béla Kun, the former president of the Federation of Foreign groups, established shortly after the 1917 revolution among the prisoners of war, with an explicit aim of spreading the proletarian revolution. The Kun regime was in turn to a great extent responsible for the third Marxist regime to emerge from the disintegration of the Austro–Hungarian empire, the Slovak Soviet Republic. Its leaders were associates of Béla Kun in Russia at the Federation.

The relationship between the two regimes is best summarized by the following account of Endre Rudnyanszky, the Hungarian Soviet Republic's representative in Moscow:

> The Hungarian proletariat had to contend with precisely the same problem as the Russian proletariat, namely, to convince

the workers of all oppressed peoples of the former Hungarian Kingdom that Hungary's proletariat had no intention whatsoever of oppressing them, and that their only means of defending themselves against foreign capitalism lay in forming a federative Soviet republic jointly with the Hungarian proletariat. Following these lines, Hungary formed her first Ukraine–Soviet Slovakia . . . Like Soviet Russia, which came to the Ukrainian Soviet government's assistance with its organizing forces, Hungary delegated out of its own party workers several capable comrades to the newly organized Slovak government[4].

The defeat of Germany at the end of the First World War deeply shocked the German nation, fed on stories of military success. In late 1918 a violent expression of discontent, reaction to German humiliation and revulsion against the authoritarian government showed itself in a fast-growing wave of strikes in the factories, a mutiny of sailors in Kiel and uprisings all over Germany. The main organizer of the movement was the German Communist Party. Numerically strong and ideologically committed, the Party was genuinely international in its character and outlook.

The influence of the movement was increased not only by the Bolshevik revolution but also by hopes of Russian assistance in utterly destroying militarism in Germany and in preparing a radical socialist revolution in the country. Workers' and Soldiers' Councils, similar to the Russian soviets, sprang up all over Germany. Among the metal-workers of Berlin and in the industrial centres of Hamburg, Bremen, the Ruhr, Munich and elsewhere there also appeared a new radical type of organization – factory councils. The Bremen and Bavarian republics were the outcome and results of this movement in which the national and internationalist aspects were closely intertwined.

The short-lived Socialist Republic of Chile does not belong to any of the suggested periods. It is important to emphasize that it remains a most interesting maverick repercussion of the Russian revolution.

The second period (see *Figure 2*) is centred on the Second World War and its aftermath in Asia and Eastern Europe. It spans the years 1939-1957 and is in turn divided into four major interrelated stages which evolved in the context of the specific post-war Asian and European political environment.

(1) The first clearly distinguishable stage is linked with the Japanese surrender in Indochina, and the disintegration of the

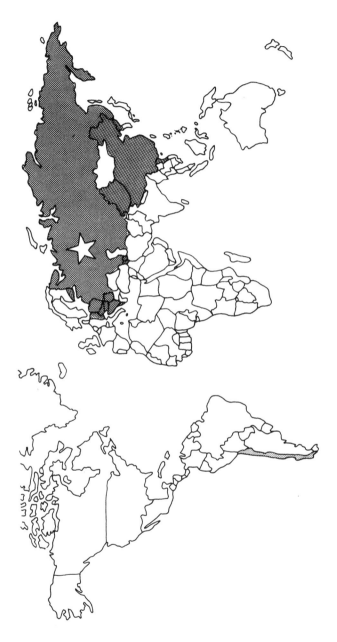

Figure 2 Second period: 1939–1957

French colonial rule in Vietnam as a result of the military and political successes of the Communist-led nationalist anti-imperialist struggle. These were the main factors that brought about the establishment of the Democratic Republic of Vietnam.

The Chinese communist victory in their twenty-two-year anti-imperialist war is an intrinsic part of this stage. It should, however, not be seen only in the context of the post-Second World War demise of imperialism but primarily as a result of the successful conclusion of the Chinese revolution.

(2) The second stage is linked with Stalin's creation of a *cordon sanitaire* in Eastern Europe and the successful conclusion of the national liberation wars in Yugoslavia and Albania, organized and led by their respective communist parties[5].

(3) The third stage is closely linked with Stalin's overall aim to secure Russia's borders after the outbreak of and during the Second World War, against Germany in Finland, Japan in Eastern Turkistan and the Western powers in Iran. Hence the encouraged creation of friendly buffer states in these areas[6].

It is worth noting, however, that the primary factor in establishing the Marxist regime in Eastern Turkistan was Muslim nationalism, which merged with local communist groups and subsequently received support from the self-interested Soviet Union.

Similar to Eastern Turkistan were the cases of the regimes in northern Iran. Although Soviet military and political support for the Azeri and Kurdish insurrections in 1945 was undoubtedly of considerable importance, the creation of these regimes derives only in part from the Red Army's presence in northern Iran. Of equal, if not greater, importance was the strong nationalism of the Azeris and Kurds and the long tradition of nationalist uprisings. The view that both regimes were neither purely the creation of the Soviet Union nor doomed simply because of the withdrawal of Soviet forces is supported by the fact that they survived with popular support for six months after the Red Army's departure and collapsed only after having been crushed by the central government troops.

In the closing months of the Second World War the Red Army became the dominant force in liberating the countries of Eastern Europe (except Albania and Yugoslavia) from Nazi occupation. The entry of the Soviet troops in the territories of Poland, Bulgaria, Romania and Hungary[7] gave the Russians a unique opportunity to promote Soviet military and political interests, in which the utilization of the small but well-organized indigenous communist parties[8] in the countries played an important part.

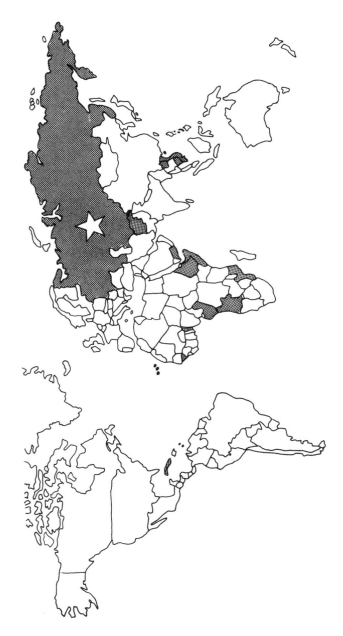

Figure 3 Third period: 1959–1979

Thus a *cordon sanitaire* was created on the west of the Soviet Union aimed at securing Russia's borders against the West.

(4) The fourth stage is linked with the height of the 'cold war' which was not limited to Europe but which had global character and consequences. It was during 1948 and 1949 that the division of Europe, and Germany in particular, between two opposing political and military blocs became final. A similar process of lasting division also took place in Korea[9].

The third period (see *Figure 3*), between 1959 and 1976, is intrinsically linked with resurgent Caribbean, Cuban, African, Arab and Asian nationalism in general and the successful conclusion of several long-drawn-out national liberation struggles in particular. Although the victories of the communist-led national liberation movements in Asia are an overall part of this period, it would seem that in a sense they form, within it, distinctive variants not so much in geographical terms but in terms of the complexities and length of the processes that finally established the Marxist regimes in Kampuchea, Laos and unified Vietnam.

All the regimes established during the third period naturally have their source in the Bolshevik revolution of 1917, but they also directly relate in several structural and organizational aspects to the Cuban Revolution, which to many was not only an inspiration but a clear military, political and ideological example and precedent. Apart from its romantic appeal to many nationalist movements in diverse parts of the world, the Cuban revolution also demonstrated a novel way of conducting and winning a nationalist, anti-imperialist war without a vanguard party. Or as Régis Debray puts it, Cuba showed that the vanguard of revolution

is not necessarily the Marxist–Leninist party; and that those who want to make the revolution have the right and the duty to constitute themselves a vanguard, independently of these parties.

It takes courage to state the facts out loud when these facts contradict a tradition. There is, then, no metaphysical equation in which vanguard = Marxist–Leninist party; there are merely dialectical conjunctions between a given function – that of the vanguard in history – and a given form of organization – that of the Marxist–Leninist party. These conjunctions arise out of prior history and depend on it[10].

The Cuban example of bypassing an over-rigid conception of 'party', like Castro's unprecedented 16 April 1961 declaration on the 'socialist' nature of his revolution, serves as an example echoed later in diverse parts of the world.

Thus, for example, in some African countries the process of establishment of some of the Marxist regimes during this period constituted an acceptance of scientific socialism by the leaders of these countries. Such a commitment appears to have been opportunistic, aimed to a great extent at securing and maintaining power. Thus the commitments of the military rulers of the Congo, Somalia, Benin and Ethiopia seem to consist primarily of pragmatic adaptations of high nationalist aspirations within the limited options available to the military–political elites.

In cases such as Somalia and Ethiopia the self-ascription as a Marxist regime appears to have been a purely instrumental act – an effort by its leaders to secure military and/or economic aid from the communist countries. Similar factors undoubtedly played an important role in the encompassing of Marxist ideology by the liberation fronts in South Yemen and Mozambique. On the other hand, countries such as the Congo and Benin, where the acceptance of Marxism was instrumental for the purposes of legitimization, were not favoured recipients of military and economic aid from communist countries in their pre-acceptance periods[11].

It would also appear that for some of the regimes established during the third period, formal identification with Marxism may have been an attempt to upgrade their status by simultaneously associating themselves with prestigious symbols and powerful, high-status regimes such as the Soviet Union, China, Cuba and Vietnam, and, at the same time, separating themselves from exclusive identification as former colonies. Similarly, on an international level, acceptance of scientific socialism provided these regimes with an opportunity of closer relationships with the 'positive references' in the international arena (the communist countries of Europe and Asia) and at the same time separation from the 'negative references', the capitalist countries of Western Europe and the United States.

Unlike the Congo, Somalia and Benin, who came to independence as constitutional nationalist movements, the Yemen, Mozambique and Angola became independent as revolutionary movement regimes, having won their independence from Britain and Portugal, respectively, after more than a decade of liberation war[12].

These liberation struggles are the first successful indigenous Marxist revolutions, accompanied by prolonged fighting, not growing directly from the conditions of international wars. In large measure the conditions produced in Russian society by the First World War ushered in the Bolshevik revolution. As has been pointed out earlier, the 1919 communist revolutions in Europe also have a direct relationship with that war. The Second World War generated situations favourable for communist revolutions in China, Vietnam, Albania and Yugoslavia. The efficacy of Marxist insurgencies, at least in Mozambique and South Yemen, forces into perspective the connection between major wars and revolution[13].

FRELIMO in Mozambique, the NLF in South Yemen and, to a lesser extent, the MPLA in Angola developed their socialist ideology independently but through similar processes of protracted internal political struggle while waging a military and political battle for liberation. The acceptance of Marxism–Leninism as a guiding ideology by the three fronts was decided before their assumption of power. Their subsequent transformation into vanguard parties appears therefore to have been the next step in their ideological and political development[14].

All the regimes established during the third period had either organized their vanguard Leninist parties after effectively establishing themselves in power or transformed their national liberation fronts into vanguard parties[15]. The exceptions are Kampuchea and Laos, where the existence of the respective communist parties was made known only after the parties' effective assumption of power.

The main reasons for the formation of the Congolese Party of Labour, the Somali Socialist Revolutionary Party and the People's Revolutionary Party of Benin appear to have been administrative, aimed at the legitimization of the radical political option of the countries' political elites. The transformation of nationalist movements into vanguard parties of the working class in Mozambique, South Yemen and Angola began during the long-drawn-out guerrilla wars and was concluded after their consolidation of power (not merely assumption of power, as was the case in the countries mentioned earlier). The main activities during this transformation span both the guerrilla war and the post-independence periods and involve fundamental changes in two essential areas. In the economic sphere they concentrate on:

(1) Widening the state sector through partial or complete nationalization.
(2) Agrarian reforms.
(3) Development of the cooperative movement.
(4) The ending of foreign economic exploitation.

The political changes required for the transformation centre on:

(1) The study of the methodology of scientific socialism, re-education of the members of the respective fronts, either in special political schools[16] and/or in the socialist countries.

(2) Selection of those members of the Front who could join the proposed new party. The factors taken into account here were candidates' ideological attitudes, class background and activities during the guerrilla war.
(3) A change in the organizational structure from one based on territorial principle to one based on workplaces.
(4) The unification of the various contingents of the national liberation movement nationalist parties, communist and left-wing groups into a single political organization.
(5) The development and deepening of relations of friendship and all round cooperation, on the principle of proletarian solidarity with the world socialist system headed by the Soviet Union and with other world revolutionary movements.

The successful accomplishment of these changes appears to have been a prerequisite for the transformation of national liberation movements into a vanguard party of the working class[17].

In Ethiopia a revolutionary-nationalist socialist movement led by the military has followed the overthrow of Haile Selassie's regime in 1974. The basic political strategy of the Ethiopian socialist revolution has few parallels in the annals of socialist and/or revolutionary politics. First, political change has followed rather than preceded the inauguration of socio–economic changes, so that it has focused more on the consolidation of initial reforms than on promising further moves, placing the Dergue itself in an ambiguous political position as a nominally provisional regime. Second, since military socialism itself has few parallels, the emerging of defence and developmental roles as outlined in the NDRP and the use of force as a surrogate for political processes raised an important problem of the reconciliation of socio–economic and political idealism with the practical problem of maintaining and exercising the power to implement such ideals. Third, the military has assigned itself the role of 'tutor' in the political phase of Ethiopian revolution, at the same time legitimizing itself by using the rhetoric and symbols of Marxism–Leninism.

It should also be emphasized that in Ethiopia, as in Angola, outside military and economic assistance of major proportions was required to establish political control and consolidate the positions of the new regimes threatened by civil war, military invasions from neighbouring countries and/or secessionist movements. The assistance came mostly from Cuba, the Soviet Union and other socialist countries[18].

The end of the war in Vietnam meant also an end to several successive wars of national liberation not only for the Vietnamese but also the other peoples of Indochina. The Communist Party of

Kampuchea and the Lao People's Revolutionary Party emerged for the first time publicly, to take charge of the new regimes. Many of their leaders were veterans of the Indochinese Communist Party founded by Ho Chi Minh in 1930. The shared revolutionary experience of three decades of struggle forged what was termed a 'militant solidarity' between the three Indochinese states, a special relationship which allowed them to enjoy (for only a short time, however) and benefit from peace and security. Soon after their victories in 1975, national interests began to strain relations between them. For the Kampucheans, always in the background has been the memory of Vietnamese conquests and occupations. Laos, on the other hand, which has traditionally been drawn to Vietnam in order to protect itself from the other powerful neighbour, Thailand, this time also fitted into an old historical pattern. It would seem that the same nationalism, which was the driving force for the recently ended and long-drawn-out war, was still permeating the inter-party and inter-governmental relations among the three Indochinese states.

The emergence of the three latest Marxist regimes must be seen in their individual contexts.

The establishment of the Democratic Republic of Afghanistan should be seen not only in terms of a successful *coup* staged by the military members of the People's Democratic Party of Afghanistan and on its behalf but also in terms of the inroads made by the Soviet Union in Afghanistan. The geographical proximity of the two countries and traditional friendship between them brought about an increase in economic cooperation with the Russians which resulted in a series of economic agreements[19]. Over the years since the early 1950s Afghanistan also became the largest per capital recipient of Soviet aid in the non-communist world[20]. Consequently the Soviet Union enjoyed considerable prestige not only among the ruling circles of Afghanistan but also among the ordinary people, many of whom shared a common language and religion with the other side of the Soviet–Afghan border.

Another important factor in the establishment of the Marxist regime in Kabul was the fact that in Afghanistan, as in Somalia, the Soviet Union over the years became a major supplier of military hardware, and thousands of Afghan civilians and military personnel have been trained in the Soviet political and military schools. All these factors explain to an extent the ease with which the communist regime in Afghanistan was established.

The second Marxist regime in Kampuchea was imposed on the country by Vietnam in order to offset Chinese influence in

South-east Asia and it should be seen as an offshoot of the Sino–Soviet dispute.

The new regime in Grenada should be seen in the context of the radicalization of the Caribbean Black Power movement which, drawing directly on the revolutionary example and ideological content of Cuba, assumed its own dynamics and structures. The process of the development of these structures is unlikely to be concluded for some time yet. The mixture of revolutionary Castroism and African pragmatism is a new and stimulating example of the convergence of thus far unconnected components of the same movement.

This chapter has analysed the establishment of the Marxist regimes in historical retrospect and has looked at them as a continuing process, a movement that began with the Russian revolution of 1917. It does seem that such a perspective offers a most fruitful, coherent and intellectually stimulating set of propositions for understanding and analysing the spread and growth of the Marxist regimes. Looking at the establishment of these regimes makes more sense in historical terms than the somewhat crude approach offered so far, which mainly concentrates on the techniques of takeovers.

It has suggested three main periods in the establishment of the Marxist regimes. The first, between 1917 and 1924, is centred on the direct aftermath of the Bolshevik revolution, its attitudes to the national minorities in Russia and the consequences of the First World War in Germany and Austria–Hungary. All of them form a chain of events in terms of the establishment of Marxist regimes during this period, rather than separate incidents. The second period, between 1939 and 1957, is centred on Stalin's concern with Soviet security, his policies in that respect, the growth of nationalism in Asia, the end of the Second World War, the disintegration of the French empire and, finally, the outbreak of the cold war. Again these were a chain of interrelated and spiralling events. The third period, between 1959 and 1975, is closely linked· to the aftermath of the Cuban revolution and its decisions concerning ideological questions and internal and foreign policy areas; the victories of the national liberation movements in Africa and South Yemen. Lastly, during this period the final victory of the national liberation anti-imperialist struggle for the peoples of Indochina was achieved. The spiralling of events can also be quite clearly detected in this period.

The emergence of these regimes was to a large extent a consequence of major international events such as wars or events

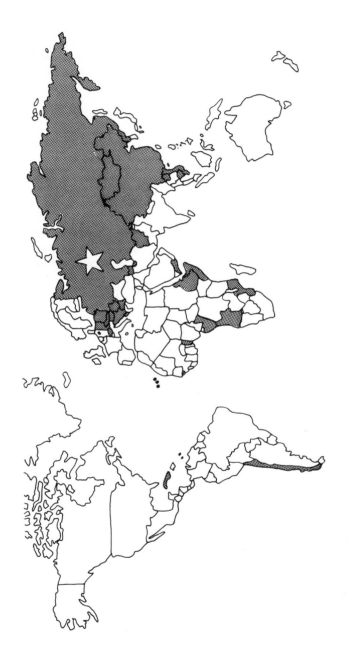

Figure 4 Marxist regimes: 1917–1979

which subsequently acquired global significance, such as the assumption of power by Castro or the April 1974 military coup in Portugal, and such events undoubtedly activated nationalist forces and/or communist groups. Nevertheless it should be emphasized that it was the actions of the latter which were directly responsible for the establishment of the fifty-three Marxist regimes (see *Figure 4*).

The image of a two-dimensional spiral has been suggested as being perhaps the most useful illustration of the process which is described and analysed chronologically in Chapters 4, 5 and 6, and in global terms in Chapter 7. Such an image, from both a descriptive and an analytical point of view, is much more comprehensive in illustrating what should be conveyed in the study of the establishment of the Marxist regimes.

It would seem that, central to the understanding of the study of the establishment of these regimes, are two of its essential aspects. First, it is a continuing process which assumes different forms and shapes depending on the social and political conditions of different societies at different times. It is also increasingly influenced by the societies' ethno–cultural characteristics and even more so by the international environment of great power politics. Second, in spite of its complexity it is not possible to detach the process from the Russian revolution of 1917. As Lenin asserted in 1920:

> . . . certain fundamental features of our revolution have a significance which is not local, not peculiarly national, not Russian only, but international. I speak here of international significance not in the broad sense of the term; not some, but all the fundamental and many of the secondary features of our revolution are of international significance in the sense that the revolution influences all countries. No, taking it in the narrowest sense, i.e. understanding international significance to mean the internationality of a repetition on an international scale of what has taken place in our country . . .[21]

1 See Y. Akhapkin (ed.), *First Decrees of Soviet Power*, pp. 31–32
2 See Eudin and North, *Soviet Russia and the East 1920–1927. A Documentary Survey*, p. 65; and Spector, *The Soviet Union and The Muslim World, 1917–1958*, pp. 288–298
3 It is perhaps worth recalling here the aims of the Jangalis movement, which can be summarized as follows: (1) The overthrow of imperialist domination; (2) The confiscation of foreign enterprises and banks; (3) Unity of the country with recognition of the right of each nationality to self-determination; (4) Confiscation of all lands of big landlords. This was to be for the peasants and soldiers; and (5) Alliance with Soviet Russia and the world proletarian movement
4 Tökés, *Béla Kun and the Hungarian Soviet Republic*, p. 191

5 It should perhaps be emphasized that there was a close political and military cooperation between the two partisan movements during the war. The extent of collaboration is illustrated by the fact that Yugoslav partisan units fought with the Albanians under Albanian command. Also, from December 1944 two Albanian divisions fought in Montenegro and Bosnia under Yugoslav command until the liberation of the country

6 The same pattern of securing Russia's borders can be seen in the absorption of the Baltic States, Estonia, Latvia and Lithuania

7 The Red Army also swept across Czechoslovakia during 1944 and 1945 and Communist inlfuence in the country was undoubtedly greatly enhanced by that. However, for reasons suggested in the section on Czechoslovakia (see Chapter 5), the Czechoslovak case belongs to the fourth stage discussed below

8 It should be stressed that in our view the generally upheld assumption that the communist parties of Eastern European countries were totally dependent on the Soviet Union and acted on the CPSU's behalf is a vast oversimplification. It might have seemed to be the case in 1945. But in historical retrospect, which perhaps allows a more balanced and fruitful appraisal, it is clear that the relationships at least between the Polish, Bulgarian and Romanian Parties were far from that of complete dependence on either the CPSU or the Soviet government

9 For background and useful discussion of the diverse impact of the cold war see, for example, D. F. Fleming, *The Cold War and its Origins, 1917–1960*; R. Frelek, *Historia zimnej wojny*; J. Lukacs, *History of the Cold War*, 2 vols; P. Tompkins, *American-Russian Relations in the Far East*

10 R. Debray, *Revolution in the Revolution?* pp. 96–97

11 See C. Legum, 'The African Environment', *Problems of Communism*, January/February 1978, 1–19; D. E. Allbright, 'Soviet Policy', ibid., 20–39; G. T. Yu, 'China's Impact', ibid., 40–50

12 It should be emphasized, however, that the victory in Angola was much less clearcut because the massive Soviet–Cuban assistance assured the control of the capital Luanda and its surrounding areas by the Marxist and pro-Soviet movement

13 The Cuban case must be excluded here because a strong argument can be made that the revolution was not Marxist until after Castro achieved power

14 The processes accompanying this transformation are discussed below

15 Ethiopia is still in the process of forming its vanguard party. Also the NJM in Grenada is in the process of building its structures on the vanguard party principles

16 Such schools for the training of proposed party cadres were organized in advance of party formation

17 This conclusion is drawn on the basis of detailed analysis of the following: 'Frelimo Third Congress, Maputo 3–7 February, 1977', *People's Power*, Nos. 7 and 8 (June 1977), 16–43; *Central Committee Report to the Third Congress of FRELIMO; MPLA Central Committee Plenary 23–29 October 1976*; A. F. Ismail 'A New Vanguard Party', *World Marxist Review*, **22**, No. 1 (January 1979), 14–21

18 See, for example, H. Thomas 'Cuba In Africa', *Survey*, **23**, No. 4 (105), Autumn (1977–78), 181–188 and D. W. Albright, ibid.

19 See F. Halliday, 'Revolution in Afghanistan', *New Left Review*, November-December 1978, 16–17

20 The origins of Soviet aid to Afghanistan go back to subsidies granted in 1919. The aid increased considerably since the 1950s. Between 1954 and 1976, the Soviet Union gave Afghanistan $1.3 billion, the third largest amount given to any non-communist developing country after India and Turkey

21 V. I. Lenin, *'Left Wing' Communism, an Infantile Disorder*, pp. 1–2

Bibliography

ADAMS, Nina and McCOY, Alfred W. (eds), *Laos: War and Revolution*, Harper, London, 1970

AKHAPKIN, Yuri (ed.), *First Decrees of Soviet Power*, Lawrence and Wishart, London, 1970

ALBRIGHT, David E., 'Soviet Policy', *Problems of Communism*, January-February 1978, 20–39

ALI, Mohammed H., 'Land Reforms in Southern Yemen', *World Marxist Review*, **15**, No. 2 (February), 1972, 29

ANONYMOUS, 'Revolutions in Ethiopia', *Monthly Review*, **29**, No. 3, July-August 1977

Area Handbook for People's Republic of the Congo (Congo-Brazzaville), US Government Printing Office, Washington, DC, 1971

Area Handbook for the Peripheral States of Arabian Peninsula, US Government Printing Office, Washington, DC, 1971

Area Handbook for Somalia, US Government Printing Office, Washington, DC, 1977

ARFA, Hassan, *The Kurds: An Historical and Political Study*, John Murray, London, 1964

A Short History of the Bulgarian Communist Party, Sofia Press, Sofia, n.d.

'August 1944 Insurrection. Political and Military Chronology', *Lumea*, No. 31, 3–9 August 1979, 23–24

'August 1944 Insurrection. Political and Military Chronology (11)', *Lumea*, No. 32, 10–16 August 1979, 21–23

AVAKUMOVIC, Ivan, *History of the Communist Party of Yugoslavia*, Vol. 1, Aberdeen University Press, Aberdeen, 1964

BAIN, Francis J., *Beyond the Ballot Box*, Grenada Publishers, St George's, 1980

BALAJ, Teofil, *Romania: The Land and the People*, Meridiane Publishing House, Bucharest, 1972, p. 55

BALLARD, John, 'Four Equatorial States' in *National Unity and Regionalism in Eight African States* (ed. by G. Carter), Cornell University Press, Ithaca, New York, 1966, pp. 378–392

BALLIS, William B., 'Soviet Russia's Asiatic Frontier Techniques: Tannu Tuva', *Pacific Affairs*, Vancouver, **xiv**, March 1941, 91–96

BARGHOORN, Frederick C., 'The Critique of American Foreign Policy', *Columbia Journal of International Affairs*, New York, Winter 1951, 5–15

BEKER, Seymour, *Russia's Protectorates in Central Asia: Bukhara and Kiva, 1865–1924*, Harvard University Press, Cambridge, Mass., 1968

BENNIGSEN, Alexandre and LEMERCIER-QUELQUEJAY, Chantal, *Islam in the Soviet Union*, Praeger, New York, 1967

BENNIGSEN, Alexandre, 'The Bolshevik Conquest of the Moslem Borderlands' in *The Anatomy of Communist Takeovers* (ed. by Thomas T. Hammond), pp. 61–70

BETHELL, Nicholas, *Gomulka, His Poland and his Communism*, Longman, London, 1969

BIERUT, Bolesław, *O Partii* (On the Party), Książka i Wiedza, Warsaw, 1952

BILMANIS, Alfred, *A History of Latvia*, Greenwood Press, Westport, Connecticut, 1970

BISHOP, Maurice, *Forward Ever! Against Imperialism and Towards Genuine National Independence and People's Power*, Political Publishers, Havana, 1980

BLACK, Cyril E., 'The Anticipation of Communist Revolutions' in *Communism and Revolution* (ed. by Cyril E. Black and Thomas P. Thornton), Princeton University Press, Princeton, NJ, 1964

BLACK, Cyril E. and THORNTON, Thomas P., (eds), *Communism and Revolution: the Strategic Uses of Political Violence*, Princeton, NJ, 1964

BOORSTEIN, Edward, *The Economic Transformation of Cuba*, Monthly Review Press, New York, 1968

BRAND, Conrad, SCHWARTZ, Benjamin and FAIRBANK, John K., *A Documentary History of Chinese Communism*, Harvard University Press, Cambridge, Mass., 1952

BRAYTON, Abbott A., 'Soviet Involvement in Africa', *Journal of Modern African Studies*, **17**, No. 2, 1979, 253–269

BROWN, Joseph F., *Bulgaria under Communist Rule*, Pall Mall Press, London, 1970

BROWN, MacAlister and ZASLOFF, Joseph, 'Laos in 1975: People's Democratic Revolution – Lao Style', *Asian Survey*, **xvi**, No. 2, 1976, 193–9

BROWN, William A. and ONON, Urgunge, *History of the Mongolian People's Republic*, Harvard University Press, Cambridge, Mass., 1976

BURDICK, Charles B, and LUTZ, Ralph H., *The Political Institutions of the German Revolution 1918–1919*, Praeger (for the Hoover Institution), New York, 1965

BURKS, Richard V., 'Eastern Europe' in *Communism and Revolution* (ed. by Cyril E. Black and Thomas P. Thornton), pp. 77–116

CABRAL, Amilcar, *Our People Are Our Mountains*, Committee for Freedom in Mozambique, Angola and Guinea, London, 1971

CABRAL, Amilcar, *Revolution in Guinea. An African People's Struggle*, Stage 1, London, 1969

CABRAL, Amilcar, *Unity and Struggle, Speeches and Writings*, Heinemann, London, 1980

CARNEY, Timothy M., *Communist Power in Kampuchea (Cambodia): Documents and Discussion*, Southeast Asia Program Data Paper No. 106, Cornell University, Ithaca, New York, 1977

CARR, Edward H., *Socialism in One Country*, Vol. 2, Penguin, Harmondsworth, 1970

CARR, Edward H., *The Bolshevik Revolution*, Vols 1–3, Penguin, Harmondsworth, 1966

CASTRO, Fidel, 'History Will Absolve Me' in Fidel Castro and Regis Debray, *On Trial*, Lorrimer Publishing, London, 1968, pp. 9–67

Central Committee Report to the Third Congress of Frelimo, Mozambique, Angola and Guinea Information Centre, London, n.d.

CETERCHI, Ioan, TRASNEA, Ovidu and VLAD, Constantin (eds), *The Political System of the Socialist Republic of Romania*, Editura Stiintifica si Enciclopedica, Bucharest, 1979

CHEN, Jerome, *Mao and the Chinese Revolution*, Oxford University Press, London, 1965

CHILDS, David, *East Germany*, Praeger, New York, 1969

CHURCHILL, Winston, *The Second World War, Triumph and Tragedy*, Vol. 6, Cassell, London, 1954

CONQUEST, Robert (ed.), *Soviet Nationalities Policy in Practice*, The Bodley Head, London, 1967

'Constitution of the People's Democratic Republic of Yemen' in Albert P. Blaustein and Gisbert H. Flanz (eds), *Constitutions of the Countries of the World*, Vol. 10, Ocean Publications, New York, 1972

CROZIER, Brian, 'The Soviet Presence in Somalia', *Conflict Studies*, No. 54, February 1975

DAE-SOOK, Suh, 'A Preconceived Formula for Sovietization: The Communist Takeover of North Korea' in *The Anatomy of Communist Takeovers* (ed. by Thomas T. Hammond), pp. 475–489

DALLIN, Alexander and BRESLAUER, Geoge W., *Political Terror in Communist Systems*, Stanford University Press, Stanford, California, 1970

DAVIDSON, Basil, 'Cape Verde: Liberation and Progress', *People's Power*, No. 17, Spring 1981, 5–15

DAVIDSON, Basil, 'Somalia: Towards Socialism', *Race and Class*, **17**, No. 1 (Summer 1975), 19–38

DAVIDSON, Basil, *The Liberation of Guiné: Aspects of an African Revolution*, Penguin, Harmondsworth, 1969

DEBRAY, Régis, *Revolution in the Revolution?* Penguin, Harmondsworth, 1968

DECALO, Samuel, 'People's Republic of Benin' in *Marxist Governments: A World Survey* (ed. by Bogdan Szajkowski), Vol. 1, pp. 87–115

Declaration of the Provisional Military Government of Ethiopia, Addis Ababa, 20 December 1974

Documents of MPLA Central Committee Plenary, 23–29 October 1976, Mozambique, Angola and Guinea Information Centre, London, n.d.

DOMES, Jürgen, 'The Model for Revolutionary People's War: The Communist Takeover of China' in *The Anatomy of Communist Takeovers* (ed. by Thomas T. Hammond), pp. 516–533

DRAKE, Paul W., *Socialism and Populism in Chile 1932–52*, University of Illinois Press, Urbana, 1978

DRAPER, Theodore, *Castroism: Theory and Practice*, Praeger, New York, 1965

DUPREE, Louis, 'Afghanistan Under the Khalq', *Problems of Communism*, July-August 1979, 34–50

DZIEWANOWSKI, Marian K., *The Communist Party of Poland: An Outline of History*, Harvard University Press, Cambridge, Mass., 1959

Economic Achievements of Democratic Yemen, The People's Democratic Republic of Yemen Ministry of Information, Russell Press, Nottingham, 1977

Enashenifalen, London, No. 1, November 1979

ENGEL, Gerhard, 'Die Politisch–ideologische Entwicklung Johann Knieffs (1880–1919). Untersuchungen zur Geschichte der Bremen Linksradikalen' (unpublished PhD dissertation), Humbolt University, East Berlin, 1966

ERDI, Ferenc, *Information Hungary*, Pergamon, Oxford, 1968

EUDES, Dominique, *The Kapetanios: Partisans and Civil War in Greece 1943–1949*, New Left Books, London, 1965

EUDIN, Joukoff X, and NORTH, Robert C., *Soviet Russia and the East 1920–1927. A Documentary Survey*, Stanford University Press, Stanford, California, 1957

FAINSOD, Merle, *How Russia is Rules* (revised edn), Harvard University Press, Cambridge, Mass., 1970

FATEMI, Nasrollah S., *Diplomatic History of Persia 1917–1923*, Russell F. Moore, New York, 1952

FISCHER, Ruth, *Stalin and German Communism: A Study in the Origins of the State Party*, Oxford University Press, London, 1948

FISCHER-GELATI, Stephen, 'The Communist Takeover of Rumania: A Function of Soviet Power' in *The Anatomy of Communist Takeovers* (ed. by Thomas T. Hammond), pp. 310–320

FISCHER-GELATI, Stephen, *The Socialist Republic of Rumania*, The Johns Hopkins Press, Baltimore, 1969

FLEMING, Jenna F., *The Cold War and its Origins 1917–1960*, Doubleday, New York, 1961

FRELEK, Ryszard, *Historia zimnej wojny*, Panstwowe Wydawnictwo Naukowe, Warsaw, 1971

Frelimo, Estatus e Programme, Imprensa Nacional, Lourenço Marques, 1975

'Frelimo Faces the Future' – an interview with Marcelino dos Santos by Joe Slovo in *African Communist*, No. 55 (1973), 32–50

'Frelimo Third Congress, Maputo 3–7 February 1977', *People's Power*, Nos 7 and 8 (June 1977), Mozambique, Angola, and Guinea Information Centre, London, pp. 16–43

GAUZE, Rene, *The Politics of Congo-Brazzaville*, The Hoover Institution Press, Stanford, California, 1973

GERASSI, John, *Venceremos! The Speeches and Writings of Che Guevara*, Panther, London, 1972 (particularly Chapter 2, 'The Revolutionary War')

GONZALEZ, Edward, 'Cuban Foreign Policy', *Problems of Communism*, November-December 1977, 1–15

GONZALEZ, Edward, *Cuba Under Castro: The Limits of Charisma*, Houghton Mifflin, Boston; Mass., 1974

GORA, Władysław, *P.P.R. W Walce o Niepodleglosc i Wladze Ludu* (The Workers' Party in the Struggle for Independence and People's Power), Ksiązka i Wiedza, Warsaw, 1963

Grenada: Let Those Who Labour Hold the Reins. Interview with Bernard Coard of the Revolutionary Government of Grenada. A Liberation pamphlet, London, 1980

GREIG, Donald W., *International Law* (2nd edn), Butterworths, London, 1976

GRIPP, Richard C., *The Political System of Communism*, Dodd, Mead, New York, 1973

GUEVARA, Che, *Guerrilla Warfare*, Monthly Review Press, New York, 1961

HAJDU, Tibo, 'Adatok a Tranacskoztersasag Kikialtasanak Tortenetkes' (Information from the History of the Proclamation of the Soviet Republic), *Part-Torteneti Kozlemenyek*, No. 18 (3), 1972, 121–155

Halgan (The Struggle). Official monthly organ of the Somali Revolutionary Socialist Party, State Printing Agency, Mogadishu

HALLIDAY, Fred, *Arabia Without Sultans*, Penguin, Harmondsworth, 1974

HALLIDAY, Fred, 'Revolution in Afghanistan', *New Left Review*, November-December 1978, 3–44

HAMMOND, Thomas T., 'Moscow and Communist Takeovers', *Problems of Communism*, January-February 1976, 48–67

HAMMOND, Thomas T., *The Anatomy of Communist Takeovers*, Yale University Press, New Haven, 1975, pp. 638–643

HAMMOND, Thomas T., 'The Communist Takeover of Outer Mongolia: Model for Eastern Europe?' in *The Anatomy of Communist Takeover* (ed. by Thomas T. Hammond), pp. 107–144

HARSCH, Ernest, 'How the Gairy Regime was Overthrown', *Intercontinental Press*, 3 December 1979, 1187

HARRISON, E.J., *Lithuania Past and Present*, T. Fisher Unwin, London, 1922

HEEGER, Gerald, 'The Sources of Communist Political Power in Kerala' in *The Anatomy of Communist Takeovers* (ed. by Thomas T. Hammond), pp. 620–657

HEIDENHEIMER, Arnold J., *The Governments of Germany*, Thomas Y. Crowell, New York, 1966

HENRIKSEN, Thomas H., *Mozambique: A History*, Rex Collings, London, 1978

HODGSON, John H., *Communism in Finland: A History and Interpretation*, Princeton University Press, Princeton, NJ, 1967

HOLMES, Leslie, 'People's Republic of Bulgaria' in *Marxist Governments: A World Survey* (ed. by Bogdan Szajkowski), Vol. 1, pp. 116–144

HRUSOVSKY, Francis, 'This is Slovakia', *Slovakia*, No. 20 (43), 1970, 42–69

HUMBERMAN, Leo and SWEEZY, Paul M., *Cuba: Anatomy of a Revolution*, Monthly Review Press, New York, 1961

HUTCHINSON, Arnalo, 'The Long Road to Freedom', *Granma Weekly Review*, 12 July 1981, 1–16

IGNATOV, Alexander, 'Afghanistan: Three Months of Revolution', *New Times*, No. 35, August 1978, 27–30

INGRAMS, Harold, *Arabia and the Isles*, Praeger, New York, 1968

IONESCU, Ghita, *Communism in Rumania, 1944–1962*, Oxford University Press, London, 1964

ISMAEL, Tareg Y., 'People's Democratic Republic of Yemen' in *Marxist Governments: A World Survey* (ed. by Bogdan Szajkowski), Vol. 3, pp. 755–785

ISMAIL, Abdel F., 'A New Vanguard Party', *World Marxist Review*, **22**, No. 1 (January 1979), 14–21

ISMAIL, Abdel F., 'On Social Orientation', *World Marxist Review*, **20**, No. 10 (October 1977), 26–30

Istoria Alkbanskoi Partii Truda (The History of the Party of Labour of Albania), 'Naim Frasheri' Publishing House, Tirana, 1971

JANICKI, Lech, *Ustroj Polityczny Niemieckiej Republiki Demokratycznej*, Instytut Zachodni, Poznan, 1964

KADAR, Janos, 'Our Glorious Heritage: the Hungarian Republic of Councils', *Nepszabadsag*, 25 March 1979

KAYSONE, Phomvihane, 'The Victory of Creative Marxism–Leninism in Laos', *Journal of Contemporary Asia*, **vii**, No. 3, 1977, 393–401

KIM HAN GIL, *Modern History of Korea*, Foreign Languages Publishing House, Pyongyang, 1979

KIM IL-SUNG, *Works*, Vol. 1, Foreign Languages Publishing House, Pyongyang, 1980

KIRK, George, *The Middle East 1945–1950*, Oxford University Press, London, 1954, pp. 56–78

KLEIN, Donald and CLARK, Ann, *Biographic Dictionary of Chinese Communism*, 2 vols, Harvard University Press, Cambridge, Mass., 1971

KOLOMEJCZYK, Norbert and SYZDEK, Bronislaw, *Polska w latach 1944–1949*, Panstwowe Zaklady Wydawnictw Szkolnych, Warsaw, 1971

KOUSOULAS, George D., *Revolution and Defeat: The Story of the Greek Communist Party*, Oxford University Press, London, 1965

KOVAC, Istvan, *New Elements in the Evolution of Socialist Constitution*, Akademiai Kiado, Budapest, 1968

KUCKUK, Peter, 'Bremen's Linksradikale bsw. Kommunisten von der Militarrevolte im November 1981 bis zum Kapp-Putsch in März 1920', (unpublished PhD dissertation), Hamburg, 1970

KUCKUK, Peter, *Revolution und Räterepublik in Bremen*, Edition Suhrkamp 367, Frankfurt, 1969

KUSIN, Vladimir, V., 'Czechoslovakia' in *Communist Power in Europe 1944–1949* (ed. by Martin McCauley), pp. 73–94

LECZKOWSKI, George, *Russia and the West in Iran, 1918–1948*, Cornell University Press, Ithaca, NY, 1949

LEDERER, Ivo J., (ed.), *Russian Foreign Policy: Essays in Historical Perspective*, Yale University Press, New Haven, 1962

LEGUM, Colin, 'The African Environment', *Problems of Communism*, January-February 1978, 1–19

LENIN, Vladimir I., *'Left Wing' Communism, an Infantile Disorder*, Foreign Languages Press, Peking, 1970

LEONHARD, Wolfgang, *Child of the Revolution*, Henry Regnery, Chicago, 1958

LEWIS, Ioan M., *A Modern History of Somalia: Nation and State in the Horn of Africa*, Longman, London, 1980

LEWIS, Ioan M., *A Pastoral Democracy*, Oxford University Press (for the International African Institute), 1961

LEWIS, Ioan M., 'The Politics of the Somali Coup', *Journal of Modern African Studies*, **10**, No. 3 (October 1972) 383–408

LEWIS, John W., *Major Doctrines of Communist China*, W. W. Norton, New York, 1964

LITTLE, Tom, *South Arabia*, Pall Mall Press, London, 1968

LOW, Alfred J., *The Soviet Hungarian Republic and the Paris Peace Conference*, The American Philosophical Society, Philadelphia, 1963

LUCAS, Erhard, *Die Sozialdemokratie in Bremen während des Ersten Weltkrieges*, Bremen, 1969

LUGMAN, Farouk, *Democratic Yemen Today*, Bombay, India, 1971 (no publisher listed)

LUKACS, John, *History of the Cold War*, 2 vols, Doubleday, New York, 1961

MACHEL, Samora, 'Consolidating People's Power in Mozambique: Extracts from a speech made by the President at the Opening of the First People's Assembly of the People's Republic of Mozambique on August 31, 1977', *The African Communist*, No. 72, first quarter, 1978, 32–50

MALINOWSKI, Marian, *et al.*, *Polski Ruch Robotniczy w Okresie Wojny i Okupacji Hitlerowskiej* (The Polish Workers' Movement During the War and the Nazi Occupation), Książka i Wiedza, Warsaw, 1964

MAN'KOVSKI, Boris Stepanovich, *Norodno-demokraticheskie republiki Tsentral'noi i Iugo Vostochnoi Evropy – gosudarstva sotsialisticheskogo tipa* (The People's Democratic Republics of Central and South-Eastern Europe – States of the Socialist Type), Pravda, Moscow, 1950

MANSFIELD, Peter, *The Middle East: A Political and Economic Survey*, Oxford University Press, London, 1972

MANUSHEVICH, A. Ia., (ed.), *Oktiabr'skaia Revolutsiia i Zarubezhnye Slavianskie Narody* (The October Revolution and Slavs Abroad), Izdatelstvo Nauka, Moscow, 1957, 233–270

MAO ZEDONG, *Selected Works*, Vol. 1, Peking Foreign Languages Press, 1967

MARCUM, John, *The Angolan Revolution*, Vols 1 and 2, MIT Press, Cambridge, Mass., 1969 and 1978

MARKAKIS, John, 'Garrison Socialism: The Case of Ethiopia', *MERIP Reports*, No. 79, 3–17

MARKAKIS, John, and AYELE, Nega, *Class and Revolution in Ethiopia*, Spokesman Press, Nottingham, 1978

MARMULLAKU, Ramadan, *Albania and the Albanians*, C. Hurst, London, 1975

MAXWELL, Robert (ed.), *Information USSR*, Macmillan, New York, 1962

MICKEVICIUS-KAPSUKAS, Vincas, 'Borba za Sovetskuiu Vlast', *Proletarskaia Revoliutsiia*, No. 108 (1931), 65–107

MITCHELL, Alan, *Revolution in Bavaria 1918–1919. The Eisner Regime and the Soviet Republic*, Princeton University Press, Princeton, NJ, 1965

MLYNAR,, Zdenek, *K teorii socialisticke democracie* (The Theory of Socialist Democracy), Statni naklad politicke literatury, Prague, 1961

MONDLANE, Eduardo, *The Struggle for Mozambique*, Penguin, Harmondsworth, 1969

MPLA Central Committee Plenary 23–29 October 1976, Mozambique, Angola and Guinea Information Centre, London, n.d.

MURPHY, George G.S., *Soviet Mongolia: A Study of the Oldest Political Satellite*, University of California Press, Berkeley, 1966

McCAULEY, Martin (ed.), *Communist Power in Europe 1944–1949*, Macmillan, London, 1977

McCAULEY, Martin, 'East Germany' in *Communist Power in Europe 1944–1949* (ed. by Martin McCauley), pp. 58–72

NAUMKIN, Vladimir, 'Southern Yemen: The Road to Progress', *International Affairs*, No. 1, January 1978, 64–69

NEWELL, Richard S., 'Revolution and Revolt in Afghanistan', *The World Today*, November 1979, 432–452

NGOUABI, Marien, 'Scientific Socialism in Africa', *World Marxist Review*, **18**, No. 5 (May), 1975, 40–43

NORTON, Henry K., *The Far Eastern Republic of Siberia*, Allen and Unwin, London 1923

O'CONNOR, James, *The Origins of Socialism in Cuba*, Cornell University Press, Ithaca, NY, 1970

OKUMA, Thomas, *Angola in Ferment*, Beacon Press, Boston, 1962

ONON, Urgunge, 'Mongolian People's Republic' in *Marxist Governments: A World Survey*, (ed. by Bogdan Szajkowski), Vol. 2, London, Macmillan, 1980, pp. 492–523

OREN, Nissan, 'A Revolution Administered: The Sovietization of Bulgaria' in *The Anatomy of Communist Takeovers* (ed. by Thomas T. Hammond), pp. 319–338

OTTOWAY, Marina, and OTTOWAY, David, *Ethiopia: Empire in Revolution*, Africana, Holmes and Meier, New York, 1978

PAGET, Julian, *Last Post: Aden 1964–67*, Faber and Faber, London, 1969

PANO, Nicholas, O., *The People's Republic of Albania*, The Johns Hopkins Press, Baltimore, 1968

'People in the News: Nur Mohammed Taraki, Hafisullah Amin', *New Times*, No. 26, June 1978, 23

PEOPLE'S HERALD, *Ethiopia: Revolution in the Making*, Progressive Publishers, New York, 1978

PHOUMI, Vongvichit, *Laos and the Victorious Struggle of the Lao People Against US Neo-colonialism*, Neo Lao Haksat, Sam Neua, 1969

PICK, F.W., *The Baltic Nations: Estonia, Latvia and Lithuania*, Boreas Publishing, London, 1945

PIPES, Richard, *The Formation of the Soviet Union: Communism and Nationalism 1917–1923*, revised edn, Harvard University Press, Cambridge, Mass., 1964

POL POT, *The Grand Victories of the Revolution of Kampuchea Under the Correct and Clearsighted Leadership of the Communist Party of Kampuchea*, Ministry of Foreign Affairs of Democratic Kampuchea, Phnom Penh, 1978

POLYAKOU, Genrikh, and DAVYDOV, Alexander, 'Initial Steps of the Revolution', *New Times*, No. 18, April 1979, 12–13

Programme of the National Democratic Revolution of Ethiopia, Central Printing Press, n.d.

Provisional Military Government, *Declaration of Economic Policy of Socialist Ethiopia*, Addis Ababa, 7 February 1975

PULLERITS, Albert (ed.), *Estonia: Population, Cultural and Economic Life*, Tallinn, 1935

RAUCH, Georg von, *The Baltic States. The Years of Independent Latvia, Lithuania, 1917–1940*, C. Hurst, London, 1970

RAY, Sally, 'Communism in India: Ideological and Tactical Differences Among Four Parties', *Studies in Comparative Communism*, V, Nos 2 and 3, Summer/Autumn 1972, 163–180

RAY, Sally and VAN DER KROEF, Justus M., 'Communism in India: Documents', *Studies in Comparative Communism*, V, Nos 2 and 3, Summer/Autumn 1972, 181–233

'Report of the Central Committee to the First Congress of the MPLA', *Granma Weekly Review*, Havana, 8 January 1978, 11–16

RAMAZANI, Ruhollah K., 'The Autonomous Republic of Azerbaijan and the Kurdish People's Republic: Their Rise and Fall', in *The Anatomy of Communist Takeovers* (ed. by Thomas T. Hammond), pp. 145–162

'Romanian Communist Party. Decisive Role in the Historic Events of August 1944 (11)', *Lumea*, No. 34, 24–30 August 1979, 24

RUDEBECK, Lars, 'Development and Class Struggle in Guinea-Bissau', *Monthly Review*, No. 30, 1979, 14–32

RUDEBECK, Lars, 'Political Mobilisation in Guinea-Bissau', in Sam C. Sarkesian, *Revolutionary Guerrilla Warfare*, Precedent Publishing, Chicago, 1975, pp. 431–451

RUPEN, Robert A., *Mongols of the 20th Century*, Indiana University Press, Indiana, 1964

RUPEN, Robert A., 'The Absorption of Tuva' in *The Anatomy of Communist Takeovers* (ed. by Thomas T. Hammond), pp. 145–162

RYDER, Arthur J., *The German Revolution of 1918: A Study of German Socialism in War and Revolt*, Cambridge University Press, Cambridge, 1967

SADOWSKI, Michal, *The Political System of People's Poland*, Interpress, Warsaw, 1976

SASSOU-NGUESSO, Denis, 'The Congo: Key Tasks of the Current Stage' in *Free Africa Marches*, Peace and Socialism International Publishers, Prague, 1978

SCHAPIRO, Leonard, *The Communist Party of the Soviet Union*, Methuen, London, 1966

SCHOPFLIN, George, 'Hungary' in *Communist Power in Europe 1944–49* (ed. by Martin McCauley)

SCHWARTZ, Benjamin Isadore, *China and the Soviet Theory of 'People's Democracy'*, MIT Press, Cambridge, Mass., 1954

SELDEN, Mark, *The Yenan Way in Revolutionary China*, Harvard University Press, Cambridge, Mass., 1971

SENN, Alfred E., *The Emergence of Modern Lithuania*, Greenwood Press, Westport, Connecticut, 1975

SETON-WATSON, Hugh, *From Lenin to Khruschev: the History of World Communism*, Praeger, New York, 1960

SETON-WATSON, Hugh, *From Lenin to Malenkov: The History of World Communism*, Praeger, New York, 1953

SETON-WATSON, Hugh, *The Eastern European Revolution*, Methuen, London, 1950

SIAD, Barre M., *My Country and My People*, The collected speeches of Major-General Mohamed Siad Barre, President, The Supreme Revolutionary Council, Somali Democratic Republic. Ministry of Information and National Guidance, Mogadishu, 1970

SIAD, Barre M., *My Country and My People*, Vol 2, State Printing Agency, Mogadishu, 1972

SIAD, Barre M., *My Country and My People*, The collected speeches of Jalle Major-General Mohamed Siad Barre, President, The Supreme Revolutionary Council, Somali Democratic Republic, 1971–1972, Vol 3, Ministry of Information and National Guidance, Mogadishu, 1972

SIAD, Barre M., *My Country and My People*, State Printing Agency, Mogadishu, 1974

SIHANOUK, Norodom, *My War with the C.I.A.: The Memories of Prince Norodom Sihanouk*, Pantheon, New York, 1973

SMITH, Jay C., 'Soviet Russia and the Red Revolution of 1918 in Finland', in *The Anatomy of Communist Takeovers* (ed. by Thomas T. Hammond), pp. 71–93

SNOW, Edgar, *Scorched Earth*, Gollancz, London, 1941

SOBOLEV, Aleksandr Ivanovich, *People's Democracy, a New Form of Political Organization of Society*, Foreign Language Publishing House, Moscow, 1954

SOON SUNG CHO, *Korea in World Politics, 1940–1950*, University of California Press, Berkeley, 1967

SPECTATOR, 'Building the Party in Mozambique', *The African Communist*, No. 79, fourth quarter 1979, 45–63

SPECTOR, Ivar, *The Soviet Union and the Muslim World 1917–1958*, University of Washington Press, Seattle, 1959

STAAR, Richard F., *Yearbook on International Communist Affairs – 1970*, Hoover Institution Press, Stanford, California, 1971

STEELE, Jonathan, *Socialism with a German Face. The State that Came in from the Cold*, Cape, London, 1977

STERN, Carola, 'History and Politics of the SED 1945–1965' in *Communism in Europe* (ed. by W.E. Griffith), Vol III, MIT Press, Cambridge,Mass., 1966

STRONG, Anna L., *Lithuania's New Way*, Lawrence and Wishart, London, 1941

SUAREZ, Andres, *Cuba: Castroism and Communism, 1959–1966*, MIT Press, Cambridge, Mass., 1961

SVECHNIKOV, Mikhail S., *Revolyutsiya i grazhdanskaya voina v Finlyandii, 1917–1918 g.g. (Vospominaniya i materialy)* Revolution and Civil war in Finland during 1917–1918: Memoirs and documents), Moscow–Leningrad, 1923

SWORAKOWSKI, Witold S. (ed.), *World Communism: A Handbook 1918–1965*, Hoover Institution Press, Stanford, California, 1973

SZAJKOWSKI, Bogdan, *Documents in Communist Affairs – 1977*, University College Cardiff Press, Cardiff, 1978

SZAJKOWSKI, Bogdan, *Documents in Communist Affairs – 1979*, University College Cardiff Press, Cardiff, 1980

SZAJKOWSKI, Bogdan, *Documents in Communist Affairs – 1980*, Macmillan, London, 1981

SZAJKOWSKI, Bogdan (ed.), *Marxist Governments: A World Survey*, Macmillan, London, 1981
    Vol. 1 Albania–The Congo
    Vol. 2 Cuba–Mongolia
    Vol. 3 Mozambique–Yugoslavia

SZEKERES, Josef, A Fovarosi Herbiztossag' (The People's Commissariat of Budapest), *Szazadok*, No. 103 (2–3), 1969, 347–371

SZYMCZAK, Tadeusz, *Organy władzy i administracji euroejskich panstw socialistycznych* (The Executive and Administrative Organs of the European Socialist Countries), Książka i Wiedza, Warsaw, 1970

TEPLINSKY, Leonid, 'Afghanistan: The Peoples Defend Their Revolution', *New Times*, No. 14, April 1979, 10–11

The Paris Agreement on Viet Nam and the Agreement of Laos, Viet Nam Committee, Auckland, 1973

The Political Report Presented by Comrade Abdel Fattah Isma'il, Secretary-General of the Unified Political Organization, The United Front to the Unification Congress 11th to 13th October 1975, Russell Press, Nottingham, 1977

The Roles of POMOA and the Yekatit '66 Political School in the Ethiopian Revolution, Propaganda and Information Committee, Addis Ababa, Fourth Anniversary of the Ethiopian Revolution, September 1978

THOMAS, Hugh, 'Cuba in Africa', *Survey*, **23** (105), Autumn (1977–1978), 181–188

THOMAS, Jack R., 'Marmaduke Grove and the Chilean National Election of 1932', *The Historian*, **29**, No. 1, 1966, 22–23

THOMAS, Jack R., 'The Evolution of a Chilean Socialist: Marmaduke Grove', *The Hispanic American Historical Review*, **XLVII**, February 1967), 22–37

THOMAS, Jack R., 'The Socialist Republic of Chile', *Journal of Inter-American Studies*, **VI** (1962), 203–220

THOMPSON, Virginia and ADOLFF, Richard, *Historical Dictionary of the People's Republic of the Congo*, The Scarecrow Press, Metuchen, NJ, 1974

TIGRID, Pavel, 'The Prague Coup of 1948: The Elegant Takeover', in *The Anatomy of Communist Takeovers* (ed. by Thomas T. Hammond), pp. 399–432

TÖKES, Rudolf L., *Béla Kun and the Hungarian Soviet Republic*, Praeger (for the Hoover Institution), New York, 1967

TOMA, Peter R., 'The Slovak Soviet Republic of 1919', *The American Slavic and East European Review*, **17**, April 1950, 203–215

TOMPKINS, Pauline, *American–Russian Relations in the Far East*, Macmillan, New York, 1949

TOWNSEND, James R., *Political Participation in Communist China*, University of California Press, Berkeley, 1967

TREVAKIS, Kennedy, *Shades of Amber, A South Arabian Episode*, Hutchinson, London, 1967

TROTSKY, Leon, *The History of the Russian Revolution*, Vols 1–3, Sphere, London, 1967

TROYANOVSKY, Konsantin, *Vostok i Revolutsiya* (The East and Revolution), Moscow, 1918

TUCKER, Robert C., 'Paths of Communist Revolution, 1917–67' in *The Soviet Union: A Half Century of Communism* (ed. by K. London), The Johns Hopkins Press, Baltimore, 1968

Twenty Years of Socialism in Albania, Naim Frasheri Publishing House, Tirana, 1964

Tymczasowy Komitet Rewolucyiny Polski (The Provisional Revolutionary Committee of Poland), Książka i Wiedza, Warsaw, 1955

URCH, R.O.G., *Latvia: Country and People*, Allen and Unwin, London, 1938

USVATOV, A., 'Afghanistan: A Democratic Republic', *New Times*, No. 20, May 1978, 7

VARDYS, Stanley V. and MISIUNAS, Ronald J. (eds), *The Baltic States in Peace and War, 1917–1945*, Pennsylvania State University Press, University Park, 1978

Viet Nam: A Sketch, Foreign Languages Publishing House, Hanoi, 1971

VICTOR, Martin, *Slovenska Sovietskaya Republika v r. 1919* (The Slovak Republic in 1919), Slovenske Vydavatelstvo Politickej Literatury, 1955

VIVO, Raul V., *Ethiopia's Revolution*, International Publishers, New York, 1978

VOLSKY, Dimitry, 'The Target: Afghanistan's Revolution', *New Times*, No. 24, June 1979, 12–13

WALLER, Michael, 'Movement is a Movement is a Movement', *Communist Affairs*, **1**, No. 1, January 1982, pp. 40–44

WALLER, Michael, 'Problems of Comparative Communism', *Studies in Comparative Communism*, **XII**, Nos 2 and 3, Summer/Autumn 1979, 107–132

WALLER, Michael, *The Language of Communism*, The Bodley Head, London, 1972

WASSMUND, Hans, 'German Democratic Republic' in *Marxist Governments: A World Survey* (ed. by Bogdan Szajkowski), Vol. 2, pp. 320–361

WENNER, Manfred W., 'The People's Republic of South Yemen', in *Governments and Politics of the Contemporary Middle East* (ed. by Tareg Y Ismael), The Dorsey Press, Homewood, 1970, 412–429

WESSON, Robert G., *Communism and Communist Systems*, Prentice-Hall, New Jersey, 1978

WHEELER-BENNETT, John W., *Brest-Litovsk: The Forgotten Peace, March 1918*, Norton, New York, 1971

WHITING, Allen S., *Sinkiang: Pawn or Pivot?* Michigan State University Press, East Lancing, Michigan, 1958

WILSON, David, *The Long March 1935*, Hamish Hamilton, London, 1971

WOODHOUSE, Christopher M., *The Struggle for Greece 1941–1949*, Hart-Davis, London, 1976

YU, George T., 'China's Impact', *Problems of Communism*, January-February 1978, 40–50

'Zadadi i Usloviia Sostialisticheskoi Propagandy v Persii' (The Nature of the Propaganda to be Carried on in Persia), *Zhizn Natsionalnostei*, No. 19 (27), 25 May, 1919

ZAGORIA, Donald S., 'Kerala and West Bengal', *Problems of Communism*, January-February 1973, 16–27

ZASLOFF, Joseph J., *The Pathet Lao: Leadership and Organisation*, D.C. Heath, Lexington, Mass., 1973

ZASLOFF, Joseph J., and BROWN, MacAlister (eds), *Communism and Indochina*, D.C. Heath, Lexington, Mass., 1975

ZENKOVSKY, Serge, *Panturkism and Islam in Russia*, Harvard University Press, Cambridge, Mass., 1960

ZERAI, Saleh M., 'Afghanistan: The Beginning of a New Era', *World Marxist Review*, 22, No. 1, January 1979, 73–78

ZINNER, Paul E., *Communist Strategy and Tactics in Czechoslovakia 1918–1948*, Pall Mall/Greenwood Press, London, 1963

Index